Green Spirit

TREES ARE THE ANSWER

Patrick Moore

TEXT AND PHOTOGRAPHY

Greenspirit Enterprises Ltd.

Vancouver, BC, Canada

"A world without forests is as unthinkable as a day without wood"

P.M.

To Eileen, Jon and Nick

"May the Forest be With You"

For ordering information contact:

Patrick Moore
Greenspirit Enterprises Ltd.
4068 West 32nd Avenue, Vancouver, B.C. Canada V6S 1Z6
phone (604) 221-1990 *fax* (604) 222-9353
e-mail   patrickmoore@home.com
Internet: http://www.greenspirit.com

Canadian Cataloguing in Publication Data

Moore, Patrick Albert, 1947-
  Green spirit : trees are the answer

Includes bibliographical references and index.

ISBN 0-9686404-0-0

1. Forest ecology. 2. Forest renewal. 3. Forest environment. 4. Trees. 5. Reforestation. 6. Title.

Contents

Cover: *The pioneer wildflowers pearly everlasting and fireweed thrive in the sun among young subalpine fir and Engleman spruce growing back after logging in the Slocan Valley, British Columbia.*

Overleaf: *A second growth Ponderosa pine thrusts skyward in an area logged 40 years ago in northern Idaho.*

Back Cover: *The author stands beside a second growth Sitka spruce that is about 100 years old near his home at Winter Harbour on northern Vancouver Island.*

Introduction

 In recent years, there has been a high-profile battle over the future of the forests of the Pacific Northwest of the United States and Canada, which includes the largest area of temperate rainforest in the world. Environmentalists have been locked in confrontation with forest companies, and in many instances with governments, over a variety of forest management issues, the most contentious concerning clearcut logging and old growth forests. These campaigns have had some very positive effects. They have increased public awareness of the value of old growth coastal rainforest, and greater support for the creation of more protected parks and wilderness areas. Environmentalists have pressed for, and often achieved, higher standards for forest management. Unfortunately, these campaigns have also spread misinformation and confusion about forests and forestry.

This book gives an alternative view of the environmental arguments used to support a drastic reduction in forest harvesting, not only in the Pacific Northwest, but also around the world. It is my belief that this is exactly the opposite of what we should be doing to improve the environment. Rather than cutting fewer trees and using less wood we should be growing more trees and using more wood. And contrary to conventional environmental wisdom I argue, for example, that clearcutting of some forests is beneficial for them and for humans, rather than harmful. To help understand this I explain how misconceptions arose from popular myths about deforestation, forest life cycles, and endangered species.

I believe that much of the environmental movement has gone astray and lost its perspective on the subject of forests. All human activity has an impact on the environment, but forestry is the most sustainable of all the primary industries that provide us with energy and materials. Indeed, wood is the most renewable material used in large quantities to build and maintain our civilization. The only viable substitutes are non-renewable materials such as fossil fuels, steel, cement, and plastic, all of which result in severe impacts to the environment.

As a lifelong environmentalist, I feel the need to speak out because I cannot agree with claims made to the world by some of my environmentalist colleagues about the "totally destructive and irreversible impact" of forestry in general and clearcutting in particular. This book expresses my conviction, backed by experience from birth, an education in forest ecology, and a career in environmental activism, that the forests of the Pacific Northwest, and of North America in general, are as healthy and sustainable as any in the world. I am dismayed by campaigns that employ misinformation and selective images to support extreme positions such as boycotts and bans. There is simply no justification to single out the forest practices of this region for special sanctions. To the contrary, leadership in both protection of forest wilderness and the practice of forestry is clearly evident. An element of the environmental movement has become seriously misguided in its effort to convince the world otherwise.

There is no doubt that some of the forestry practices that were used in the past are no longer acceptable due to changing values about the environment. Huge clearcuts with little or no concern for fish-bearing streams or other wildlife were once common throughout the Pacific Northwest.* The various codes of forest practice that have been adopted in each of the jurisdictions have changed this dramatically. Today, the trend is towards smaller, more carefully

---

* Throughout the book, the Pacific Northwest refers to northern California, Oregon, Washington, Idaho, western Montana, British Columbia and south-east Alaska.

contoured clearings with mandatory stream protection and consideration for other species. Single trees and patches of trees are often left standing within the clearings to provide habitat for birds and other wildlife. Public recreation and aesthetics are part of the planning process and governments play a major role in making the rules and enforcing them. These changes are occurring all across North America and are part of a worldwide trend to manage forests on a sustainable basis.

Despite these changes, there are still many people within the environmental community who do not accept these new standards. Their demands would appear to require an end to large-scale forestry operations over much of the land; based on the assumption that logging is so destructive to the environment that it must be drastically curtailed.

Perhaps the most dangerous myth that has been created in the war of words over the environment is that human activity is somehow "unnatural," that we are not really part of nature but apart from it. Human intervention in nature is portrayed as fundamentally negative while other species can do no wrong. This gives rise to the perception that humans are not really part of nature, that we are like a cancer on the earth.[1] There could be no more unfortunate teaching for our children than to further alienate them from an understanding of their place in the natural world. It is difficult enough for the masses of people in cities to understand their connection to the rest of creation without reinforcing a feeling of separation.

The central teaching of ecology is that we are part of nature and interdependent with it. All our acts are "natural" in this sense. If there is a place for the word "unnatural" it is certainly not as a definition of all human activity as opposed to non-human activity. This is a clear case of a word being used in a way that was never intended. The word "unnatural" is a moral word that is meant to distinguish certain socially unacceptable types of behavior from acceptable behavior. Practices such as incest are considered unnatural because we have moral codes against them. Ask yourself if whales and trees are capable of unnatural acts. They are not because we don't apply moral principles to species other than our own.

I hope to demonstrate that this false dualism, that humans are unnatural and everything else is natural, is particularly inappropriate in relation to forests. Forests are able to respond to disturbance caused by humans in the same manner as they respond to disturbance from fire, disease, and climate change. Some severe forest fires cause far greater damage to the forest ecosystem than would have been caused by logging. Some fires cause less damage, for example when they burn only the grass and shrubs beneath the trees but leave many of the trees alive.

The central purpose of this book is to show how important sustainable forest management is for the future of humanity and all life on Earth. Many environmental groups have adopted policies that would curtail forestry and bring about a drastic reduction in the use of wood. I believe this is the wrong approach for a number of reasons, including the implications for climate change and nature conservation. From a strictly environmental perspective, setting aside social and economic issues, I believe it is better to focus policy on growing more trees, and using more wood rather than less. Before entering into this minefield, however, I would like to share a bit of personal history by way of introduction.

I was born into the remote, windswept fjords of northern Vancouver Island in British Columbia. My childhood was spent living in a logging community on the edge of a rugged rainforest wilderness. A few hardy pioneer families, the remnants of the native community, and a crew of loggers were the only inhabitants of the float camp and tiny fishing village of Winter Harbour that was home for my first 15 years.

My grandfather, Albert Moore, arrived in Quatsino Sound in 1915 as chief timber cruiser for the Whelan Brothers who were building northern Vancouver Island's first pulp mill at Port Alice. He mapped many of the region's forests for the first time, surveying the topography and taking an inventory of the trees. When that task was completed in 1923 he went out on his own as

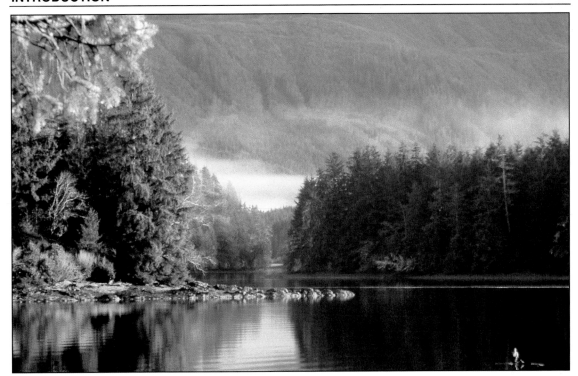

The view looking east from my home at Winter Harbour on the northwest coast of Vancouver Island.

a contract logger. He hired some men, set up a small float camp, and began to cut the old growth hemlock and cedar growing near the water's edge.

The original Kwakiutl inhabitants of Winter Harbour called their village Klayina. They had survived for thousands of years on the abundant salmon, clams, and berries, and built their houses of cedar planks taken from the forest behind them. Over the years, in common with many aboriginal communities, the people of Klayina were decimated by measles, smallpox, and other diseases introduced by Europeans. By the time my grandfather established his float camp in Winter Harbour in 1936 the village site had long been abandoned, the survivors having relocated to the nearby community of Quatsino. I was born into that float camp in 1947, spending my first seven years in a bulky life jacket that was compulsory dress outside the house.

There were no frills in the life of a west coast logger in those early years. Four men bunked in each 12-by-24-foot shack, one to a corner, with a 45-gallon oil drum woodstove in the center where rain soaked clothes were hung to dry. They worked six or seven days a week, getting up in the dark, working in the rain and wrestling in the mud trying to fix broken machinery. It was hard, relentless work, falling the huge trees, winching them down the mountain to the sea where they could be boomed to the mill, all the while staying alert to escape being slashed by a snapping cable or crushed by a run-away log. When the loggers were not working there was nothing much to do back at the bunkhouse but play cards or listen to the radio. It was a lonely and sometimes miserable existence.[2]

Until as late as the 1970s there was not much concern for the environmental effects of logging. Entire valleys and mountainsides of timber were clearcut with little regard for salmon streams, wildlife habitat, or reforestation. This was not done maliciously; it was simply assumed that the forest would grow back in time. Words such as environment, ecology, and biodiversity, and the concepts they represent, were absent from everyday conversation.

The early float camp era was ending during my boyhood. As the merchantable trees along the water's edge had all been cut, my father, Bill Moore, who had taken over from his dad, obtained a lease in 1954 from the Kwakiutl to establish a permanent community on the original

3

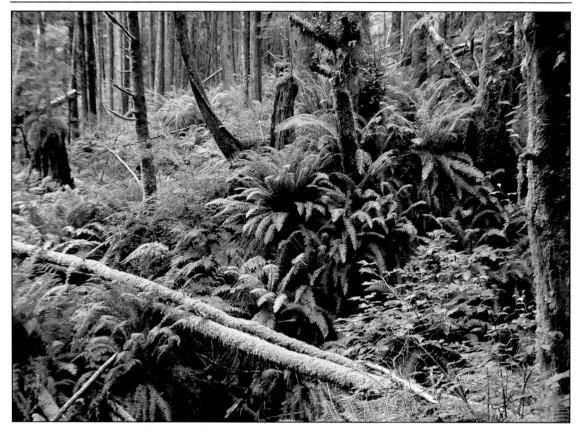

This area was clearcut by my grandfather in 1939. There was no reforestation and yet the forest has recovered naturally and the lush growth of trees, shrubs, mosses and ferns typical of the coastal rainforest now supports the full diversity of wildlife.

native village site. Roads were built to access timber farther up the valleys. Diesel had replaced steam some years before but it was the introduction of the motorized chainsaw, replacing double-bitted axes and crosscut handsaws, that revolutionized logging. Productivity increased dramatically with improvements in technology. Loggers and their families shared in the post-war boom in material culture and working class affluence. It was a wonderful time to live in the rainforest.

I didn't know I lived in a rainforest; to us it was the "woods" and it rained a lot. When it rained for 30 days straight we began to miss the sun. My playground and backyard was a recent clearcut across the road from our house. We didn't call it a clearcut because the word wasn't known; it was simply an "opening" or the "slash." The slash was a better place to play than the deep dark of the old growth forest surrounding us. It was brighter and when the sun shone it was warmer and drier. The only other places where the sun came out were down at the dock and on the tide flats. In the clearing you could sit on a stump in the sun and all summer long the berries grew; first the salmon berries, then thimble berries, then huckleberries and finally the salal berries. They were all deliciously different and we shared them with birds, deer and bears. As time went on new trees came up and added year-round green to the logged area. Hemlocks, cedars, and firs competing for the sunlight eventually crowded out the berry bushes. It was time to move on to a more recent clearcut. From this experience I developed a very different impression of clearcut logging than one might gain in the popular press today.

Today I can walk through forests where my grandfather clearcut logged 60 and 70 years ago and if it weren't for the presence of rotting, moss-covered stumps you would never know it had once been cleared. The new forest is so lush and full of shrubs and ferns that all evidence of disturbance has been removed. Bears, wolves, cougars, ravens and all the other forest-dwellers roam there. The trees are straight and tall and although they have not yet reached the great size of some of their predecessors they form a dense and growing cover on land once cleared bare. The marvel of this renewal is that it took place entirely on its own, without the slightest help from human hands. There had been no thought given to reforestation or any other aspect of restoration. Nature has regenerated almost in spite of human disturbance and is rapidly returning to its original condition.

When I was shipped down to Vancouver for four years of boarding school (Winter Harbour had no high school and no road out to the nearest one), I was thankful that my new school was beside a substantial forest that had grown back from logging early in the century. Then known as the University Endowment Lands associated with the University of British Columbia, most of this forest is now part of Pacific Spirit Park. Next to the forests of Winter Harbour I have become most familiar with the Douglas-fir-dominated forest of Pacific Spirit Park. After boarding school I attended the University of British Columbia for eight years, set in these same woods. For most of my adult life since then I have lived close to these woods, watching them grow into a magnificent new forest.

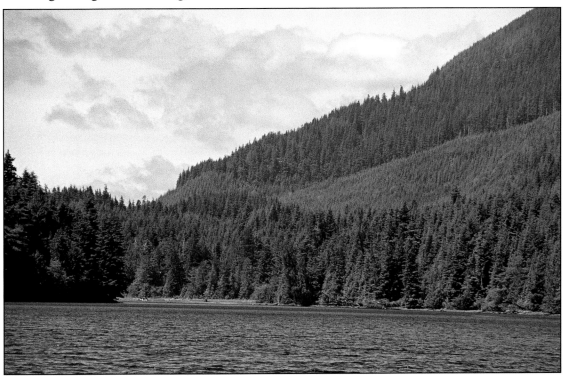

This scene of forests recovering from clearcutting in Ahwhichoalta Inlet on northern Vancouver Island is typical of the coastal rainforest in British Columbia. My grandfather clearcut the forest in the foreground in 1940 and now it is beginning to resemble the original forest. The area in the center was clearcut by my father in 1975 and is now a thriving young forest. The higher slopes in the background are original forest where the trees are of various ages ranging up to 500 years.

It was not until one day in my second year of university (in the Faculty of Forestry, naturally) that I began to gain an intellectual understanding of the great web of life I had been immersed in all my childhood. The occasion was a noon-hour lecture by Dr. Vladimir Krajina, the founder of the British Columbia Ecological Reserves and the author of the classification system for all British Columbia's ecosystems. It was a lecture that changed my life.

Vladimir Krajina had fled from Czechoslovakia in 1949, a freedom fighter and refugee from the Communist purges after the war. He eventually made his way to British Columbia where he joined the Faculty of Forestry at the University of British Columbia. Krajina brought with him a deep knowledge of the science of forest ecology. He also brought to the forestry faculty his tendency to stand up for his beliefs. Soon Krajina aroused the ire of the forestry establishment when he became the leading opponent of the widespread practice of slash burning in coastal forests after logging. Under political pressure he was transferred to the Faculty of Science where he continued to teach ecology for more than 20 years. Gradually foresters adopted his classification system but it was not until 1988 that the system he developed 20 years earlier became the legally required basis for forest planning in the province. Now, due to continuing environmental concerns, slash burning is used less and less as alternative methods are adopted where practical.

That noon-hour Krajina painted a word picture of the relationship among the species of the forest and their environment that shocked me to attention. It was as if I had never realized who I was or what I knew. In a few moments his words transformed my intuitive, almost subconscious thoughts about the natural world into a realization that ecology was not just about food chains and nutrient cycles. It was a new way of seeing the world and the miracle of living creation of which we are a part. I realized ecology was capable of linking rational thought with spiritual wonder, that through a holistic appreciation of nature one could gain insight into the meaning of life. This was a rather large thought for someone who had been raised an agnostic and who, until that moment, thought science was a purely technical subject.

There was no turning back. I devoured every book and paper on ecology and the environment I could find. With help from the late Dr. Oscar Sziklai, a UBC forest geneticist, I fashioned a more academic program of study that gave me access to biology courses in the science faculty as well as in forestry. This led to a combined degree in biology and forest biology after which I was accepted into a doctoral program in the UBC Institute of Resource Ecology.

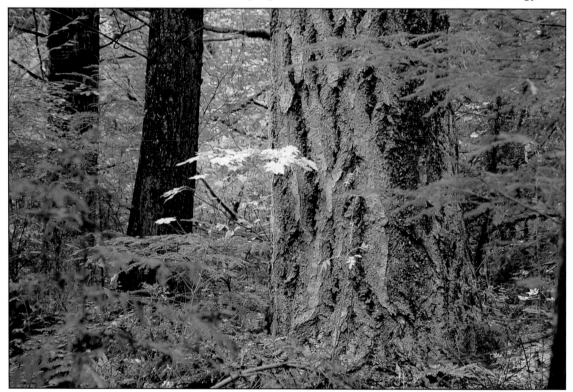

The forest that is now called Pacific Spirit Park was a refuge from the city while I attended high school and university in Vancouver.

I had chosen as my Ph.D. thesis topic the case of a huge copper mine project that proposed to dump its waste into Rupert Inlet, part of Quatsino Sound near my home at Winter Harbour. The US-based mining company stated publicly that the waters of Rupert Inlet were stratified in layers of differing density and that the mine waste would sink to the bottom and have no effect on the productive surface waters. A few days of research on my part revealed data from previous oceanographic surveys that virtually proved the opposite case. The waters of Rupert

Inlet were thoroughly mixed from top to bottom and any waste injected into the inlet would surely be carried into the surface waters by ocean currents. I challenged the mining company in public hearings only to find that the public process had little or no impact on the final decision. To top it off, my professors informed me that they had been advised that if I ever wanted a job when I graduated perhaps I should change the nature of my inquiry. This was 1969 and I rebelled against such blatant coercion. In my Ph.D. thesis I proved conclusively that the mine waste was carried into the surface waters and that the government's pollution control process was essentially immune to truth. I had become, through an entirely academic process, a radical environmental activist.[3]

This experience led to my involvement in the founding of the Greenpeace movement in early 1971. Meeting regularly in the basement of the Unitarian Church in Vancouver, we planned the first Greenpeace campaign, a protest voyage against US nuclear testing in the Aleutian Islands. For the next 15 years I helped lead Greenpeace as it grew into the world's largest environmental activist group, with branches in 26 countries and an annual budget of more than $100 million.[4]

Those were heady years and sometimes looking back it is hard to believe what we did and what we accomplished. They were frightening times too. In the early 1970s the Vietnam War was raging and the prospect of nuclear holocaust loomed. Rachel Carson's "Silent Spring"[5] had warned of toxic chemicals in the environment and Paul Ehrlich's "Population Bomb" predicted mass starvation and ecosystem collapse.[6] The great whales were being hunted to extinction. We believed "The Third World War will be the war to save the environment."[7] Our ragtag band of Greenpeace volunteers pledged to be the shock troops in that war. We adopted a philosophy linking the tradition of non-violent protest with the newly emerging awareness of ecology and the environment, and used our knowledge of communications media to create events that television news could not resist. Images of daring environmentalists dodging whale harpoons and blocking nuclear tests filled the front pages and evening newscasts. There was no stopping us as we broadened our campaigns to include baby seal killing, toxic discharges, nuclear waste dumping, supertanker traffic, driftnet fishing, kangaroo hunting, and the protection of Antarctica.

I was the leader of many of those campaigns and a participant in many more. During my years with Greenpeace I was always a member of the top committee as we evolved from a loose-knit group of volunteers to an international board of directors. For two years, from 1977 to 1979, I headed the organization and was instrumental in creating Greenpeace International. We worked tirelessly and the only reward was the sweet success of achieving first awareness and then change. Moratoriums were declared on hydrogen bomb tests. The International Whaling Commission outlawed whaling in the North Pacific in 1979. Canada called off the baby seal slaughter in 1981. The London Dumping Convention voted to forbid the practice of dumping nuclear waste into the North Atlantic in 1984. By the mid-eighties the environmental agenda previously considered radical was being widely adopted by the mainstream of western society. In 1989 the combined impact of the Chernobyl nuclear disaster, the Exxon Valdez oil spill, the threat of global warming, and the hole in the ozone layer clinched the debate. All but a reactionary minority had joined the call for sustainable development and environmental protection.

In 1986 I left Greenpeace. Fifteen years in the eco-trenches had worn me out; I needed a rest as well as a change — and I wanted to see more of my two young boys who were growing up with a father who was seldom home. But I also left satisfied that, in my view, we had largely accomplished the task we set out for ourselves. For me, Greenpeace was really about ringing an ecological fire alarm, awakening people to the true dimensions of our global predicament. Greenpeace could define the problems, but did not necessarily have the solutions nor was it equipped to put them into practice. That requires the combined efforts of governments, corporations, public institutions, *and* environmentalists. The war, it seemed to me, was over.

Whereas previously the leaders of the environmental movement found themselves on the outside railing at the gates of power, they were now invited to the table in boardrooms and caucuses around the world. It was time to move from confrontation to cooperation. I now believed that a consensus approach promised to give environmental issues their fair consideration in relation to the traditional economic and social priorities — and to lead to solid progress in resolving the problems.

That is not how some of my former colleagues and other environmentalists saw it. There had always been a minority of extremists who took a "No Compromise in Defense of Mother Nature" position. They were the monkey-wrenchers, tree-spikers, and boat-scuttlers of the Earth First! and Paul Watson variety. They had always been considered totally unacceptable by the mainstream of the movement, who subscribed to a philosophy that was "trans-political, trans-ideological, and trans-national." For Greenpeace, the Cree legend "Warriors of the Rainbow"[8] referred to people of all colors and creeds working together for a greener planet. The traditional sharp division between left and right was rendered meaningless by the common desire to protect our life support systems. Non-violent direct action and peaceful civil disobedience were the hallmarks, violence against people and property the only taboos. Truth mattered and science was respected for the knowledge it brought to the debate.

In recent years, this original broad-based vision has become increasingly threatened by a new philosophy of radical environmentalism. Faced with the widespread adoption of the environmental agenda by the mainstream of business and government, environmentalists had to choose between switching to working with their former "enemies" or always adopting more extreme positions. Many chose to become more hard-line. The fall of the Berlin Wall and its aftermath also had an impact on this trend. Suddenly, pro-Soviet groups were discredited and the international peace movement was redundant. Many members of the left moved into the environmental movement bringing with them their eco-Marxism and anti-establishment sentiments. In the name of "deep ecology," much of the environmental movement has since taken a sharp turn to the ultra-left, ushering in a mood of extremism and intolerance. As a clear signal of this new agenda, Greenpeace in 1990 called for a "grassroots revolution against pragmatism and compromise."[9]

As an environmentalist in the political center, I found myself branded a traitor and a sellout by this new breed of saviors. My name appeared in Greenpeace's "Guide to Anti-Environmental Organizations." Fellow Greenpeace founder, Bob Hunter, referred to me as the "eco-Judas." It's true that I have been trying to help the forest industry improve its environmental performance. As chair of the Sustainable Forestry Committee of the Forest Alliance of BC, I helped draft the Principles of Sustainable Forestry that have been adopted by a majority of the industry in my home province. These principles establish goals for environmental protection, forest management, and public involvement. They are providing a framework for dialogue and action towards improvements in forest practices.

I hope this book will help broaden public understanding of the process of forest renewal, and in this way will counter the misinformation being spread by environmental extremists. In their campaigns to save old growth forests, environmentalists commonly publish photographs of ugly and allegedly bad forest practices to indicate the fate of the forest if it is not protected. These scenes are invariably of areas recently cut and are depicted in the worst possible manner — bare clearcuts full of stumps and debris. Where forestry is practiced the trees must be cut and the land managed to create new forests. This inevitably involves periods of time where the land looks rather ugly to most observers.

Many environmentalists convey the simplistic, and wrong, impression to the public that the choice is between preservation and devastation, between saving pristine natural ecosystems or allowing their complete destruction by clearcutting. What trees do grow back after logging, we are told, are genetically deprived monocultures good for nothing but pulp. The "monoculture fiber farm," as they call it, is depicted as forever lacking in biodiversity and devoid of any aesthetic or spiritual value.

A stand of mountain ash in southern Australia illustrates the way in which the living trees create a new environment. The canopy and the interior of the forest provide thousands of habitats for plants, animals and insects. The majority of all living species can be found in forested environments. This stand has grown back after a devastating fire in the 1930's.

The casualty in this war of words and pictures is the truth that, in most cases in forest ecosystems, the new forest that grows back after logging is as diverse and beautiful in its own way as the one it replaced. This is the central theme that I elaborate in this book. Photographs and text referring to specific forest lands in the Pacific Northwest and British Columbia challenge the basic idea promoted by extreme environmentalists that once a forest is cut the ecosystem is "gone forever."[10] This is also supported by evidence of how forests have recovered through the ages from fire, ice, wind, volcanic eruption, disease, and human disturbance. With visual and factual evidence I hope to demonstrate that neither the biodiversity nor the spiritual quality of the original forest need be lost when a new forest returns. New forests can be purposefully managed to resemble the original forest in species composition and structure. But the process of renewal takes time, much more time than it takes to cut the trees in the first place. The time-scale of forest growth extends beyond the human lifetime, something difficult to communicate or appreciate in a world of 30-second news clips.

It is true that in many parts of the world, managed forests are very different from the original forests. In New Zealand the managed forests are mainly plantations of radiata pine, a species imported from California. In Germany, plantations of Scots pine and Norway spruce predominate. In Brazil, eucalyptus from Australia and pines from North America are the plantation species of choice. But in the Pacific Northwest, in fact in most of North America, the second-growth forests are composed entirely of the native tree and plant species that were in the original forest. These second-growth forests are as natural in terms of species composition as the original forests they have replaced. So long as they are either left alone or helped along by foresters the forests will return and can eventually be as beautiful in their own right as the forests they replace.

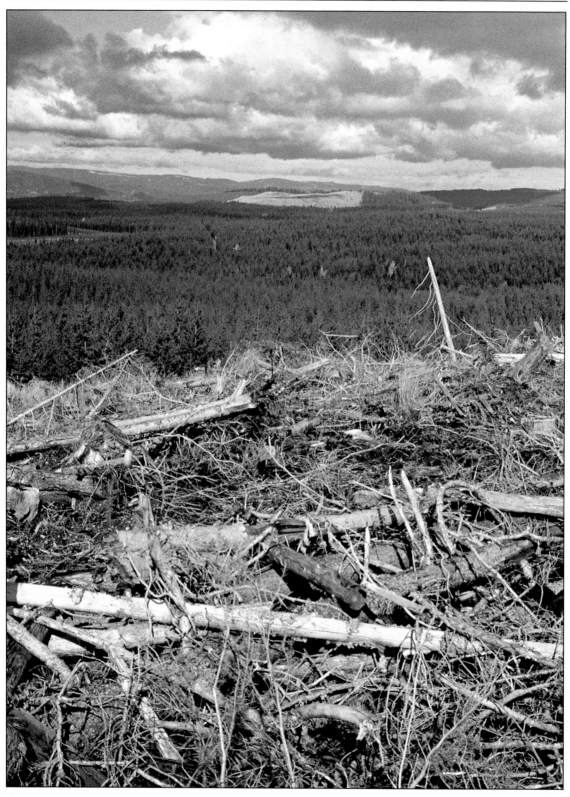

Contrasting images of clearcuts in British Columbia. The recently logged area near Kelowna (above) looks raw and devastated while the fireweed growing in a clearcut near New Denver (facing page), only four years after logging, looks beautiful as it recovers. The ecological health of landscapes cannot be judged by visual aesthetics alone. Beauty and ugliness are subjective human values and often have little or nothing to do with the state of the environment.

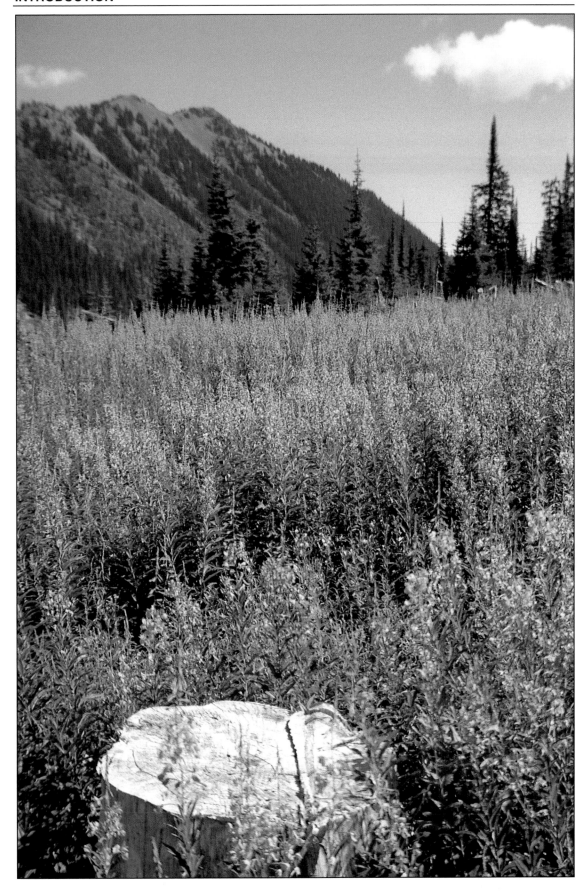

All forests, no matter how old they are, are growing on land that was once treeless. As climates have changed over the millennia, forests have come and gone, ever changing themselves as they respond to a changing environment. Even where forested land is stripped to bedrock by glaciers the forest will return if the climate becomes suitable again. This is equally true of forests cut by humans. The only way to stop forests from growing back is by purposefully interfering with the process of renewal: by plowing the land every year and planting crops, by setting so many livestock on it they eat every tree seedling that tries to grow, or by covering the land with cement and buildings.

While life began in the sea most of it has ended up in forests. From the tropical rainforests of Asia, Africa, and Latin America to the broad sweep of boreal forest around the Northern Hemisphere, the majority of today's species live in environments dominated by trees.[11]

This is a recent development in the scale of geological time. Life emerged more than three billion years ago yet it was *only* 350 million years ago that forests began their conquest of the land. During little more than 10 percent of the history of life, forests have become home to most of the species of plants, animals, and insects known today. The trees themselves generate the conditions that allow this diversity of life to flourish.

When plants evolved the ability to grow long wooden stems, and hence to become what we call trees, they did so for a single purpose. The taller the tree, the better to monopolize the energy of the sun for photosynthesis and growth. Trees are basically plants that want to grow in full sunlight. This is one of the reasons foresters often prefer to create clearings in which to grow new tree seedlings.

The great height of trees adds a third dimension to the landscape and creates new interior environments in and beneath the forest canopy. This three-dimensional nature of forests has enabled species to develop that could never exist in the two-dimensional world of meadows, plains, and deserts. The canopy of the forest above is now home to millions of birds and insects where there was once thin air; and the interior of the forest below is now protected from frost, sun and wind. This, in combination with the vast surface areas and foodstuff provided by the leaves, fruits, and wood of the trees creates thousands of new habitats into which new species can evolve — species that could never exist if it weren't for the presence of the trees.

The tallest, largest, and most long-lived species of trees on the planet have evolved in the forests of the Pacific Northwest of North America. From the giant sequoias and redwoods of California to the red cedars, Douglas-firs, and Sitka spruce of British Columbia and Alaska, nothing rivals the vegetative power of these giants. They are the largest organisms ever to exist on earth.

Since all ecosystems have unique qualities, it may seem presumptuous to claim exceptional merit for the deep green forests of the Pacific coast of North America. There is as much reason to give special status to the forests of the Amazon, the high Himalayas, and the Australian outback. Other writers have done so. But for me, there is nothing like the fern-thick deep of the Pacific coastal rainforest to bring on a feeling of inner peace and a sense of wonder at the lush, primeval beauty of it all. This is the landscape that I have come to know and love through a lifetime of experience. It is unique to me, but from an ecological point of view it is very much a forest like any other.

Despite the unique mix of species and the widely varying climates found in the world's many types of forests, it is surprising how much all forests have in common from an environmental perspective. The underlying ecological principles are very similar in all forested landscapes, even though the species may be entirely different. The basic laws of nature, from the sun's energy as it passes through the food chain to the competition and co-operation among species, are universal. This also holds true for many of the political and social issues surrounding forests and their management. Even though individual forests may be very different, the debates about their conservation and management are similar the world over. Partly because of these common features, many foresters and ecologists believe it would be possible, and desirable, to develop an international agreement on sustainable forest management and the certification of products produced from sustainably managed forests. There are many initiatives now underway to develop standards that can be used to measure progress towards a style of forestry that protects the environment and biodiversity while providing society with that most renewable of materials, wood.

The following chapters set out to provide readers with an alternative interpretation of the environmental issues in forestry. In brief:

- The chapter on **Beauty and the Beholder** shows through photographs and text that natural beauty returns to clearcut areas soon after logging and that the new forest can be as beautiful as the one it replaced. It also demonstrates that aesthetics -- or the "look" of a forest -- is not a good measure of whether a particular practice is right or wrong.

- The chapter on **Biological Diversity** challenges the contention that logging destroys biological diversity and causes species extinction, presents evidence that new forests are as diverse in their own way as the original, and refutes the charge that second-growth forests are always "monocultures" that produce inferior trees.

- The chapter on **Time and Change** discusses the multitude of factors involved in the succession of forests as they grow from tiny seedlings to giant trees. It explores as well such key issues as the causes of deforestation and soil erosion, the role of clearcutting and selective logging, the impact of ice ages, fire and volcanic eruptions, and the nature of sustainable forestry. Environmentalists often claim that "the ancient forest is a cathedral".

- In the chapter on **The Spirit of the Ancient Forest** this metaphor is examined along with the whole question of spiritual qualities attributed to forests.

- The final chapter titled **Trees are the Answer** deals with the alternate visions of how forests might contribute to the environment and society over the next hundreds of years. The critical question of how to communicate forest issues to a skeptical public is explored. It concludes that there are grounds for optimism - in programs to preserve wilderness areas and in new forestry practices - that we may finally be learning to manage forests on a sustainable basis.

REFERENCES

1 W. M. Hern, Is Human Culture Oncogenic for Uncontrolled Population Growth and Ecological Destruction? Human Evolution Vol. 12, N. 1-2, pp. 97-105, 1997.

2 Raincoast Chronicles Issues 1-16, Harbour Publishing, Howard White editor, 1972-1995.

3 Patrick Moore, The Administration of Pollution Control in British Columbia: A Focus on the Mining Industry, Ph.D. Thesis, University of British Columbia, May 1973.

4 Michael Brown and John May, The Greenpeace Story, Prentice-Hall Canada Inc., Scarborough, Ontario, 1989, and Robert Hunter, Warriors of the Rainbow, Holt, Rinehart and Winston, New York, 1979.

5 Rachel Carson, Silent Spring, Houghton Mifflin, New York, 1962.

6 Paul Ehrlich, Population Bomb, Ballantine, New York, 1968.

7 Robert Hunter, Warriors of the Rainbow, Holt, Rinehart and Winston, New York, 1979.

8 Willoya and Brown, Warriors of the Rainbow, Naturegraph, 1962.

9 Martin W. Lewis, Green Delusions: An Environmentalist Critique of Radical Environmentalism, Duke University Press, Durham, 1992.

10 Alan Drengson, Remembering the Moral and Spiritual Dimensions of Forests, in Clearcut, The Tragedy of Industrial Forestry, Sierra Club Books/Earth Island Press, 1993, p.21.

11 E. O. Wilson, The Diversity of Life, W.W. Norton, New York, 1992.

Beauty and the Beholder

Everyone has an opinion about what is beautiful and what is not. Aesthetic appeal is a basic human value and one of the most mysterious. Individuals widely disagree on what is beautiful in art, in architecture, or in women and men. Despite this, few deny the beauty of trees.

Forests symbolize natural beauty to many people. Graceful, majestic, luxuriant, colorful, they elicit powerful positive feelings. Through the ages countless painters, poets, song-writers, and photographers have extolled their beauty. City-dwellers everywhere import trees from around the world to adorn their homes and residential neighborhoods. The most livable cities have forested parks and woodlands close by for the enjoyment of residents. Many of us become attached to trees and forests as we do to friends. When they die from fire, old age, or by human hands we miss them and even mourn their passing.

It is as much the sheer beauty of forests as anything else that spurs public support for their preservation. Whether it is the view from a home or highway or the appearance of a river or lakeshore, aesthetics play a major role in the emotional side of the forest debate. Regardless of arguments about ecology, wood supply, and employment, concern over the way the land looks to the human eye is often at the root of disagreements about its use. When presented with the choice of a fully forested vista or a view of a fresh clearcut there are few today who would chose a clearcut. Felice Page expresses this perspective clearly in his essay on the sociology of timber communities: "Clearcuts are ugly. People who see them, even children, know instinctively that they are wrong, an outrage, a sacrilege."[1]

This was not always the case. In earlier times there was a premium on cleared land. The forest was seen as an obstacle to be overcome. The forest was dark and inhospitable, particularly in northern climes, and crops could not be grown there. The only way to establish towns and farms was to clear away the forest. Land that was cleared of forest was "improved" and worth much more for the labor of opening it to the sun. A new clearing in a pioneer homestead looked good to the eyes of hard working people trying to survive in a new land.

It is commonly believed that the aboriginal people of the Pacific Northwest lived in the forest. It would be more accurate to say that they lived on the edge of the forest. They lived with their backs to the rainforest facing the sea, the lakes, and the rivers that were open to the sun. They made extensive use of fire to clear away forest so the sun could reach the ground and wild game would have more forage. They too valued open spaces in a land that is inhospitable to humans in the absence of clearings.

Why then, is a newly cleared forest now seen as an eyesore? There are a number of elements that combine to explain this recent change in public perception. First, there is a widely held belief that we have already cleared too much forest and that it would be wise to clear no more. The distinction between forest land that is permanently converted to other uses, and land that is reforested after logging, is often lost because of the immediate impression of destruction.

Second, most people now live in urban environments where they have become accustomed to a world of paved streets and buildings. Where trees and gardens grow they are pruned and tended with individual care. The jagged and jumbled appearance of a recently logged-over area is foreign to the eye and looks unkempt and disorderly. Stumps, broken pieces of wood, and bared soil are seen as raw wounds on the earth. All manner of metaphors linking the look of the land with loss and pain reinforce this impression.

Third, and perhaps most influential, is the regular presentation through the media of powerful imagery linking recent clearcut areas with desolation and total destruction. For example, in an article on Canadian forest practices, the German newsmagazine Der Spiegel wrote: "After the massive deforestation, all that remains of the complex forest structure that has developed since the last Ice Age, is a desert of tree stumps and debris."[2] With sensational descriptions like this, the news media frequently convey the impression that the landscape after logging is one of a battlefield where fallen corpses of the forest lie defeated at the hands of men. Mist from moisture and smoke from fire conjure up photographic images straight from hell: nature raped, ruined, and rendered permanently devoid of beauty.

We have all been taught since we were children that you should not judge a book by its cover, or to put it another way, that beauty is only skin deep. Yet most of us are easily fooled into thinking that if we like what we see with our eyes it is good, and if we don't like the look of something it is bad. This tendency to judge whether something is right or wrong by the way it looks is fine when it comes to appreciating art, or beauty in its own right. But the visual appearance of a landscape is not sufficient information to make judgments about ecology or environmental health.

The Aesthetics of Comparative Landscapes

A taste for rural scenes, in the present state of society, appears to be very often an artificial sentiment, rather inspired by poetry and romances, than a real appreciation of the beauties of nature.

Wollstonecraft, 1759-1797, On Poetry and our Relish for the Beauties of Nature

Some landscapes appeal to the eye while others do not; it greatly depends on whose eyes do the viewing. For people born on the prairies, the lofty landscape of the Rocky Mountains can arouse feelings of claustrophobia, while people raised in steep country often see only emptiness in the vast plains. For some the experience of being alone deep in the forest would elicit fear, even panic, while for others it might evoke a feeling of spiritual union with nature. The aesthetics of comparative landscapes, as this subject might be described, is clearly very subjective in nature.

People often take what looks good to their eyes as evidence that something is good as opposed to bad. But the individual perception of beauty or lack thereof is not always an accurate indicator of environmental health. The opposite is so often the case that it is wise to begin with the premise that the visual aesthetics of a scene are not a good indicator of whether a particular environment is healthy from an ecological perspective.

Perhaps the best illustration of this principle is shown by two pairs of contrasting images. First, compare a scene of a magnificent stand of old growth trees with the scene of a recent clearcut on a hillside. The old growth scene is almost universally perceived as more pleasing to the eye. Second, compare the same clearcut with a scene of a shiny new car parked at the entrance to a grand hotel. Virtually everyone would prefer the image of the car. It is more pleasing to the eye than a mess of stumps and broken wood even though the automobile is arguably one of the most environmentally destructive human inventions and must travel on pavement where all vestiges of nature have been obliterated. At least the clearcut is still rich in plants and roots and seeds, waiting for rain and the warmth of spring to begin the cycle of renewal. This is an extreme

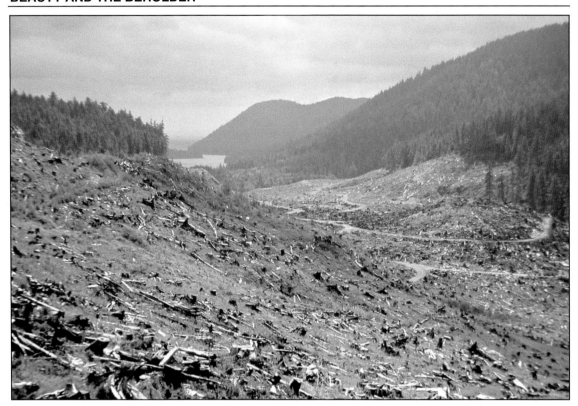

Most people would find this scene of a recent clearcut (above) rather ugly and offensive to the eye while the more pastoral farm landscape (below) is visually attractive by comparison. Yet the farmlands represent permanent deforestation and loss of biological diversity while the clearcut is beginning to grow back into a forest with native species of trees, plants and animals. Our eyes don't always tell us the truth about the environmental condition of a landscape.

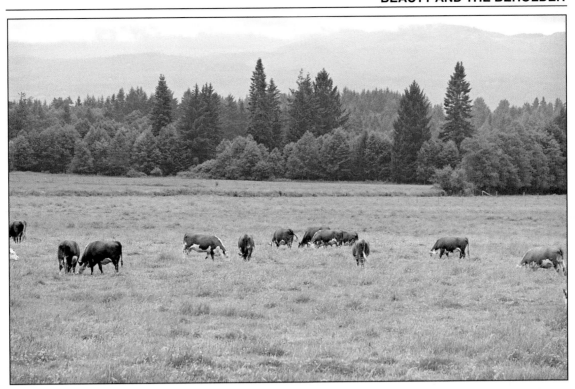

Usually thought of as peaceful and beautiful this really is a scene of deforestation where there was once a coastal rainforest. These cow pastures, in the Pacific Northwest, are now almost devoid of native species. While we usually associate deforestation with tropical countries, most of our farmland has been deforested in the same way.

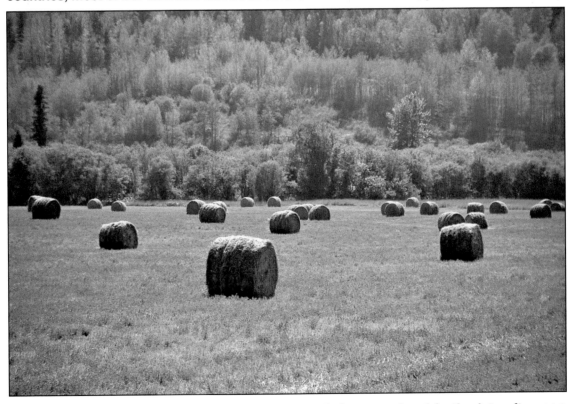

These large bales of hay look picturesque enough for a postcard in the late afternoon light. They are really just large lumps of dead cellulose grown specifically as fodder for domestic animals. They are sitting on deforested land. The forest in the background looks rather plain but it is where nearly all the native biodiversity can be found.

example but it is sobering to consider the third possible pairing of these images. How many people, in an urban consumer society, would prefer the image of the car over the old growth forest?

The case need not be stated in the extreme to demonstrate that perceived beauty and environmental health are not always synonymous. For many people one of the most beautiful scenes is the pastoral, typified by the English countryside where sheep graze peacefully beside meandering streams. The pastoral scene is calming and draws one to sit in contemplation in a sunny spot overlooking the valley. The fact that one is viewing a deforested area that has been clearcut right to the river's edge and is now occupied by a single, highly bred, domestic animal is not the usual first impression. The artificial meadow of grass and clover looks green and luxuriant on the rolling land despite its extreme biological simplicity compared to the forest it replaced.

Taken in the right light, even clearcuts can be beautiful. These recently harvested areas in the Cariboo Mountains near Barkerville, British Columbia illustrate the meadow-like nature of clearcuts. But these meadows are temporary; soon a new forest will begin to grow back on these fertile slopes.

Why do deforested areas that have been converted to permanent agricultural uses nearly always have greater aesthetic appeal than clearcuts that are about to return to native forest? One of my favorite examples of this bias is the scene of a hayfield with the newly baled hay stacked in neat bundles over the land, compared to the look of a recent clearcut. The hayfield is a deforested area predominated by a single species of domestic plant such as alfalfa. The bales of hay are large lumps of dead cellulose fiber that will be fed to domestic animals. The clearcut, on the other hand, is an area about to be rejuvenated with native plants, animals, and trees. The stumps are large pieces of dead organic matter that will rot and provide nutrition for the soil. From an ecological perspective it is simple to decide which scene is closest to the wild, native environment. From an aesthetic perspective the hayfield will invariably win out in a public beauty contest.

This prejudice applies to virtually all agricultural landscapes. Whether a cornfield, cabbage patch, sugar cane plantation, cattle ranch, or rice paddy, the appearance of neatly laid-out fields with monoculture crops is more attractive to the eye than a jumble of woody debris.

18

Perhaps the knowledge that the land is being used to produce food for human sustenance influences visual appreciation. Perhaps it is simply that more people have grown up in the vicinity of farms than managed forests. Or perhaps it is tied to our evolutionary development as creatures of the savanna where open grasslands predominate and trees are widely dispersed. Whatever the underlying cause of this bias in perception, it suggests that neither innate nor learned impressions necessarily lead to accurate ecological interpretation.

Our appreciation of urban environments gives more weight to the argument that the sense of beauty is not to be trusted as a measure of ecosystem health. All manner of city sights and scenery are more pleasing to the eye than any number of rural settings, particularly to the urban dweller. The revulsion and disgust that some people now often feel with scenes of logging are rarely experienced on viewing the demolition of a city building. Despite the entirely altered landscape of roads and structures decorated with exotic trees and shrubs, it is easy to feel at home in the concrete jungle. If home is where the heart is, the vast majority of humans feel more comfortable in cities and on farms than they do in the woods.

The Clearcut as a Temporary Meadow

Nature, I say, covers her slime, her muck, her ruins, with garments that to us, are beautiful. She conceals the skeleton, the framework, the intestinal thick of life, and makes fair the outside of things.

Walt Whitman – Poets of America

 After logging or other disturbance, the long process of forest renewal begins with re-colonization by new vegetation. Foresters call this "ecological succession" because as time goes on various groups of species succeed each other as a new forest develops from the cleared area. During the first stage light-loving plants dominate the land. They spring up from seeds that lay dormant under the shade of the forest, are blown in on the wind, or are carried in by birds and mammals from adjacent areas. Many of these plants are profuse with nectar-laden blossoms and nutritious berry crops. They attract insects, birds, and animals that feed on the abundance of low-lying forage provided. Think, for just a moment, of the clearcut as a temporary meadow. It is temporary because it will soon become a forest again. But it is meadow-like for the time being because the trees have been removed and now the sun can reach directly to the ground and foster the growth of light-loving plants.

Most people are surprised to see the words clearcut and meadow used in the same sentence. After all, meadows are pleasant places that you can walk across easily in the open sunlight, find a smooth dry place and put your blanket down and have a lovely picnic in the afternoon. On the other hand, clearcuts are ugly places, full of broken wood, stumps and mud. You might break your ankle falling in a hole and there is no smooth dry place to lay down a picnic blanket. These differences between a meadow and a clearcut have nothing to do with science and everything to do with aesthetics. A deeper look reveals that our immediate impression of what is beautiful and what is not can be thoroughly misleading.

Visual perceptions of what is beautiful - and right - about a landscape are not innate but are learned from regular exposure to ideas and images that are portrayed in a certain light. Where cleared land was once seen as the promise of a home-site and garden, it is now seen as the destruction of nature. What was once considered a sight to behold is now among the ugliest scenes imaginable. Some scenes that look bad are indeed ecologically negative. But it is equally true that some landscapes that would be called ugly are perfectly healthy from an environmental perspective. And perhaps most important, many landscapes that look perfectly fine actually represent total deforestation and the destruction of the original ecosystem.

What, actually, is the nature of a meadow? It is an area of land that is naturally open, often a relatively small area surrounded by forested land. The reason the meadow is not forested is because it is not capable of growing trees. This is invariably due to the fact that the area occupied by the meadow is too dry, too wet, or too cold for trees. In other words, its climate is too extreme to support a forest. Meadows are just one type of the general class of naturally non-forested lands. Among these, we usually call areas that are open because they are too wet "bogs," areas that are too cold "alpine" or "tundra", and areas that are hot and too dry "desert." We also tend to confuse the issue by viewing pasture lands that have been deforested for domestic grazing animals as meadows. Pastures carved out of the forest would eventually return to forest given the opportunity.

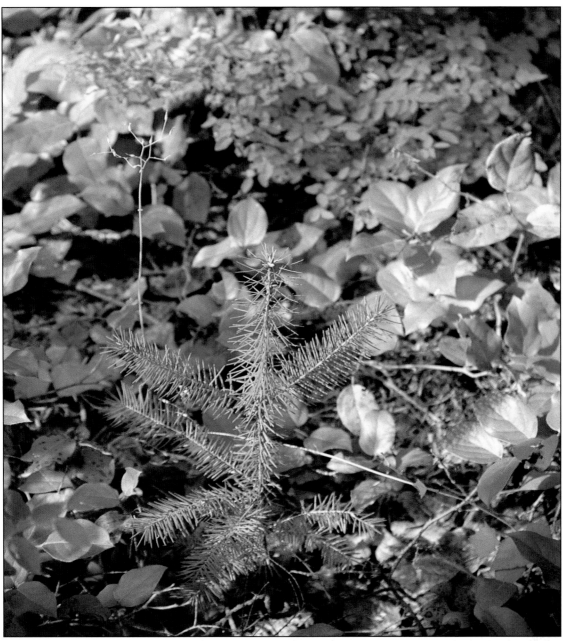

This Douglas-fir seeding is hardly visible at first among the thick growth of shrubs. It begins the process of transforming the clearcut from a temporary meadow back to a forest again.

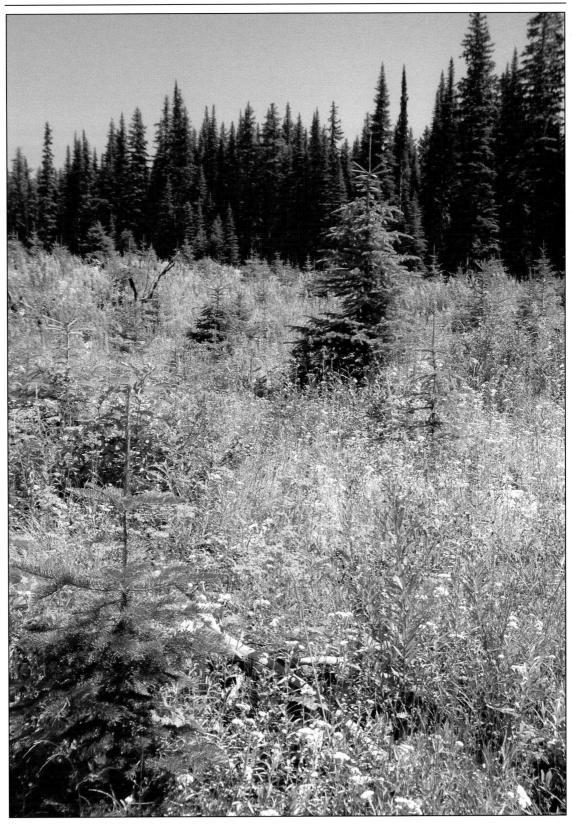

Young subalpine fir are now well established and as they continue to grow will gradually shade out the many flowering plants typical of alpine meadows. The older forest in the background has very few plants growing beneath the trees.

All one need do to demonstrate that the early stages of forest recovery are very meadow-like is to visit an area that was clearcut three to five years previously. The spring and summer are the most pleasant as the annual plants, flowers, and berries are at their best.

Once a clearcut has been taken over by the cover of sun-loving plants it becomes as pleasant a place to be on a warm day as a natural meadow. The main difference between the two is the presence of stumps and woody debris in the clearcut area. The larger pieces of wood can make hiking a bit difficult but the stumps offer a dry place to sit, take a break and eat some wild berries growing from the fresh soil. In time the woody debris will decompose to form soil for the new stand of trees that at this early stage are barely noticeable among the profusion of new growth.

What clearcuts lack in ease of passage compared to natural meadows they more than make up in ecological terms. The woody debris itself adds a dimension not present in the flat, two-dimensional world of the meadow. Wood left behind in clearcuts offers habitat for a myriad of species, from insects to fungi, to liverworts and mosses. Small mammals can hide from birds of prey beneath decaying branches and find protection from the rain there. Rotting wood is like a slow-release fertilizer, the larger the piece the longer it will provide nutrients to a growing forest. Wood soaks up water like a sponge, holds it over dry periods, and protects the soil from wind and sun.

Even more significant is the greater diversity of plants, animals, and insects that thrive in recent clearcuts as opposed to natural meadows. This is due to the less extreme climate in areas that are capable of growing trees as well as the presence of structures such as stumps and pieces of wood. This is particularly true when compared to natural meadows that are too dry to support trees. Many herbs and shrubs need more moisture than the meadow can provide. Species such as fireweed, blueberry, and swordfern thrive in clearcuts but will not grow in dry natural meadows.

Beauty and Morality

The whole world recognizes the beautiful as the beautiful, yet this is only the ugly; the whole world recognizes the good as the good, yet this is only the bad.

Lao-Tzu – Tao Te Ching

The way things look or feel, and our perception of events and situations, are often equated with whether or not these are good or bad. Statements of fact like "the tree was cut down" are confused with value judgments like "it was wrong to cut the tree down." Words like ecology have "good" connotations and words like clearcut have "bad" connotations. When otherwise objective words are codified into value judgments it becomes very difficult to engage in a rational discussion.

Sometimes the discussion becomes completely absurd. This is the case with the Sierra Club/Earth Island publication, *Clearcut: The Tragedy of Industrial Forestry.* Possibly the first coffee table book that is intended to be ugly, it is full of photographs of scenes of allegedly destructive clearcutting in which the worst possible interpretation, visual and verbal, is presented to shock the reader. On page 64, in large, bold type is a quote that is repeated a number of times elsewhere in the text. Attributed to Gordon Robinson, the Sierra Club's chief forestry spokesman from 1966-79, the statement is shocking in a different way. It is intended to capture the main thesis of the book, and is even more revealing about environmentalists' thinking:

"Anyone can identify destructive forestry practices. You don't have to be a professional forester to recognize bad forestry any more than you have to be a doctor to recognize ill health. If logging looks bad, it is bad. If a forest appears to be mismanaged, it is mismanaged".[3]

The Sierra Club clearly would have the public equate their aesthetic perception, the "look" of forestry, with their moral judgment about whether it is good or bad. Surely it is unreasonable to maintain that the good or bad of a forest situation can be determined merely by looking at it. This is an equally unreliable way of making medical diagnoses.

The perceived connection between beauty and goodness is made all the more confusing by what might be termed the "urban aesthetic." The rough and jumble of stumps and woody debris just doesn't look very neat and tidy to people who are familiar with clean streets and perpendicular building lines. Their perception of the clearcut as a bombed-out moonscape is reinforced by statements that encourage people to make judgments based on their own sense of aesthetics.

A sharp contrast with the Sierra Club approach is offered from a quite different source, a seminal 1969 essay on environmentalism titled, "The Tragedy of the Commons." In it, environmentalist Garrett Hardin explored the historical and cultural roots of environmental degradation on public land and concluded that the only lasting solution is control of the human population. One of the more enlightening passages in the paper states that:

"The morality of an act cannot be determined from a photograph. One does not know whether a man killing an elephant or setting fire to a grassland is harming others until one knows the total system in which his act occurs. It is tempting to ecologists as it is to reformers in general to try to persuade others via the photographic shortcut. But the guts of an argument can't be photographed: they must be presented rationally -- in words."[4]

As tempting as it is to equate visual appearances with moral judgments we must guard against such simplistic conclusions. While there is no doubt that the beauty of nature is worthy of our attention there are deeper issues involved. Ecological health cannot be measured by aesthetic standards alone.

It is interesting to note the power of cultural influences in determining public opinion about changing landscapes. In a number of countries where forests were long ago cleared for agriculture and grazing there is opposition to reforestation of those same lands. In Scotland, where the land has been deforested for centuries due to sheep grazing, many citizens are opposed to the establishment of new forests because they like the "natural" landscape of rock, heather, and grass. In parts of Germany there are nature conservation groups who want the forest cleared away for sheep so as to promote certain types of flowers that will not grow under the cover of trees. This is rationalized in terms of preserving the natural ecology of the region even though it was entirely forested in historical times. In Sweden one can see protest signs by the roadside stating "this beautiful meadow will be covered by a dark spruce forest if we do not stop it." Swedes have become familiar with the look of the land cleared for farming even though the natural condition was virtually total forest cover. This same attitude can be found in New Zealand where native forest was cleared for sheep during European colonization. Now some of these pastures are being planted with pine trees that originate in California. The pine trees are no more foreign than the sheep yet many people find the trees offensive whereas they are quite content with the sheep.

These examples tend to prove that change is often the common factor in determining public opinion about the beauty of landscapes. Once people become familiar with a particular use of the land they will resist its conversion to other uses even when this would result in conditions closer to the original ecology. Urban environments that are completely dominated by concrete structures can become perfectly acceptable, especially if there are a few exotic, decorative plants in view.

My boys made me stop and take a picture of this pumpkin patch. Even though it is a monoculture farm crop where there was once a lush forest of cottonwood, the very sight of it brings a smile to the face of children young and old.

It is clear that we must look beyond the immediate aesthetic impression of landscapes if we are to accurately judge their relative health as ecosystems. The clearcut looks ugly but it will soon begin recovery to a healthy, diverse forest ecosystem. The hayfield looks pleasant but it is a deforested area with little diversity and is dominated by exotic species of plants and animals.

The challenge for foresters and educators is to help give the general public a new pair of eyes with which to view landscapes. People must be given the tools to get beyond and behind the immediate visual impression and to understand some basic principles of ecology and science. These concepts are not all that difficult to grasp but they must be presented clearly because they are not intuitively obvious. It is my belief that this problem with aesthetics is the single largest obstacle to public understanding of forestry. If people pre-judge landscapes by how they look, no amount of technical or scientific information will convince them to change their opinion. If there is one thing I might accomplish with Green Spirit, it would be to help give readers that new pair of eyes.

If we cannot rely on our sense of beauty to tell us about ecological health what more reliable measures are there? In the next two chapters we will explore the ways in which biological diversity and other measurable factors can be used as indicators of the relative integrity of ecosystems.

Before moving into these topics, it's important to consider the principle of relativity as it applies to environmental issues. The simplest way to state that principle is: "There is no perfect ecosystem for any given landscape." While it is often possible to determine absolute values for, say, the number of deer living in a given area at a particular time, it is not possible to make an absolute judgment on whether or not this is the right number for that area. If the region is known to have supported deer and now there are none, concern may be warranted. If there are so many deer that they over-browse and destroy all the tree seedlings, it might be reasonable to conclude that there are too many deer. In between these extremes are a wide range of possibilities, none of which are necessarily ideal and many of which may be reasonable.

We have a tendency to idealize nature and to assume there is a perfect state of things that is the "natural" state for a given piece of land. The key to understanding nature is to realize that nothing in nature is permanent. All life changes through time in all places. No two environments are ever identical. It is a mistake to look for *the* natural condition of the land as there are many natural conditions; in a way all conditions are natural or they couldn't exist. There is no Garden of Eden in the sense of an original ecology that is the correct ecology for a given region.

While there is no such thing as a perfect ecology there are countless actual historical conditions ranging from volcanic destruction to lush forests to ice ages to deserts, all of which are perfectly natural. In many regions all of these environments will have prevailed at one time or another. Our judgments of the good or bad of given environmental situations must be tempered by these relatively large changes the land goes through in time. These changes occur with or without human involvement and cannot be foreseen in detail into the distant future. For the same reasons the weather cannot be predicted beyond about eight days it is impossible to determine future ecological conditions with much accuracy. There are too many variables, intertwined among each other, for a scientific proof of what will become of a particular place.

For me, the word that best sums up a common sense approach to ecology is "balance." Balance of human and non-human interests, balance of environment and economy, balance of reason and emotion. We cannot deny that we must consume to survive any more than we can deny that over-consumption would lead to our demise. A world without beauty is as unthinkable as a world without food, and a world without forests is as unthinkable as a day without wood. Finding the balance that allows all these apparent contradictions to exist is the challenge for modern thinkers. Absolutist or black-and-white approaches based on simplistic dogma will only compromise our ability to steer a sustainable course between human survival and general ecological health. There are no easy answers, only intelligent choices.

REFERENCES

1 Felice Page, Cultural Clearcuts: The Sociology of Timber Communities in the Pacific Northwest, in Clearcut, the Tragedy of Industrial Forestry San Francisco, Sierra Club Books/Earth Island Press, 1993.

2 Der Spiegel, "Pillagers of the North", Issue 46, November 15, 1993.

3 Devall, B. (Ed.) (1993). Clearcut: The tragedy of industrial forestry. San Francisco, CA: Sierra Club Books/Earth Island Press, 1993.

4 Hardin, Garrett. The Tragedy of the Commons, Science, 162:1243-1248, 1968.

Biological Diversity

Variety is the spice of life.
Anonymous

Throughout the ages students of nature have understood that some environments have more species and are more varied than others. Rainforests are richer in life than deserts. Coral reefs have many more species of fish than the abyss of the deep sea. While these differences were generally recognized it was not until recently that scientists began to measure and describe the diversity of ecosystems in a systematic fashion.

The term "biological diversity" or "biodiversity" is now widely used to indicate the variety of living things. In a general sense, biodiversity is used as a synonym for "nature" or "the living world". In a technical sense, biodiversity is used to describe a large number of situations in the environment.

One of the difficulties in understanding the concept of biological diversity is the fact that there are, so to speak, a diversity of diversities. In trying to keep it simple I have chosen only the three most important measures of diversity within living systems. These are genetic diversity, species diversity and landscape diversity.

Genetic diversity is an indicator of the degree of variation in the genetic make-up of individuals within a species. The basis of genetic differences is contained in the DNA in the genes of an individual organism. The genes are responsible for passing on the traits of the parents to the offspring during reproduction. Often, but not always, genetic differences can be seen in the features of the individual animal or plant. One of the best examples is the domestic dog. From the Chihuahua to the Great Dane, the great variety of breeds are all part of the same species, all derived from the wild wolf. Thousands of years of breeding by selecting particular traits has resulted in this amazing display of genetic diversity.[1] In humans, we recognize the expression of genetic diversity as differences such as those among races, facial features, and the color of eyes and hair. Underlying many of these differences are specific differences in the genetic material in the DNA of each person. Genetic diversity is higher in multi-racial communities than in communities of a single race.

Genetic diversity in humans, as in all species, is reduced, maintained, or increased depending on patterns of breeding over time. Inbreeding among members of the same family tree causes a reduction in genetic diversity. Outbreeding with new families and races causes an increase in genetic diversity.

Genetic diversity is not something you can measure by walking into a forest with a ruler and clipboard in hand. While the concept is based on theoretically measurable differences in DNA, in practice it is impossible to determine the full range of these differences for every species in a particular ecosystem. It is usually necessary to deal in generalities and comparative measures rather than actual measures of specific genetic differences. The factors affecting genetic diversity within a given species are themselves very diverse, ranging from the manner in which plant seeds are fertilized and dispersed to the social behavior of birds and mammals.

Species diversity is the type of biological diversity that most people would associate with the term. It is simply a count of the number of distinct species in a given ecosystem. This is fairly easy for the larger species of plants and animals but becomes a more difficult and expensive task if we want to count all the smaller and microscopic forms of insects, fungi, and bacteria that live in the trees and the soil. While the species count can give us a lot of useful information it doesn't tell us about the relative abundance of each species. That requires a count of the population of each species, an even more difficult task than cataloguing the number of species. Even if we knew all the species and their populations, meaningful comparisons within and among different ecosystems are not always easy to make.

Landscape diversity, also known as ecosystem diversity, refers to the variety of distinct ecosystems within a given landscape or geographic area. Some landscapes are very uniform such as the vast stretches of lodgepole pine forest growing back after wildfire. Other landscapes are more varied with a mosaic of different plant associations in close proximity. A more diverse landscape usually supports higher species diversity across that landscape. Landscape diversity is generally measured in comparative terms rather than numerically. There is no logical way to give an exact measure of the number of distinct ecosystems in a given landscape, or for that matter even to define "landscape" or "ecosystem" with precision. It is important to recognize that these terms are conceptual, they are not precise units of measurement.

All three types of biological diversity are relevant to the discussion of new forests growing back after logging. Comparisons of similarities and differences can be made between the diversity of the new forest and the one it has replaced. Comparisons are possible among new forests that have resulted from different types of disturbance such as fire, insect attack, and logging.

When they are young these Douglas-fir seedlings look identical but they have been collected and grown from a wide variety of wild trees and are therefore genetically diverse.

A forest dominated by a single tree species will often be more susceptible to catastrophic insect attack than one with a variety of tree species. The same is true of a forest where all the trees are the same age compared to a forest where there are patches of trees of different ages.

Environmentalists often contend that logging an old growth forest automatically results in the loss of biological diversity. This has become a major point in their campaigns to preserve forests in their native state. We are warned "Ecologically, clearcutting causes irreparable damage to biological diversity."[2] Unfortunately, this is one of those "half-truths" that makes it difficult to see the issue clearly.

Every individual of every species, when produced by sexual reproduction, is genetically unique. Therefore, every time an individual of any species dies, whether by disease, fire, volcanic eruption or logging, some genetic diversity is lost. It is equally true that every time an individual of any species is born that there is an increase in genetic diversity. So, it is true in a sense, that every time an ecosystem is disturbed there is a "loss" of biodiversity. It is equally true that as the ecosystem recovers from disturbance there is new biodiversity created.

The word "disturbance" is used by ecologists to mean relatively rapid change in an ecosystem. This always involves the death of individuals of some of the species in that ecosystem. But disturbance also creates the conditions necessary for new life to flourish. Fire sometimes kills nearly everything in its path and leaves the land barren, ready for new life to grow. Logging usually leaves many plants and animals alive but results in the death of others, particularly the trees! But so long as there is an abundant seed source either in the soil or in the surrounding forests, there will be no net loss of genetic diversity over time.

Considering this point in another way, if genetic diversity were permanently lost every time there was a major disturbance in an ecosystem, there wouldn't be much diversity left in this world. Disturbance is so common, even in the absence of human activity, that species must be able to flourish and maintain their diversity in the face of constant change. In fact, the conditions created by disturbance provide the opportunity for the development of new diversity.

Let us consider the three main types of biodiversity in more detail.

Genetic Diversity

There is no bush on the face of the globe exactly like another bush; there are no two trees in the forest whose boughs bend into the same network, nor two leaves on the same tree which could not be told one from the other.

John Ruskin, Modern Painters

For the multitude of plants, animals and insects living in British Columbia and Pacific Northwest forests, there is no reason to believe that logging or the many forms of natural disturbance result in a net loss of genetic diversity. The numerous species of ferns, mosses, lichen, and fungi are so prolific and widespread that it is hard to imagine inbreeding or temporary local loss of habitat as a serious threat. For the trees and other plants there are nearly always some seeds or seedlings ready to spring back to replace the old forest. These contain the genetic material of their parents. Most birds, mammals, and other animals either escape to surrounding forest or adapt to the new environment. Some species, such as salamanders, will survive in reduced numbers initially but there is no evidence that their genetic diversity is lost as they eventually recover in the new forest. Other species, such as field mice, will increase in numbers after logging but there is no reason to suspect significant change in the genetic make-up of the population.

There is a notion among some environmentalists that when native forests are cut and replaced by tree seedlings grown in nurseries that there is a loss of genetic diversity in the newly planted forest.[3] The uniform appearance of nursery seedlings suggests to the observer that they are genetically identical. In fact, in most cases in Pacific Northwest forests there is actually an increase in the genetic diversity of the planted tree species when harvested areas are replanted with seedlings grown in nurseries.[4]

When an area of forest is cleared of trees by fire, windstorm, or logging, and left to regenerate on its own, the new forest will be composed mainly of trees from seed that was on the site or blown in from trees growing close by. This means that a certain amount of inbreeding will occur over time and the trees in a given area will tend to be related to one another. When seedlings from nurseries are used they are from seeds that were collected over a far wider area than the area that is replanted. The strategy in nursery production is to increase genetic diversity by outbreeding and to use selective breeding to enhance desirable traits such as growth rate and disease resistance. As a result, there is usually a higher genetic diversity in a given species that is planted than in the same species that is naturally regenerated.

The use of the word 'genetic' is often confusing because there are so many ways of influencing the genetic composition of an individual or population. The impression is sometimes given that plantation seedlings have been "genetically engineered" when this is not the case. Most genetic work with trees simply involves controlled breeding programs using normal sexual reproduction by fertilizing seeds with pollen. The only difference between this and what occurs in the wild is the conscious effort to avoid inbreeding while at the same time selecting individuals with desirable traits.

Another word that is often misinterpreted is 'clone'. The term tends to conjure up images of test-tube babies and armies of androids ruled by evil masters. As it is applied to the breeding of plants and trees, the use of clones is not quite so sensational. Anyone who has taken a cutting from a house-plant and rooted it in a glass of water has created a clone. Much of agriculture and horticulture has always been based on the use of cloning in order to ensure uniformity of food and garden plants. All the beautiful varieties of roses and rhododendrons are the result of first breeding and then cloning the desired offspring. Staple foods such as potatoes are also grown using cloning techniques. With cloning there is a real potential to reduce genetic diversity as each clone is genetically identical to the other. This is easily avoided by appropriate selection of clones and planting programs.

Reforestation is supported by seed orchards such as this one in Washington State where trees are bred for desirable qualities such as rapid growth, disease resistance, and hardiness.

The use of clones is not nearly as common in forestry as in food and garden plants but there are some notable examples where this technique is used. The most advanced and widespread use of cloning in forestry is practiced with eucalyptus in tropical and sub-tropical climates. While all species of eucalyptus originally derive from Australia, some are now grown for timber production in many other parts of the world including Brazil, Chile, Portugal, and California. The most successful programs involve highly controlled breeding and cloning through rooted cuttings. The result has been a very high quality of wood and phenomenal growth rates.

In the Pacific Northwest there are two tree species that are cloned for forest planting. The largest program involves hybrid poplar trees that are grown on river flood plains for pulpwood. At a more experimental stage there are field trials underway with yellow-cedar (Alaska-cedar) in south-coastal British Columbia. In all tree cloning programs a great deal of attention is paid to ensuring genetic diversity both in breeding stock and in the production forest by using clones from a large number of parent plants.

Species Diversity

The impact of major disturbance on species diversity is a very different subject than the impact on genetic diversity. When a forest is severely burned or clearcut a large number of species are temporarily eliminated or drastically reduced in number on the site. In this sense it is possible to state that logging results in extensive temporary loss of biological diversity, as this is a fact for species diversity in the immediate aftermath of the disturbance. Indeed, the relative severity of a disturbance, either human or non-human in origin, is often best measured by the degree of species-loss immediately following the event.

While it is one thing to note the loss of species diversity at the time and place of a disturbance, it is quite another to determine the total impact on species diversity over time and over the entire landscape. The impression that logging invariably causes permanent loss of species diversity is widespread despite the fact that this is not so. In many cases forestry actually results in an increase in species diversity on the disturbed site as well as an overall increase in species diversity over the landscape.[5]

As with beauty, species diversity begins to increase shortly after a major disturbance, the time required being dependent on the condition of the soil, availability of seed, and severity of climate. In many cases the diversity of plant species will surpass that of the original forest within a few years of disturbance. This is due to the many light-loving and light-requiring plants that soon invade areas that lose their forest cover. This includes many species of trees, in particular pioneer hardwoods such as alder, maple, birch, aspen, cottonwood, and willow.

This early stage of forest recovery, described earlier as a "temporary meadow," is characterized by a proliferation of flowering and fruit-bearing plants. Some common examples of these are fireweed, pearly everlasting, blueberries and huckleberries, salmon berry, salal, elderberries, grasses, asters, lupines, and thimbleberry. In general, the wetter and milder the climate the richer the vegetation that grows in to renew the disturbance left by landslide, logging, or firestorm. In drier forests, such as those found in the interior, grasses predominate. On the coast and in moist high elevations there is lusher growth with a great number of mosses, herbs, and shrubs in the mix.

As much as in any old forest, the power of this natural process of renewal shows the resilience and apparent determination of ecosystems to recreate themselves. The beauty and diversity of a mature forest can be appreciated instantly as can the stark contrast of the clearcut. These images are communicated easily with snapshots in time, reinforcing the perception of nature as static. The impression often conveyed by environmentalists is that as surely as the old forest will always remain beautiful the clearcut will never recover from total destruction.

The appreciation of the healing process whereby diversity returns is not gained so easily. It is necessary to watch the change over time; to revisit the same site as it develops; to feel the progression of the seasons. There is really no substitute for the sight, smell, sound, and feel of the environment as it transforms over the years from an apparent wasteland to a lush forested landscape. It is extremely difficult to communicate this experience in written words or even in multi-media presentations. What is probably needed is a time-lapse photography sequence (similar to those familiar ones of flowers opening to sun) summing up decades of forest development. While this is not practical due to the long time frame of forest growth, the new digital technologies could be used to produce a virtual forest, shrinking 100 years into 60 seconds.

The way land is managed (or mismanaged) can permanently reduce species diversity. Converting a forest to a large oil refinery complex with attendant petrochemical and plastic industries does this quite thoroughly. In a less extreme case the removal of native vegetation for agricultural production eliminates most of the species present in the original environment. By contrast, even intensively managed forests continue to provide habitat for many native species of plants, animals, and birds. In the Pacific Northwest the low-intensity style of forest management has had even less impact on species diversity but it has changed their pattern of distribution and relative abundance.[6]

A gray jay, known as "Whiskey Jack" by woodsmen, poses on a young mountain hemlock in a clearcut full of new growth.

To understand why this is so, it is necessary to consider the way forests have been managed. A number of factors have contributed to the pattern of development of forested lands and the composition of the new forests growing back after logging.

Where they have been allowed to grow back on their own, our new forests are very similar to the original forests partly due to the lack of intervention after logging. In most areas the second growth has been given the chance to grow back exactly as it would after any major disturbance. In areas where trees have been planted they are nearly always the same species that were on the site originally. Other native tree species and the large number of local mosses, ferns, herbs, and shrubs are free to move back onto the site as time passes. In a relatively small area, vegetation is controlled by herbicides and mechanical weeding in order to give the trees enough light to get started and get above competing vegetation. Replanting with large tree seedlings immediately after harvesting has proven effective in reducing reliance on chemicals.

We can also be thankful that the European and Asian pioneers of western North America were less fond of sheep and goats than many of their predecessors in their native lands. It would have been, and still is, perfectly feasible to deforest vast tracts of low- and mid-elevation land for grazing domestic animals. Partly because large areas of the land base are publicly owned, and partly due to the commercial value of western softwood species, a larger percentage of the land remains in forest than in most parts of the world.

We have been fortunate in North America to learn from the successes and failures in regions where forests have been cut for centuries. Our ancestors recognized relatively early the benefits of protecting large areas of forest land as wilderness. The national parks systems in both the United States and Canada have been particularly effective in protecting western forests. More recently the growing concern that additional areas need to be protected is leading to further protection of many areas of National Forest in the US Pacific Northwest and a doubling of parks and wilderness areas in British Columbia (to 12 percent of the land). In both regions it has been possible to protect large areas of forest that have never been logged or developed. This system of protected areas in itself largely guarantees the survival of species diversity in the protected areas. Equally important, the protected areas are a reservoir of genetic and species diversity that can re-colonize managed areas around them.

The lack of such large protected areas is responsible for much of the reduction in species diversity in other parts of the world. In Europe, urban and farm development has virtually eliminated large predators such as wolves and bears, and reduced other species of birds, animals, and plants. These losses have resulted from forest habitat reductions and from officially sanctioned hunting. Significantly, Europeans have retained large grazing animals like moose and deer because they have purposefully made sure they were not eliminated. They valued these animals as a source of food and today it is much more common to find venison on restaurant menus in Europe than in North America. If Europeans had earlier valued large predators and old growth dependent species as much as we do today these species would still be abundant on the Continent.

In recent years, European foresters and environmentalists have realized they can learn something about protecting species diversity by studying the North American example. They have launched a movement to increase protection of critical habitats and to reform forestry practices to ensure survival of species that suffer from intensively managed monoculture plantations. As hard as Europeans may try, it will be difficult to reverse the impact of centuries of over-exploitation. There is a good possibility, though, that species not yet extinct can be brought back to healthy populations.

In the Pacific Northwest of the United States and Canada we are fortunate in having many species of native trees that are suitable for forestry. There are more than 20 species of coniferous trees and about a dozen hardwoods that are commercially valuable and readily grown. This means there is little incentive to grow exotic species for the timber or pulp and paper industries. Compare this to New Zealand where not one of the many native tree species is suitable for forestry, mainly because they are so slow growing. Consequently, the forest industry in New Zealand is based on vast plantations of radiata pine, a species imported from California, resulting in a commercial forest very different from the original native forest.

In northern Europe there are far fewer commercially valuable native tree species. Even so it has been possible to develop a successful forest economy based primarily on native trees. In Germany there are extensive Norway spruce and Scots pine plantations in a region that was originally a mixed forest of predominantly beech, oak and other hardwoods. Many people consider the spruce and pine forests to be unnatural even though these species are abundant to the north in the forests of Scandinavia. Sweden has extensive plantations of lodgepole pine grown from seed collected in northern British Columbia. Lodgepole pine is similar to the native Scots pine but grows about 50 percent faster. Some Swedish environmental groups are against the importation of lodgepole pine on the basis that it is an exotic species.

In western North America the diversity of tree species as well as other plant and animal species is richer than in any other temperate forest on the planet. So far as we know there is no exotic tree species that would perform better for forestry than the native species. It would certainly be possible to establish plantations of many exotic trees ranging from eastern North American hardwoods such as red oak to Chinese larch to cedars from Lebanon. This has not been done, mainly because the native species are seen as superior for providing fast growth and desirable characteristics. The more recent environmental arguments about maintaining native ecology will no doubt ensure that in future, only native trees are planted on public lands in North America.

All of the above factors add up to a style of forestry that has without a doubt produced new forests that are as close to the original as any other region on earth where forestry is practiced. No known species has gone extinct primarily due to forestry in the Pacific Northwest, or for that matter, in North America. Species that have suffered, such as grizzly bears and wolves, have borne the brunt of agricultural and urban development as well as over-hunting and eradication efforts. There are no biological reasons to prevent grizzlies and wolves from being re-introduced to forested areas from which they have been eliminated. The recent success in re-introducing wolves to Yellowstone National Park clearly demonstrates this. The opposition to such efforts is social and political and stems from concerns that re-introduction of predators will cause economic damage to livestock.

Landscape Diversity

Modern forest management and logging sometimes increases landscape diversity. In turn, higher landscape diversity generally leads to higher species diversity. The following section explains how and why this can occur.

Landscape diversity, often called ecosystem diversity, is an expression of the variability of ecosystem types over an area of land. Whereas the idea of species diversity is reasonably well defined, landscape diversity is a much more general concept. There is no precise definition of a "landscape" or an "ecosystem" as there is for an individual species. A landscape is usually defined as an expanse of scenery that can be seen in a single view. This can vary greatly depending on the topography and where one is standing. An ecosystem is an even more general concept and can range from a small pool to an entire watershed or even a large group of watersheds. Despite the generality of the concept, landscape diversity is a very important indicator of overall biological diversity.

If a given forested landscape is very uniform over a large area in terms of species, topography, the age of the forest, and so on; it can be described as low in landscape diversity. In many interior valleys there are vast expanses of lodgepole pine forests where the trees are all the same age. These landscapes have usually resulted from a fire that swept through the area which then grew back as an even-aged forest dominated by a single pioneer tree species.

If a landscape is composed of a mosaic of many different mixtures of species and many age classes then it is high in landscape diversity. In many areas the topography and history combine to produce a much more varied pattern of tree associations and age classes. Rapid change of elevation in mountainous regions results in a change of species with altitude. Many small disturbances over time from fire and wind produce patches of forest of different ages. Dry exposed areas support a different variety of vegetation than wet areas. Even more variety is added by a landscape dotted with lakes and bogs.

In general an area of higher landscape diversity will also have higher species diversity. This is simply because there are more kinds of habitat available to support various species where there are a larger variety of forest types and age classes. Modern forest management and timber harvesting, as noted earlier, often increase landscape diversity because of a number of factors, the most significant being the suppression of large forest fires and the pattern of logging.

Before the introduction of effective fire fighting it was more common for fires caused by lightening and human carelessness to sweep through vast areas of dry forest. The forests that grew back after these fires were often uniform and dominated by pioneer species of trees nearly all the same age. In contrast, the widespread uniformity of rainforests along the outer west coast is due to these areas being undisturbed for hundreds of years, mainly because they are too wet to burn even in the driest of summers. This resulted in landscapes dominated by old growth forests of cedar and hemlock with very few open areas.

In both the dry interior forests and the wet coastal forests one of the effects of forestry has been the creation of a more patchy looking landscape. Viewed from an aircraft this can give a somewhat tattered appearance that is not as pleasing to the eye as a continuous sea of green. This is another case where the look of the land is not necessarily a good indicator of the state of the ecosystem. The mosaic appearance caused by logging results in a much more diverse landscape with many different age classes of forest and many open areas where light loving species that can't live in the shade find a place to grow. In some areas the history of logging and forest renewal has resulted in higher populations of deer, black bear, wolf, and cougar than were present before forests were cut for timber. The increase in wildlife numbers is due largely to the opening up of some of the forest to sunlight, thus providing forage on the ground for deer and bear and in turn more prey for wolves and cougar.

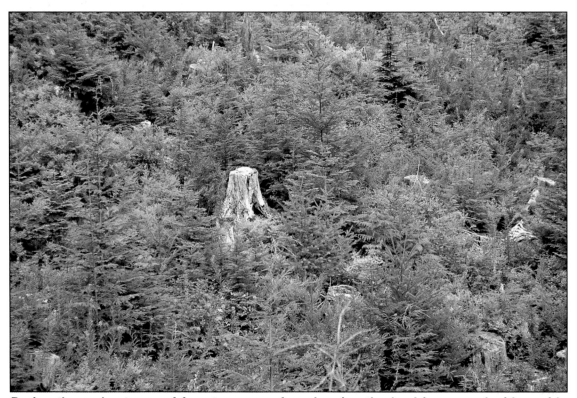

During the early stages of forest recovery from logging the land is covered with a wide variety of shrubs, many of which produce berries that provide food for birds, animals and insects.

Two points of exception should be noted here. One is the practice of "progressive clearcutting" where the clearcut begins at one end of a valley and progresses continuously to the other. This form of clearcutting was practiced extensively in coastal forests over the years and was still the method used in some areas until the late 1980s. It was not uncommon that areas in excess of 1,000 hectares (2,500 acres) would be clearcut in three to five years. Progressive clearcutting does not result in the same increase in landscape diversity that can occur when clearcuts are smaller and surrounded by standing forests of various stages of development. When clearcuts are made continuously they are closer in their impact to a large forest fire as they remove all the forest over a large area in a relatively short time. This form of clearcutting is no longer practiced so it can be expected that future landscapes will continue to become more diverse as a result of forest management.

The second point concerns the importance of maintaining habitat that is critical to certain species. The most well known example is the need to protect some older, low elevation forest, for deer and elk winter range. During winters of heavy snowfall the forage for deer and elk is covered so the only food available are lichens growing on the trunks of older trees. The practice of leaving areas of forest at low elevation as winter range for these animals has been successful in maintaining healthy populations. The increase in forage in the clearcuts when it is available during the rest of the year and in mild winters has added to this success.

There are a number of other examples of critical habitats ranging from standing dead trees, required as nesting sites by woodpeckers and owls, to clean streams required by spawning salmon. Some species, such as black bears, seem happy to live in every type of forest and can eat nearly anything including berries, skunk cabbage roots, anthills, and fresh or rotten meat. Other species, such as salmon, have an absolute need for clean gravel spawning beds in streams with clear fresh water or their eggs will not survive.

When discussing landscape diversity it is essential to consider the subject of forest fragmentation. There is a concern that some species will suffer if the original forest is changed to a patchwork of clearcuts and forests. The metaphor often used is that logging results in "islands" of forest surrounded by a sea of clearcuts.[7] Related to this is the concern about the number of edges between forest and open areas that are created by clearcutting. There is evidence that some species of birds suffer heavier predation by other birds along the edge of forest than in the forest's interior.

In order to determine the relevance of these concepts to the Pacific Northwest, and North America in general, it is important to understand their origin. Conservation biologists have correctly determined that tropical deforestation has resulted in species loss due to the conversion of vast areas to agricultural use. This has left relatively small fragments of original forest surrounded by large areas of farm crops and grazing lands. The biologists have noted that as these forest fragments become smaller, fewer and fewer species are able to survive in them. This is particularly true for the big predators that need a large territory to support a viable breeding population. To study this problem further a lot of research has been done on islands surrounded by ocean to verify the idea that the smaller the island the fewer species it will support. The theory of "island biogeography" has resulted from these investigations which demonstrated a direct correlation between island area and species number.

Some environmental campaigners have used this idea to suggest that forest management in the Pacific Northwest is creating a situation similar to that caused by tropical deforestation and by islands in the sea. Despite the fact that there is no real evidence of species loss due to clearcutting the idea has made sense to many people and is even taken for granted as true by many environmentalists. Environmental philosophy professor, Alan Drengson, confirms this inaccurate impression when he states that: "The temperate and tropical forests are among the most complex and biologically diverse areas on the Earth. Industrial forestry destroys almost all of this complexity and genetic diversity."[8]

Again, there is confusion caused by the way things look as opposed to the way they really are. The metaphor of the "island" cannot be applied directly to forests that are next to clearcuts growing new forests in the same way it can to forests surrounded by seawater or even agricultural land. The logged area is not an inhospitable place for most forest animals. Many native plants prefer the open sun; some cannot live without it. Ocean water truly is a foreign environment for most island-dwelling plants and animals, except certain seabirds and marine mammals. Cleared agricultural land is not suitable habitat for most forest species although mice and rabbits live quite happily on the farm. Logged areas, by contrast, provide forage for many birds and animals and offer no barrier to travel for deer, bear, cougar, or any other animal. More important, the cleared areas are in the process of becoming forests once again whereas farmland may not and oceans never will.

It is true that major forest disturbance by any means including clearcutting results in an alteration in the distribution and population of many species. Some plants and animals will decrease in numbers while other will increase. Some patterns of landscape diversity will be changed and some species will find it more difficult to flourish on the edges of forest and clearing. If there are more hardwood trees growing back in a clearcut than there were in the original forest it goes without saying that there will be less conifers as there is only so much room for trees to grow. If the edge of a forest favors a certain species of predatory bird then there will be more pressure on its prey species. These changes in the relative abundance of species do not mean that any species will disappear altogether from the landscape. In a properly managed forest, one that includes reserves of old growth forest, no species should be eliminated but many will be affected over time and space, as they would be by other forms of disturbance even if humans never existed.

Endangered Species and Extinction

In March 1996, the World Wide Fund for Nature, known as the World Wildlife Fund in North America, (WWF) held a media conference in Geneva, Switzerland, during the first meeting of the United Nations Intergovernmental Panel on Forests. They stated that there are now 50,000 species going extinct every year due to human activity, more than at any time since the dinosaurs went extinct 65 million years ago. Most significantly, WWF stated that the main cause of these extinctions is "commercial logging".[9] This was largely due, according to WWF director-general Claude Martin, to "massive deforestation in industrialized countries." The statements made at the media conference were broadcast and printed around the world, giving millions of people the impression that forestry was the main cause of species extinction.

I have tried to determine the basis for this allegation, openly challenging the WWF to provide details of species extinctions caused by logging. To date it would appear that there is no scientific evidence on which to base such a claim. WWF has provided no list of species that have become extinct due to logging. In particular, the claim of "massive deforestation" in industrialized countries runs counter to information provided by the Food and Agriculture Organization of the United Nations. According to the FAO, the area of forest in the industrialized world is actually growing by about 0.2% per year, due to the reforestation of land that was previously cleared for farming.[10]

In May 1996, I wrote to Prince Philip, the Duke of Edinburgh, in his capacity as President of WWF. I stated in part:

"Myself and many colleagues who specialize in forest science are distressed at recent statements made by WWF regarding the environmental impact of forestry. These statements indicate a break with WWF's strong tradition of basing their policies on science and reason. To the best of our knowledge, not a single species has become extinct in North America due to forestry."[11]

Prince Philip replied:

"I have to admit I did not see the draft of the statement that (WWF spokesperson) Jean-Paul Jeanrenaud was to make at the meeting of the Intergovernmental Panel on Forestry in Geneva. The first two of his comments (50,000 species per year and the dinosaur comparison) are open to question, but they are not seriously relevant to the issue. However, I quite agree that his third

statement (logging being the main cause of extinction) *is certainly contentious and the points that you make are all good ones. All I can say is that he was probably thinking of tropical forests when he made the comment.*"[12]

Since this exchange of correspondence, WWF has changed the way they characterize the impact of forestry in relation to species extinction. At their "Forests for Life" conference in San Francisco in May 1997, there was no mention made of forestry being the main cause of species extinction. Instead, WWF unveiled a report stating that *"three quarters of the continent's forest ecoregions are threatened with extinction, showing for the first time that it is not just individual species but entire ecosystems that are at risk in North America."*[13] The word 'extinction' is normally used to mean that something has been completely eliminated. It is entirely beyond reason to suggest that three quarters of the forested areas of North America will become 'extinct' yet this is what WWF is proclaiming to the public.

In August 1998, again using a United Nations forest conference as a platform, WWF held a media conference at which they declared that 8,753 species of trees, 10% of the world total, are "endangered with extinction".[14] This statement was based on a report titled "World List of Threatened Trees" produced by the World Conservation Monitoring Center with funding from the Dutch government. A reading of the report reveals that of the 8,753 tree species that WWF declared "endangered with extinction", fully 6,969 are not classified as 'endangered' but rather as 'vulnerable', 'lower risk', or 'data deficient'.[15]

Two days after the WWF press conference a feature story appeared in the largest British Columbia daily newspaper declaring that "Three Trees Native to BC Face Extinction".[16] The three species named were; a variety of mountain hemlock, whitebark pine, and western yew. None of these species is actually listed as endangered in the report. The mountain hemlock is listed as 'data deficient', western yew as 'lower risk', and whitebark pine as 'vulnerable' due to an outbreak of fungus that is killing many of the trees in part of their natural range. In a subsequent newspaper article the Chief Forester for British Columbia stated that "The report doesn't define any of the B.C. species as in danger of extinction the way the news article noted. So to imply they are at risk of extinction is absolutely incorrect."[17] A spokesperson for WWF responded to the Chief Forester, stating "Inevitably some flexibility slips in."[18]

The credibility of the entire report is brought into question by the inclusion of species such as the California redwood and the giant sequoia. They are listed as 'lower risk' and 'vulnerable', respectively. It is hard to imagine how anyone could interpret the California redwood or the giant sequoia to be at the slightest risk of extinction. Redwood is prolific and flourishes in the coastal zone from southern Oregon to Big Sur, California. The giant sequoia is heavily protected throughout its natural range in the Sierra Nevada mountains, and is grown extensively on streets and in parks and gardens from southern California to northern Vancouver Island.

WWF is not the only environmental group that has greatly exaggerated the extent of endangerment and extinction of species. In June 1997, Greenpeace released a report at the United Nations Earth Summit 2 in New York that predicts "mass extinctions" and the loss of 50% of the species in British Columbia under current land use policies.[19] Authored by an environmental studies professor from the University of California, Santa Cruz, the report uses island biogeography theory to support these claims. One of the principles of the theory is that if an island is reduced to 10% of its original size it will only be capable of supporting 50% of the species that were supported by the larger island. The Greenpeace report concludes that if only 12% of British Columbia is totally protected as parks and wilderness areas that these will be the only "islands" of biodiversity. In other words, Greenpeace is assuming that the other 88% of the land will have zero value for biodiversity, as if it were all paved with asphalt. This is obviously absurd as less than 5% of BC has been converted to settlement and farms, the remainder is either in managed native forest or wilderness where there will always be high biodiversity values.

Most recently, Greenpeace has launched a campaign to halt logging in what it calls "The Great Bear Rainforest" on the Central Coast of British Columbia. The campaign is squarely based on allegations that "BC's coastal grizzlies will likely face extinction in the next four decades if logging operations continue to move north up the coast" and "142 stocks of salmon are now extinct" and that logging is "a primary threat" to the remaining stocks.[20] The report does not mention that logging has been taking place on the Central Coast for over 100 years or that, according to the BC Ministry of Environment logging will "have no significant impact on grizzly bear populations."[21]

It is true that 142 stocks of the 9,663 known stocks of migratory salmon and trout in British Columbia and the Yukon are considered extinct. It is also true that all but three of these stocks were either in the populated southwest corner of BC or in the Columbia River watershed where hydro dams were the cause of extinction.[22] Nearly half of them were in what is now the city of Vancouver, where the former spawning creeks have been replaced with drainage pipes. Only one of the 142 extinct stocks is in the Central Coast and there is no evidence to link that stock's demise with logging. Even the author's of the report conclude "the largest proportion of the 142 extinctions we note resulted from urbanization and hydropower development."[23] An exhaustive review of the factors influencing declines of fish stocks in the Strait of Georgia concluded that the main causes are overfishing, climate change, and urban development.[24] The report did find that logging practices had contributed to habitat loss but concluded "Now that logging standards are improved under the Forest Practices Code, it is unlikely that the type of logging-related habitat change documented . . . will be a continuing problem in the Strait of Georgia in particular, and for British Columbia generally."

The campaigns to link forestry with species extinction have been very successfully communicated through the media to the general public. The release of each report or announcement is carefully orchestrated to reach media outlets like Associated Press, CNN, and the BBC. The result is a public, often trusting in the major environmental groups, that thinks species are going extinct by the thousands and that forestry is the main culprit.

Where did WWF and other environmental groups get the idea that species were going extinct at the rate of 50,000 per year or 137 per day? It seems that this estimate stems from the work of Edward O. Wilson of Harvard University who is widely quoted as the expert on the subject.[25] Wilson's reasoning goes something like this:

Scientists have recorded and named about 1.7 million species. There are probably many more species, particularly in tropical forests, that have not been discovered, possibly as many as 50 million in all. Forests are being cleared, mainly for agriculture, and this is surely causing species to go extinct. Using the theory of island biogeography, in a computer model, as many as 50,000 species are calculated to be going extinct each year.

The problem with this theory is that the species are going extinct in a computer model and there is little actual evidence of these hypothetical extinctions in the real world. WWF takes the speculation a step further. Forestry is taking place in areas where biodiversity it richest; they argue, therefore forestry must be the main cause of biodiversity loss. They fail to consider another possibility; that the reason those areas where forestry occurs are so rich in biodiversity is because forestry causes less damage to biodiversity than other types of land use.

It is true that our species has caused the extinction of hundreds of other species. The primary causes of species extinction are quite well documented, with real lists of real species that have disappeared due to human activity. There are three broad categories into which most human-caused extinctions fall:

Over-hunting and Eradication. Many extinctions have been caused by the use of clubs, spears and guns. When humans first arrived in the Western Hemisphere over 10,000 years ago, a major extinction event followed in which many large mammals were hunted into oblivion. This pattern has been recorded in many parts of the world, most recently when the

Maoris arrived in New Zealand 1800 years ago and caused the extinction of many species, including the moas, a group of large ostrich-like birds. In North America the passenger pigeon and the Carolinian parakeet were hunted to extinction in the 19th century.

Introduced Predators and Diseases. When Europeans arrived in Australia, New Zealand, and the other Pacific Islands including Hawaii, they brought rats, cats, foxes, other domestic animals and their diseases. The result was the extinction of large numbers of flightless birds and ground-dwelling marsupials as well as other animals and plants. This is probably the largest single cause of extinction in modern times. It is interesting to note that despite the tremendous amount of development in the continental United States, only four of more than 200 species of birds have become extinct since European colonization. In Hawaii, on the other hand, at least 23 species of birds have become extinct in the past 200 years, largely due to introduced predators and diseases.[26] This highlights the vulnerability of species on islands that have been isolated from the continents for millions of years. Nearly all these bird extinctions occurred prior to 1900 before there was widespread concern for species conservation.

Vast Clearance of Forests for Agriculture. When large areas of forest or native grassland are cleared for farming the habitat is permanently altered. Many species, particularly plants, are unable to survive the conversion of the land. Some plant species occupy a fairly narrow range of habitats and can be completely displaced by large-scale agriculture. Western Australia, where the Department of Conservation and Land Management has documented extinctions, provides a good example. In the Swan River Coastal Plain, where 80% of the forest has been cleared for agriculture and urban development, 26 species have become extinct. In the Wheatbelt, where 90% of the original vegetation has been cleared, 43 species have disappeared. In the State Forests, where only two percent of the land has been permanently cleared but large areas are used for timber production, only one species has become extinct. This species, Lewin's water rail, lived in swamps and was extinct by 1932, before extensive forestry operations began. It was presumably exterminated by introduced foxes and cats.[27]

There can be no doubt that human activity has caused, and continues to cause, the extinction of species. Given the magnitude of land conversion to agriculture combined with the high species diversity in the tropics, it's almost certain there is a loss of species diversity there. But it is not valid to transfer this assumption to the Pacific Northwest where no massive deforestation is taking place. Our new forests are similar to the ones they have replaced and provide similar habitats for the species that have lived in them for millennia. There is no valid reason to assume that species extinction, whether of known or unknown species, is occurring in forests in this region of the world. Indeed, this would seem to apply to most, if not all, of North America.

We have probably discovered most of the species of large animals, birds, reptiles, amphibians, fish and plants. But it is certain there are species of insects and other microscopic life in our forests that we have not yet discovered. This likelihood puts foresters at a disadvantage when they are accused of causing the extinction of as yet undiscovered species. They can't prove these unknown species aren't in the forest and a concerned public may well think it wise to err on the side of caution.

This highlights the importance of maintaining wilderness reserves as sanctuaries for possible unknown species as well as those we have discovered. It also highlights the need to make decisions based on demonstrable facts rather than emotional claims.

I have been a subscriber to National Geographic since my father first gave it to me as a gift when I was in school. I have always looked forward to the latest edition, with all the wonders of the world between its covers. Lately, however, even this stalwart of objective science has fallen prey to the prophets of doom who believe a human-caused "mass extinction" is already underway.

The February, 1999 special edition on Biodiversity – The Fragile Web, contained a particularly unfortunate article titled "The Sixth Extinction".[28] This refers to the fact that there have been five main extinction events during the past 500 million years, the two most severe of which are believed to have been caused by meteor impacts. It may well be that all five were of extra-terrestrial origin. During the most recent mass extinction, 65 million years ago, 17 per cent of all the taxonomic families of life were lost, including the dinosaurs. An even greater extinction occurred 250 million years ago when 54 per cent of all families perished, including the trilobites. (*family* is a term used in taxonomy, two levels up from individual species, for example the cat family, the lily family, and the hummingbird family. Each family contains many, sometimes hundreds, of individual species).

The first two pages of the article contain a photo of Australian scientist, Dr. Tim Flannery, looking over a collection of stuffed and pickled small extinct mammals. The caption under the photo reads: "In the next century half of all species could be annihilated, as were these mammals seen in Tim Flannery's lab at the Australian Museum. Unlike the past five, this mass extinction is being fueled by humans." To be sure, mention is made later in the article that the Australian extinctions were caused by the introduction of cats and foxes when Europeans colonized the region over 200 years ago. This resulted in the loss of about 35 animal species,[29] mainly of flightless birds and ground-dwelling marsupials that were not able to defend themselves against these new predators. This is hardly a "mass extinction" and the cause was a one-time introduction of exotic species. The rate of extinction of Australian mammals has slowed considerably in recent decades, partly because the most vulnerable species are already extinct, and partly because people started caring about endangered species and began working to prevent them from going extinct. In Australia today there are programs to control wild cats and foxes, some of which have resulted in the recovery of native animal populations.

The use of the Australian example to justify claims that we are experiencing a mass extinction is put into focus by Brian Groombridge, editor of the IUCN* Red List of Threatened Species when he states, "around 75% of recorded extinctions . . . have occurred on islands. Very few extinctions have been recorded in continental tropical forest habitat, where mass extinction events are predicted to be underway."[30] It is clearly misleading to point to the specific and exceptional case of extinctions caused by the introduction of new species to islands as evidence of a worldwide mass extinction. The National Geographic article goes on to quote biologist Stuart Pimm; "It's not just species on islands or in rain forests or just birds or big charismatic mammals. It's everything and its everywhere. It is a worldwide epidemic of extinctions." Yet nearly every example used in the article involves islands such as Australia and Tasmania, Mauritius, Easter Island, and the many islands of the South Pacific.

On pages 48 and 49 of the Sixth Extinction article there is a graph depicting the number of taxonomic families that have existed on earth for the past 600 million years. The graph shows that despite the five great extinctions that have occurred during this period, the number of living families has risen steadily, from around 200 families 500 million years ago to over 1,000 families today. This tendency to diversify over time is one of the major features of evolution. The line of the graph is a thick, solid one until it reaches the present day whereupon it turns abruptly downward as if to indicate a loss of families due to the "mass extinction" now underway. But the line does not remain thick and solid, it turns fuzzy right at the point where it turns down. I wrote to National Geographic and asked "Why does the line turn fuzzy? Is it because there are actually no known families that have become extinct in recent times? I do not know of any families of 'beetles, amphibians, birds and large mammals' that have become extinct as implied in the text."

The reply to my inquiry came from Robin Adler, one of the researchers who worked on the article. She thanked me for "sharing my thoughts on this complicated and controversial issue" but offered no answer to my question about the graph. Instead she asked me to "Rest assured that

---

* The International Union for the Conservation of Nature and Natural Resources.

. . . the many members of our editorial team . . .worked closely with numerous experts in conservation biology, paleobiology, and related fields. The concept of a "sixth extinction" is widely discussed and, for the most part, strongly supported by our consultants and other experts in these areas, although specific details such as the time frame in which it will occur and the number of species that will be affected continues to be debated."

Nowhere in the National Geographic article is there any mention that the "sixth extinction" is a controversial subject; it is presented as if it is a known fact. It is clear from the reply that the "mass extinction" is actually in the future ("the time frame in which it **will** occur"). In other words there is no evidence that a mass extinction is actually occurring now, even though the article plainly implies that it is. The reply also refers to the sixth extinction as a "concept" implying that it is just an idea rather than a proven fact. Perhaps a better title for the article would have been "No Mass Extinction Yet, Maybe Someday."

It is very frustrating when a trusted institution such as the National Geographic resorts to sensationalism, exaggeration, and misleading illustrations. There is enough bad science and misinformation in the popular press as it is. One can only hope that the present tendency to ignore science and logic, rightly referred to as a "bad intellectual climate" by environmental philosopher Henry H. Webster, will eventually come to an end.[31]

The Spotted Owl

Species diversity cannot be discussed today without mention of the spotted owl. This little night hunter has become the symbol of forest preservation in the US Pacific Northwest. It has provided the legal basis for a major reduction in logging in the National Forests, large tracts of public land controlled from Washington, DC. The spotted owl is listed as a "threatened" species under US legislation, one step away from "endangered." As a result the species qualifies for protection under the Endangered Species Act. This has led to a virtual shutting down of logging in many National Forests, despite the fact that they were originally established as areas where forestry would be one of the main activities. In the early 1990's, about 30,000 forest workers lost their jobs due to the concern that the spotted owl would become extinct if logging continued.

This is a classic case of a species that has been deemed to be absolutely dependent on old growth forest. The theory is that each pair of owls requires about 3,500 acres (1,500 hectares) of old growth forest to survive and that logging any old growth will result in a reduction in the population. As this contravenes the Endangered Species Act it has been successfully argued in court that logging should be curtailed.

The restrictions on logging and the debate about the owl have resulted in a tremendous increase in research on the species. Contrary to environmentalists' claims, it has been found that spotted owls are quite capable of surviving in second-growth forests as well as old growth.[32] This finding was initially greeted with disbelief. When it was irrefutably demonstrated that owls were not only living, but also breeding, in second growth, they were deemed to be "surplus owls" on the assumption that they were not viable in the long term. It now appears that these owls are as viable as those that live in old growth and that in some cases logging may actually be beneficial to the owl.

In coastal forests from southern Oregon to northern California the main prey species for spotted owls is the dusky-footed woodrat. The rat reaches its highest population density in 10 to 15 year-old forest after which its numbers decline as the forest ages. So long as there are surrounding forests over 40 years old the owl does best when there is a mixture of forest ages. On Simpson Timber's 500,000 acres (200,000 hectares) of private forest near Eureka, California there are more than 370 territorial spotted owls with a stable breeding population even though there is virtually no old growth forest remaining in the area. There have been over 1000 pairs of owls counted on private forest land alone in northern California, and not all the land has been surveyed.[33]

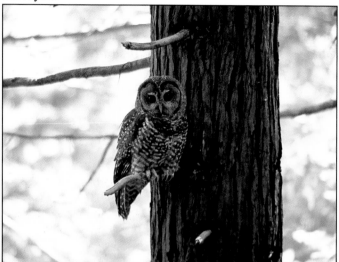

Spotted owls thrive in 40 year-old second-growth redwood forests near Eureka, California. This female is taking a break from feeding her hatchling high in the canopy, safe from predators and photographers alike.

In more northern forest in Oregon, Washington and British Columbia, the spotted owl's main prey is flying squirrels. Here the owls are more dependent on old growth as the flying squirrel does best in mature forests. But even in these regions researchers have found that owl numbers are far higher than originally predicted. In 1990 a team of scientists published the Thomas Report,[34] which estimated there were 136 pairs of spotted owls on 750,000 acres (300,000 hectares) of public forest land on the Olympic Peninsula in Washington. This included Olympic National Park, Olympic National Forest, and state lands managed by the Department of Natural Resources. The scientists also predicted that the maximum number of owls that could be supported in the area under ideal conditions in the future was 143 pairs or one pair for every 5,200 acres (2,100 hectares). In 1994, scientists working for the same federal agencies reported documented existence of 234 pairs in the same area and estimated there are between 282 and 321 pairs in the region.[35] In other words, it is now acknowledged that there are more than twice as many owls as was considered the theoretical maximum only four years earlier. Now it is believed that a pair of owls requires only 2,300 acres (935 hectares) rather than the previous estimate 5,200 acres (of 2,100 hectares). In all likelihood, even these more recent estimates are conservative. It seems the more we look for them, the more owls we discover.

Despite these findings, which prove there are far more owls than were thought to exist when logging was curtailed, environmentalists continue to demand that logging be outlawed. The "Zero Cut" campaign led by the Sierra Club, and supported by many other groups, takes the position that there should be no commercial forestry on any public land in the US.[36] Much of the reasoning behind this policy is based on the false assertion that species are threatened with extinction from logging.

The news media isn't helping much with the public's understanding of the relationship between spotted owls and forestry. In an article about redwood forests in March 1999, the New York Times reported that the spotted owl was a "nearly extinct species"[37] No evidence was provided for this statement; it was made as if it was an obvious fact. No wonder people believe that forestry must be stopped to protect species from extinction!

The issue of species protection offers an interesting contrast between approaches taken in the US Pacific Northwest compared to British Columbia. The 49th parallel that divides the two regions is entirely artificial geographically but it is the starting point in defining radically different political and legal systems on either side of the border. Whereas the ecosystems are virtually identical, especially near the boundary, the similarity ends at the level of forest ecology.

The ownership of forest lands in the US Pacific Northwest is a complex checkerboard of federal, state, and private interests. Lands in the National Parks, the National Forests and Bureau of Land Management are under federal jurisdiction. There are also large tracts of state-owned forests that are managed for timber and other resources. Much of the most productive, low-elevation forest land is owned privately by individuals and companies. Each of these jurisdictions comes under a different set of regulations.

In British Columbia, by contrast, over 95 percent of the forest land is owned and controlled directly by the provincial government. The provincial Forest Practices Code (1995) brings the small percentage of managed, privately held forest land under similar regulations as public land. There is little federal ownership in forest land other than national parks so the federal government of Canada has minimal involvement in the management of forest for timber. The main role of the federal government is the protection of salmon streams, a role that has had considerable influence on forest practice near rivers. The result is that commercially managed forest land in British Columbia is essentially under one set of regulations whereas there are three distinct types of jurisdiction in the US Pacific Northwest.

The most interesting comparison is between the National Forest lands in the US Pacific Northwest and the provincial forest lands in British Columbia. They are similar in these respects: both are publicly-owned, dedicated to timber harvesting (among many other uses), contain considerable old growth and other stages of original forest, support the economies of many communities, and are subject to the growing demands and values of an increasingly urban population. In recent years these similarities have been overshadowed by entirely different approaches to resolving the conflict between preservationists and pro-forestry interests.

On the US side, a combination of the Endangered Species Act, the protection of the spotted owl as a threatened species, and the individual citizen's right to sue the government have resulted in the cessation of most timber harvesting in National Forests. The result has been economic disaster for local forestry communities and few effective government programs to assist in developing other forms of economic activity. In this case, the legal rights of a listed owl species have been rated higher than those of humans, making the spotted owl a symbol of both preservation and devastation. It has been a classic example of land use conflict based on confrontation and litigation where the losers get little or no compensation.

In British Columbia, land use conflicts that focus on preservation of old growth forests have been equally intense. But there has been no simple legal route to force one side's agenda on the other. As a result, the conflict -- after some dramatic logging site demonstrations -- has settled down to being resolved largely through negotiation rather than legal action. All sides in the debate (environmental, forestry, tourism, labour, fish, wildlife, and communities) have engaged in round table forums and have had a surprising amount of success in reaching agreements that accommodate all interests and create win-win solutions.

A Tale of Two Woodpeckers

When it comes to endangered species and forests, there are few more interesting examples than the contrasting fates of two woodpecker species from the southeastern United States. In one case the story is a sad reminder of how species can be lost forever, in the other the story is one of hope and survival.

The ivory-billed woodpecker was a large bird that lived in the forests of the southeastern United States and some Caribbean islands including Cuba. It was never abundant, possibly because both aboriginal people and European settlers hunted it for its plumage. As the land was cleared and converted to agriculture the ivory billed woodpecker disappeared from much of its former range and by 1940 was confined to a 120-square-mile section along the Tensas River in Louisiana known as the Singer Tract.[38] This area was cleared for agriculture in 1948, apparently sealing the fate of the species forever. There were isolated sightings afterwards, in the US and in Cuba, but by the 1980's the bird was declared officially extinct. It is likely we will never see this woodpecker again.

A similar fate may have befallen the red-cockaded woodpecker, a much smaller bird but in some ways more specialized in its habitat requirements than its ivory-billed cousin. Unique among woodpeckers, the red-cockaded makes its nest in living trees, preferably old longleaf pines that have rotten centers in their tops. Among the southern pines, the longleaf is also the longest lived, surviving over 300 years, in part due to its thick bark which makes it resistant to fire. As the southern forests were cleared for timber and converted to cattle pastures and cotton plantations, the longleaf pine was diminished, thus reducing suitable habitat for the woodpeckers. Where forests were renewed it was more often with other species of pine such as loblolly and slash which were more easily cultivated. Populations of the red-cockaded woodpecker dwindled and it was declared an endangered species by the US Fish and Wildlife Service in 1970.

Fortunately for the woodpeckers, a number of stands of old growth longleaf pine survived, some on private land and others on public land in National Forests and on Military Reserves. Over the past ten years the US Fish and Wildlife Service has developed a program that allows private landowners to adopt Habitat Conservation Plans for species listed under the Endangered Species Act. Many forest companies, including Georgia-Pacific, International Paper, Champion International, and Temple-Inland have joined this program. They are working to enhance and increase the longleaf pine habitat on their forest lands and to relocate woodpeckers to more suitable areas of public land. This co-operative approach is proving far more successful than the adversarial approach that characterized the spotted owl controversy in the Pacific Northwest. And as with the spotted owl, it is virtually certain that the red-cockaded woodpecker will continue to survive and thrive in southern US forests from Texas to Florida and north into the Carolinas.

Monoculture

One of the constant themes of anti-forestry activists is that most forests growing back after logging are monoculture plantations that will produce inferior trees and inferior wood compared to the original forest. They also convey the impression that the new forest is not a suitable home for the many species that lived in the original forest. In the extreme case, they characterize the new forest as an "ecological desert" that has been permanently destroyed and where "the forest" will never return.[39] For the new forests of the Pacific Northwest, this is simply not true.

The use of the word monoculture to describe managed forests has resulted in a great deal of misunderstanding. It may seem to be a fairly precise term but this is not the case, particularly as applied to forests composed of native species, whether natural or managed. The term monoculture, as it is used in forestry, was borrowed from agriculture. As an agricultural term, monoculture refers to the planting and cultivation of a single plant species over an extensive area. Typical examples are the vast cornfields of the US Midwest, wheat fields of the Canadian prairies, and sugar cane plantations of the tropics. In these kinds of monoculture the original ecology is eliminated in its entirety and replaced with the desired crop species, usually an exotic, highly hybridized variety. The objective of management is to remove all competing animals, plants, insects, and fungi, often with the use of chemical pesticides.

Many kinds of trees are farmed in the manner of agricultural crops and therefore fit the agricultural definition of monoculture. Examples include banana, coconut, and oil palm plantations, orange groves, and apple orchards. There are also a number of examples of trees grown for the pulp and paper industry in the style of monoculture crops. Some of the eucalyptus plantations of Brazil, especially where they have been established on former farmland, are pure clonal monocultures. In the Pacific Northwest there are a growing number of plantations of hybrid poplars (cottonwood) planted as monocultures, although these are often grown in habitats where cottonwood was the native species and where it would occur normally as a near-monoculture forest.

There is often a real difference in the meaning of the term monoculture, as it is applied to agriculture and to forestry respectively. Whereas in agriculture the term means that the land is occupied by a single, usually exotic, hybridized crop species, in forestry the term is used to describe a forest that is dominated by a single tree species, often of native, naturally regenerated stock. A "monoculture" forest usually contains many species of shrubs, herbs, ferns, grasses, animals, birds, insects, and other species associated with a forest.

It would be far more instructive to define the difference between a monoculture tree plantation and a forest dominated by a single tree species. There is a huge difference between an apple orchard and a monoculture lodgepole pine forest that has regenerated naturally after logging or fire. Even then there is a gray area as the most rigid of monocultures always have some other species living among the intended crop.

The purest monoculture tree plantation has more biodiversity than a field of annual food crops as there is more habitat provided by a stand of trees and a far longer period of rotation even in the fastest growing pulp plantations. From the perspective of biodiversity, forests of any species are superior to annual crops.

There are many native forests that are dominated by a single species of tree, so many that it is reasonable to use the word "natural" to describe them. Great tracts of the original forests of redwood, Douglas-fir, lodgepole pine, subalpine fir, white spruce, aspen, and Engelmann spruce are composed almost entirely of those trees alone. Over an even greater area, there is a mixture of tree species such as the western hemlock/red cedar association in the coastal rainforest and the lodgepole pine/Engelmann spruce/subalpine fir association at mid to high elevations throughout the mountains of the Pacific Northwest. But whether we like it or not, forests dominated by a single tree species are just as "normal" and "natural" as those containing two or more species.

If it is normal for the original forest to contain a single dominant tree species is it not reasonable to replace those forests with the same single species after logging? There are many areas where natural regeneration after disturbance results in monoculture forest growing back. It is very misleading for critics of forest policy to complain about "monoculture plantations" when they are referring either to single tree species forests that are naturally regenerated or single tree species forests that are replanted with the species that was growing there in the first place. In particular, it is confusing to borrow the word monoculture from farming and apply it to a forest composed of native trees filled with a host of other plant, animal, and insect species, all of which are part of the original biodiversity.

But, you might ask, surely most new forests are less diverse in tree species than the original forest they replace. Again, while this may be true in other parts of the world, it is not the case in the Pacific Northwest. A thorough study done in British Columbia by the BC Ministry of Forests of all lands logged between 1970 and 1990 shows that tree species diversity had increased slightly in the new forests as compared with the original forest.[40] Whereas 32 percent of forests were identified as monocultures before harvesting, only 29 percent of new forests were monocultures 5-15 years after harvesting. About 50 percent of the clearcuts in the province have

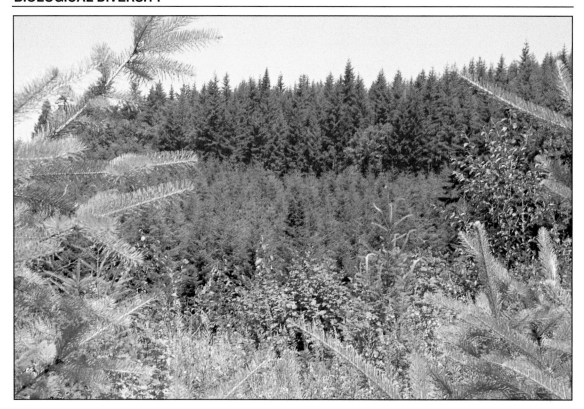

This Douglas-fir plantation on private land in southern Washington is an example of monoculture plantation forestry. Even though these forests are dominated by a single species of tree there is a rich diversity of other native plants, shrubs and wildlife.

been reforested by natural regeneration and about 50 percent have been reforested by planting one or more species of trees that were present in the original forest. Average tree species diversity has been maintained or increased in both naturally regenerated and replanted forests.

The tree species diversity has remained high for two main reasons. First, the Ministry of Forests pursues a conscious strategy to make sure that the new forest, whether naturally regenerated or planted, has similar tree species diversity to the one it replaces. In British Columbia there is a legal requirement to determine the forest renewal strategy prior to harvesting. The Pre-Harvest Silvicultural Prescription must state which species of seedlings will be planted after harvesting in cases where it is determined that natural regeneration alone is insufficient for rapid renewal. In some cases, up to four species of trees are planted on a single site and natural in-filling by other species occurs after planting. Where there was only one species in the original forest there is often only one species planted. In other areas, for example where massive areas of pine and spruce forest have been killed by bark beetles and salvage-logged, two or more species are sometimes planted in order to provide more diversity and hopefully more resistance to catastrophic insect attack.

The second reason that new forests often have as high or higher tree species diversity than the original forest is due to the greater incidence of pioneer hardwood species such as alder, maple, willow, aspen, birch, and poplar growing in young forests. Many of these species are adapted to grow back after disturbance. They are not as long-lived as the coniferous trees and not as tall so they are eventually shaded out and crowded out by the conifers as the forest ages.

In the past the tendency of hardwoods to come in aggressively after logging was considered a nuisance as these species had no commercial value. This view is now changing rapidly as alder, aspen and poplar have become valued for a wide range of products. The acceptance of the hardwood species as a valuable part of the commercial forest has a positive effect on biodiversity and ecosystem health. The pioneer species of hardwoods are good soil- builders

This is what a real monoculture tree plantation looks like. Fast growing eucalyptus, planted on lands cleared for farming decades ago, provides the basis for improved living standards on the Atlantic coast of Brazil. Even here there are more habitats for other species than in a field of annual food crops.

This 35-year-old second growth Douglas-fir forest is the result of natural regeneration after logging near Sproat Lake in central Vancouver Island. This is a natural forest monoculture as the trees are all Douglas-fir. It is not a monoculture in the sense that this term is used in agriculture, as there are many other species including plants, birds, animals and insects living in and beneath the forest canopy.

and are often preferred by birds for nesting and as food sources. Alders are particularly beneficial as they are nitrogen-fixers and add fertility to the soil in the same way as clover and alfalfa do in farming. The fact that these species are definitely more common in new forests than in the original forests provides further evidence that the younger forests may add to the biological diversity of the landscape rather than detract from it. This is certainly the case given that many of the unique features of old growth forests have been protected in parks and wilderness as well as in other areas that will not be logged due to economic or environmental considerations.

Exotic Species – Curse Or Benefit?

There is a growing movement to target exotic species, those that have been introduced to new regions as a result of human activity, as a threat to the environment. They are often referred to as "alien species", or "invasive species" in order to give a negative impression. Extreme language is used in campaigns designed to recruit public support for a war against these aliens, almost as if they were invaders from another planet. A group of environmental scientists issued a statement in February 1997 claiming that "A rapidly spreading invasion of exotic plants and animals is destroying our nation's biological diversity."[41]

The examples given to support the case against exotics are invariably species that cause harm to forests, farm crops, or compete successfully against native species that are considered desirable.

This is a classic example of our ability to take what was once a positive connotation and turn it into a negative one. The word "exotic" has normally been associated with ideas like "exotic paradise" and "exotic pleasures". Over the centuries exotic plants have been sought after by gardeners to add beauty and diversity to both public and private landscapes. While Californians were busy importing eucalyptus trees and other Australian plants, Australians were lining their streets with cedars from Lebanon and maples from Japan and North America. Botanical gardens pride themselves in the number of rare and exotic plants they have on display for the pleasure of an appreciative public.

Now it is fashionable to favor "native" plants and animals and to perceive exotics as undesirables that should be uprooted and otherwise driven from the land. The language employed is akin to that used by white supremacists and supporters of "ethnic cleansing" to spread dislike of other races and cultures. Could it be that the campaign against exotic species is just another form of racism, in this case against other species rather than against different races and cultures of our own species?

I was inspired to include a section about exotic species when I heard a news story from Washington DC in the spring of 1999. The citizens of the Capitol were distressed to find that a family of beavers had taken up residence there and were busy felling the Japanese cherry trees that adorned the banks of the Potomac River. It became a national emergency of sorts and a great effort was made to trap every last beaver; only then were the townspeople put at ease. There was no mention made of the fact that the beaver is a native North American species whereas the cherry trees are exotics, imported from Japan. Yet there was no question which species the public favored.

This example gets to the heart of the debate over exotic species. The reason we dislike certain species and like others has nothing to do with whether or not they are exotic. By playing on people's natural suspicion of all things foreign, environmentalists confuse the issue and give the public a misleading picture. There are actually thousands of exotic species that are not only beneficial, they are the mainstay of our daily lives. Food crops like wheat, rice, and cabbage are all exotics when grown in North America. Vegetables that originated in the Americas such as beans, corn and potatoes are exotics when they are grown in Europe. All around the world, agriculture is largely based on species that originated somewhere else. This is also the case for domestic animals, garden plants and street trees.

There are also hundreds of native species of plants and animals that we consider undesirable. For centuries we have referred to them as weeds, pests, vermin and disease. There are also many exotic species that fall into this category. And, of course, there are many native species that are considered extremely beneficial, especially those that provide food for a growing population. The point is, both exotic and native species can be desirable or undesirable from a human perspective, depending on how they effect our lives. Our almost innate dislike of rats and spiders has nothing to do with whether or not they are native or exotic, it is due to the possibility of deadly disease or a fatal bite. And even though dandelions in the lawn are hardly a life-and-death issue, millions are spent each year to rid lawns of these "weeds".

Certain exotic species have resulted in severe negative impacts. The most notorious case involved the introduction of European species of animals to Australia, New Zealand, and the Pacific Islands when Europeans colonized these regions beginning about 225 years ago. Many native species, flightless birds and ground-dwelling marsupials in particular, were not able to survive the introduction of predators such as rats, cats and foxes. As a result, hundreds of native species were eliminated. Another well known exotic is Dutch elm disease, a fungus that actually originated in Asia, came through Europe and on to North America where it has resulted in the death of many native elms in the US and Canada.[42]

There can be no doubt that we should always be careful when considering the introduction of a new species, and that regulations are needed to prevent undesirable accidental introductions. At the same time we must not lose sight of the fact that introduced species play a vital, even essential, role in modern society. Each species must be evaluated on its own merits. The introduction of some species may be desirable in one region and yet undesirable in others. Islands are particularly susceptible to introductions because they are isolated and their native species are not subjected to as wide a variety of predators and diseases. When rats are introduced to islands that support large bird rookeries there is often a precipitous decline in bird populations due to predation on eggs and nestlings.

There is really no difference when considering the use of an exotic species of tree for managed forests. As mentioned previously, one of the reasons we tend to use native species of trees for forestry in North America is because they are the best available in terms of productivity and wood quality. In other regions this is not the case. Radiata pine from California has been very successful in New Zealand, Australia, and Chile. Eucalyptus from Australia is the forestry species of choice in many parts of Brazil, Portugal and South Africa. Douglas-fir from Oregon has become the number two species of softwood produced in France. And Chinese larch is a favorite for reforestation in Scotland where forest cover was lost centuries ago to sheep farming.

A Challenge to Foresters – Protect Biodiversity and Produce More Wood

There is a tendency among foresters to believe that strategies to increase wood production will automatically result in a loss of biodiversity. As we move from forests that are naturally regenerated to forests that are managed by planting, weeding, fertilizing, thinning and pruning we select in favor of the trees and against other species. Biodiversity certainly is lost when the traditional agricultural model is simply borrowed and adapted to forestry. It is my belief, after many years of field observations around the world, that biodiversity protection and high-yield wood production need not be mutually exclusive.

In the traditional model, wood production is increased by creating a fast growing monoculture over a wide area, eliminating competition through the application of herbicides, and focussing entirely on the trees as an agricultural crop. There is no doubt that this approach works from the perspective of maximizing wood production, but it is nearly always at the expense of biodiversity and the habitat required by many species of birds and animals. By adopting creative strategies at both the level of the individual stands of trees and at the level of the larger landscape, this apparent conflict between production and biodiversity can be overcome.

We can begin with a very simple example. In many areas of Germany, Austria and Switzerland, private forest owners have found that planted spruce monocultures provide the best financial return for their families. These forests tend to be very simplified and in particular they have few potential nesting sites for birds that need holes in dead trees. In Austria there is a regulation requiring that private forest owners provide eight wooden birdhouses per hectare (three per acre), nailed to the sides of the spruce trees. Even though this is a very easy and inexpensive obligation, it results in a tremendous increase in bird populations and breeding success in these forests.

Moving to a more complex situation, consider a typical pine plantation such as those found in many regions of the world today. Following harvesting, usually by some form of clearcutting, the site is commonly disc plowed and planted with genetically improved nursery stock in nice neat rows. A herbicide application is often used to reduce competition from herbs and shrubs and at age five to ten a pre-commercial weeding and thinning establishes the desirable number of stems per acre. Other tree species such as pioneer hardwoods that regenerate from native seed are removed in favor of the pines. In intensive cultivation there may be several herbicide applications during the growing cycle, effectively eliminating the understory shrubs and many flowering plants. If the trees are grown close together to maximize production not much sunlight gets through to the ground. Not many plants can survive in the deep shade so biodiversity is reduced to those that can. While not all plantation forests are this extreme there is a tendency to move in this direction with a number of species including pines, spruce, eucalyptus, and poplar.

One of the keys to maintaining a high level of biodiversity is the recognition that in a given ecosystem there are usually some species that have evolved to take advantage of all the successional states in that ecosystem. Some species will prefer recently disturbed areas while others will prefer middle-aged or older forests. Some birds will nest in dead trees while others nest in shrubs and still others nest in live trees. The best way to make sure that all these features are present in an ecosystem at any given time is, in the words of wildlife ecologist Fred Bunnell, "Don't do the same thing everywhere."[43] If forests are managed by blanket prescription; doing the same thing everywhere, some habitats and structures will tend to be lost. This can result in considerable loss of biodiversity at the local or even regional level.

The black bear is indicative of healthy forests throughout much of North America. Can we make sure there are forested areas large enough to allow this species to flourish in the face of urban encroachment?

There are a number of strategies to avoid the loss of biodiversity that can result from intensive plantation management over large tracts of land. These can be accomplished both at the stand level and at the landscape level.

At the stand level the key to creating higher biodiversity without much compromise to wood production involves the retention of key structural elements in the stand. Some examples are:

- Where herbicides are used to reduce competition from shrubs it is possible to establish small areas in the stand that are avoided during herbicide application. Even though this might be as low as 2-5% of the total area of the stand, it will allow for shrubs to become established and for shrub-nesting birds and other species dependent on shrubs to remain in the stand.

- Small patches of forest can be designated as reserves within the stand to maintain living and standing dead trees throughout the growing cycle. These mini-reserves can be established around small wetlands that are naturally low in productivity but high in biodiversity.

- During weeding and thinning operations a small percentage of non-plantation species of trees can be retained to provide a wider variety of habitat. For example, in a pine plantation, a few stems of naturally regenerated hardwood trees could be retained. These trees may be commercially valuable in the future and they will increase bird and insect biodiversity in the stand.

- Individual dead or dying trees can be retained in the stand for cavity nesting birds and mammals. Even one standing dead tree per acre can result in a considerable increase in biodiversity. This can often be accomplished with no loss of wood production.

- During site preparation for planting, woody debris can be piled or windrowed to provide habitat for birds, mammals and reptiles. This kind of structural diversity on the land can make a big difference to biodiversity without effecting productivity.

At the landscape level the key to creating higher biodiversity is to zone the landscape so that all elements of the forest are retained at all times. Some examples are:

- Perhaps the most important landscape level strategy for protecting biodiversity is the streamside reserve zone or streamside management zone, otherwise known as the riparian reserve zone or riparian management zone. "Streamside" and "riparian" are synonyms referring to the area of land immediately adjacent to a stream or river. A 'reserve zone" is an area where no active management occurs whereas a "management zone" is an area where management does occur, but with special consideration for the stream or river. By establishing streamside reserves and management zones it is possible to protect a wide variety of species, including fish and other aquatic life.

- At the landscape level permanent reserves can be established for the protection of native species of wildlife. This is particularly effective when exotic species of trees are used for production plantations. In Brazil, where eucalyptus is used for fast growing monoculture pulp plantations, it is common to establish a network of streamside reserve zones and one large core reserve zone where native plants and animals can flourish. This results in a landscape where 75-80% of the area is planted in eucalyptus and 20-25% is in reserves of native forest. This produces a landscape that has far higher biodiversity than if it was a 100% eucalyptus plantation.

- Another feature that can be employed at the landscape level is the "corridor". For example, corridors of native forest can be used to join streamside reserve zones by connecting them over the height of land. A network of streamside reserves and corridors can result in a mosaic of plantations surrounded on all sides by native forest. During the growing cycle of the plantation species, native plants, animals and birds will disperse into the plantation, thus making it much more biodiverse than if the surrounding native forest was absent.

It is impossible to manage forests intensively for timber production without having some impact on biodiversity. By adopting strategies such as those recommended above, it is possible to minimize negative impacts on biodiversity while maintaining a high level of wood production. To a considerable degree, we can have our cake and eat it when it comes to sustainable forestry.

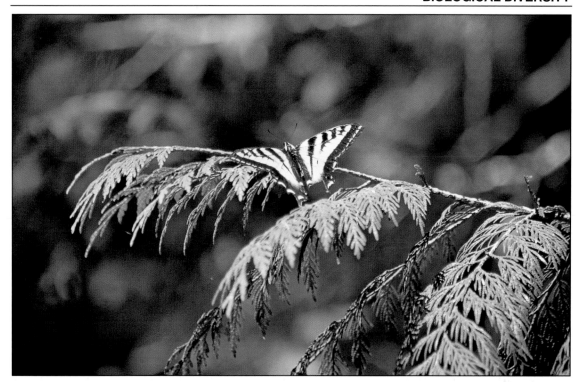

A swallow-tail butterfly rests briefly on a red cedar bough in the coastal forest. Butterflies at once symbolize the fragility and the resilience of nature. So long as their desired habitats remain suitable for their needs, the swallow-tails will survive and flourish.

REFERENCES

1 Stephen Jay Gould, Revising and Extending Darwin, in: Eight Little Piggies, W.W. Norton & Company, New York, 1993. This is a readable introduction to some of the principles of genetic diversity.

2 Herb Hammond, Clearcutting: Ecological and Economic Flaws, in: Clearcutting: the Tragedy of Industrial Forestry.

3 Elizabeth May, At the Cutting Edge – The Crisis in Canada's Forests, Key Porter Books, Toronto, 1998, p. 19.

4 Hamish Kimmins, Balancing Act – Environmental Issues in Forestry, UBC Press, Vancouver, 1992, p. 160.

5 R.J Keenan, and J.P. Kimmins, The Ecological Effects of Clear-cutting. Environ. Rev.. 1: 121-144. 1993. also see P.J. Burton, et al, The value of managing for biodiversity. For. Chron. 68: 225-237, 1992.

6 Lee E. Harding and Emily McCullum (Ed.) Biodiversity in British Columbia: Our Changing Environment, Environment Canada and Canadian Wildlife Service, 1994.

7 Herb Hammond. Clearcutting: Ecological and Economic Flaws, in: Clearcut, the Tragedy of Industrial Forestry.

8 Alan Drengson. Remembering the Moral and Spiritual Dimensions of Forests in: Clearcut, the Tragedy of Industrial Forestry.

9 Vancouver Province, Associated Press Wire Story, March 12, 1996, p. A16

10 State of the World's Forests '97. FAO,
    http://www.fao.org/waicent/faoinfo/forestry/SOFOTOC.htm

11 Correspondence, Patrick Moore to HRH the Duke of Edinburgh, May 14, 1996.

12 Correspondence, Prince Philip to Patrick Moore, May 27, 1996.

13 Forests for Life – WWF's Annual Global Forest Report for 1997,
    http://www.panda.org/forests4life/report97/forestw5.doc

14 WWF News Release, August 25, 1998, http://www.panda.org/forests4life/news/news_4.htm

15 The World List of Threatened Trees, World Conservation Monitoring Center, World
    Conservation Press, 1998.

16 Vancouver Sun, August 27, 1998, p. A3

17 Vancouver Sun, September 2, 1998, p. A3

18 Ibid.

19 M.A. Sanjayan and M.E. Soulé., Moving Beyond Brundtland: The Conservation Value of British
    Columbia's 12 Percent Protected Areas Strategy, Greenpeace, June 1997.

20 The Great Bear Rainforest, Greenpeace, June 1997, p. 21 and p.8.

21 Ministry of Environment, Lands and Parks, Internet Site,
    http://www.env.gov.bc.ca/wld/his/grizhist.doc

22 T. L. Slaney et al, Status of Anadromous Salmon and Trout in British Columbia and Yukon,
    Fisheries, Vol. 21, No. 10, October 1996, pp.20-35.

23 Ibid. p. 31.

24 D.A. Levy et al, Strait of Georgia Fisheries Sustainability Review, Hatfield Consultants Ltd.,
    West Vancouver, January 1996.

25 E. O. Wilson, The Diversity of Life, W.W. Norton, New York, 1992.

26 See: http://biology.usgs.gov/s+t/frame/t017.htm

27 Ian Abbott and Per Christensen, Living With Logging, Landscope, Western Australia's
    Conservation, Forests and Wildlife Magazine, Summer, 1995-96, pp. 21-27.

28 Virginia Morell and Frans Lanting, The Sixth Extinction, National Geographic Vol.195, No. 2,
    February 1999, pp. 42-59.

29 See: http://www.wcmc.org.uk/species/animals/table4.html

30 B. Groombridge, ed., 1994 IUCN Red List of Threatened Animals (Gland, Switzerland: IUCN,
    1993).

31 Henry H. Webster, Some Sources of Persistent Error in Thinking About Resources, Forestry
    Chronicle, January/February 1999, Vol. 75, No. 1.

32 Personal communication, Lowell Diller, biologist with Simpson Redwood Inc. Arcata, California,
    May 1995.

33 Personal communication, Lowell Diller, biologist with Simpson Redwood Inc. Arcata, California,
    November 1999.

34 Jack Ward Thomas et al, A Conservation Strategy for the Northern Spotted Owl. Interagency
    Scientific Committee to Address the Conservation of the Northern Spotted Owl, Portland
    Oregon, May 1990.

35 Richard S Holthausen, et al, The Contribution of Federal and Nonfederal Habitat to Persistence
    of the Northern Spotted Owl on the Olympic Peninsula, Washington, Report of the Reanalysis
    Team, U.S. D.A Forest Service and National Biological Survey, October, 1994.

36 See: http://www.emagazine.com/july-august_1996/0796ibsierr.html

37 New York Times, December 8, 1998.

38 American Bird Conservancy's Field Guide - All The Birds Of North America, Harper Perennial Press, 1997

39 Christoph Theis and Thomas Kunz, Greenpeace Germany fundraising pamphlet, March/April 1992.

40 British Columbia's Forests: Monocultures or Mixed Forests? Province of British Columbia, Ministry of Forests, May 1992.

41 Environment News Service, February 19, 1997.

42 See: http://www.ksu.edu/plantpath/extension/facts/tree3.html

43 Fred Bunnell, et al, An Ecological Rationale for Changing Management Practices on MacMillan Bloedel's Forest Tenures, Centre for Applied Conservation Biology, University of British Columbia, June, 1998.

The late summer light silhouettes Mittlenatch Island, a bird sanctuary in the Strait of Georgia. Biodiversity can often be protected in relatively small areas that are critical to nesting and feeding. The mountains of Vancouver Island loom in the background.

Time and Change

All is in a continuous flux upon earth. Nothing keeps a constant and fixed form.
   Jean-Jacques Rousseau, Reveries of a Solitary Stroller

One of the keys to understanding forests is to appreciate the time-scale of their existence. Individuals of the shortest-lived tree species live about as long as the average human while the oldest can survive for more than 100 human generations. The forests in which they live have been evolving over even longer spans of time, constantly changing as climates have changed for more than 400 million years. Over the past 1.5 million years the changes have been dramatic as ice ages have come and gone.

Trees are highly adaptable and have evolved to grow over a wide range of climatic conditions. From the searing heat of the tropics to the frigid northern boreal reaches, tree species have developed that can withstand these extremes. It is easier to list the environments that trees cannot grow in than those they have evolved to survive.

The primary limits for trees are set by environments that are too dry, too cold or a combination of the two. In general, trees require more water than smaller plants because they use the evaporation of water from their leaves to draw nutrients dissolved in water up their stems from their roots. Even so, there are species such as the Ponderosa pine of the dry interior and the Joshua tree of the California desert that can live in areas with very little rainfall. The northern boundary of the boreal forest that circles the globe through Canada, Scandinavia, Russia, and Alaska is determined by the cold climate. Beyond this only scrub willow and a few hardy low-lying plants persist in the vast northern tundra.

Given sufficient rainfall or irrigation, there is no climate on earth that is too hot for forests. Very few places are too wet for trees. Lodgepole pine will grow in a saturated peat bog. In the tropics mangroves grow in shallow seawater. In the southeastern US the bald cypress grows in knee-deep watery swamps.

One of the more interesting exceptions to limits set by dry and cold climates occurs on islands surrounded by cool seas. The Aleutian Islands off Alaska remain treeless even though it seldom freezes and there is ample rainfall. Compared to the boreal forest of the Canadian north the climate is very warm. The limit here is not too cold a temperature in winter, but that it never gets warm enough in the summer for trees to produce viable seed. This is clear from the evidence that spruce trees grow quite nicely where they have been planted in and around villages. The failure to produce seed thus limits the range of trees even though they are quite capable of growing when planted outside their normal territory.

Another interesting example of this phenomenon is the ability of the giant sequoia from the Sierra Nevada mountains in California to grow as far north as northern Vancouver Island.[1] The natural range of the giant sequoia is restricted to a few pockets where it is capable of reproducing in the wild. But seedlings will take and grow into large, healthy trees when planted far beyond this natural range. Their inability to reproduce successfully may be due to lack of viable seed or at least the inability of any seed produced to germinate and become established anywhere but those areas where they are found in the wild. The significant point is that many plant species, including trees, can be successfully grown far beyond their natural range with a little assistance.

These *are* the Ice Ages

You may drive out nature with a pitchfork, yet she will always hasten back

Horace, 65 BC - 8 BC

Forests, particularly old growth forests, are often described as if they have existed in their present state for millions of years. While it is true that individual tree species have existed for millions of years, the forests they make up have been in a constant state of change. Even the vast Amazon rainforest is a recent phenomenon on the time-scale of evolution. Only 9,000 years ago the Amazon basin was largely savanna with scattered trees and only patches of closed forest. It was the change in climate caused by the passing of the last ice age that influenced the development of the vast forest present there today.

During the last ice age, which lasted thousands of years, nearly the whole of Canada, part of the northern United States, and northern Europe and Russia were covered by a massive sheet of ice. This resulted in a dramatic shifting in forest types, causing every species of plant and animal to migrate south at the onset of the ice age and return north again at its conclusion 8,000 years ago. Four times during the past million and a half years this wholesale change in geographical distribution of forest cover has occurred, as succeeding ice ages advanced and retreated. Known to scientists as the Pleistocene, this era featured some of the most rapid fluctuations in climate since the beginning of life on earth three and a half billion years ago. There is no reason to believe we are not still in the Pleistocene and that there will be another ice age thousands of years from now.

10,000 years ago, nearly all of Canada and Russia were still covered by a sheet of ice. Nothing lived under the ice and when it retreated it left barren rock in its wake. Yet today, Canada and Russia account for 30% of the world's forests. In Alaska, where the glaciers continue to retreat due to the present global warming trend, it is only about 100 years from when the rock is bared to the sun until a new forest ecosystem becomes established. Forests are not only capable of recovering from complete destruction but they can recover quickly, given the right conditions.

A comparison between northwestern North America and northern Europe illustrates the powerful influence the ice ages had on the composition of forests in those regions. The two areas are comparable as they occupy similar latitudes, have similar temperate climates, and a range of topographies including high mountains. Here the similarity ends as they have quite different forests, the main distinction being the greater number of tree species, particularly conifers, in the North American temperate forests. This has come about largely because of the ice age migrations.

A quick look at the topographic maps of the two continents shows a clear distinction in the alignment of the major features. In northwestern North America the mountain ranges all run more or less from north to south with continuous valleys between them. The Coast Range and the Cascades, the Selkirks, the Purcells and the Rockies parallel each other as they cross the US-Canada border. This configuration allowed an easy migration of trees and other plants as the ice moved south and then north again. Over the thousands of years these movements took, it was not difficult for species to seed ahead of themselves as the climate gradually changed.

In Europe the main mountain chain of the Alps runs from west to east. In addition there are two seas, the Mediterranean and the Baltic, that also run west to east. These three features present a formidable barrier to the migration of trees and other plants. By the time the southward-moving ice had reached the northern shores of the Mediterranean the only refuge for most tree species was in northern Africa. Many of these species had migrated all the way south from Scandinavia. As the ice then receded, these plants would have faced the challenge of first crossing the Mediterranean, then getting over the Alps, and finally crossing the Baltic if they were ever to become re-established in Scandinavia. In fact, for many species this was impossible and the only route of migration was along the eastern shores of the Mediterranean, up through Eastern Europe, and across the straits between Denmark and Sweden. Even on this trek, the Carpathian and Caucasus mountains, again running west to east, are difficult barriers.

One of the results of this geographical obstacle course is a present-day forest in Scandinavia that has only two species of large coniferous trees, Scots pine and Norway spruce. The broadleaf trees faired somewhat better, as most of southern Scandinavia and the great lowlands of Germany, France, and the Benelux countries are dominated today by forests of beech, oak, maple, and birch. This product of topographical circumstance and changing climate brings to light some interesting questions.

It has been discovered by analysis of pollen samples preserved in peat bogs that during an earlier period between glaciers the forests of northern Europe contained Douglas-fir, a species now found only in western North America. It would seem that Douglas-fir was eliminated from Europe as a result of its inability to cope with the constant need to move at the whim of mile-thick ice sheets. In North America the species survived because it was much easier to migrate up and down the valleys running north and south.

In 1827 the Scottish botanist, David Douglas, introduced Douglas-fir to England.[2] During the past 150 years a large number of Douglas-fir seeds have been collected in North America by other botanists and foresters and planted in Europe. They do very well there, growing about as fast as they do in North America, putting the European species of conifers to shame. The question is, as has been suggested by some environmental groups, is Douglas-fir an exotic species as far as Europe is concerned? Is there a sound ecological reason to keep it out or is it valid to bring it back as a native species that has suffered a long absence due to climate change?

The particular case of Douglas fir leads to the more general issue of the "naturalness" of particular forest types. As each of the successive ice sheets retreated, it was followed back north by many tree species that had been pushed south by advancing ice. The pollen record shows that even though the climate returned to "normal" after each ice age, the composition of the forests in the same locations was usually different each time. This can be explained by a number of factors and is actually what should be expected. Each time the plants migrated back circumstances were a little different. The ice would recede at a different rate and in different patterns. Some plant species would just get lucky and be blown ahead on the wind or be carried by birds. The first ones to colonize a new area would have an advantage and would help create the environment that might make it easier or harder for subsequent species to flourish there. In the end, the pattern of species distribution and forest types was as much influenced by circumstance as by the variety of plants that were capable of growing in a particular region.

The lesson to be taken from these historical facts is that, as much as we might have an idealized vision of what is natural and what is not, there is no perfect ecosystem for any particular time or landscape. The way we find things today is not the only natural way for them to be. Environments were different in the past even when conditions were the same and they will be different in the future regardless of human activity. This is the same message imparted by Stephen Jay Gould in his book, "Wonderful Life",[3] where he demonstrates, through studying the fossil record dating back 530 million years, that chance circumstance is as important as natural selection in determining the outcome of evolution. Using the analogy of a cassette tape, he concludes that no matter how many times you wind the tape back in time and play it forward again, things will never come out the same as they are today. In other words, as far as our present understanding goes, there is no master plan for life on earth. Evolution is not a triumphant march towards the creation of the perfect species, nor is it predictable as it proceeds according to the fascinating rules of chaos theory.[4]

Gould does not conclude from this that we are justified in doing whatever we like to ecosystems and their species. Rather he points out correctly, in the sense that the present species could only happen once, that they are all miracles, including ourselves. This insight gives us the opportunity to view all of living creation as a "secular miracle." It makes us realize that we are not perfect, just miraculous. It also gives further weight to the slogan "Extinction is Forever". Once a species becomes extinct, whether caused by humans or not, an identical species will never appear on the earth again.

More specifically, the history of the ice ages tells us some important things about the evolution and composition of forests. First, there is no ideal forest composition for any given climate or region. In the absence of human intervention a fairly wide range of conditions are capable of occurring and of sustaining themselves over long time periods. This may mean there is no need to be terribly rigid in defining what constitutes a native or "natural" forest for a given area. Second, geographical features, such as those in Europe, greatly influenced the composition of forests after each ice age. Perhaps it is reasonable to re-introduce species that have been lost, or even similar species found elsewhere, as a way of increasing biological diversity. Third, and perhaps most significant for the subject of this book, every time the vast forested regions of the north have been totally denuded by ice the forests have returned in splendor as the ice receded.

None of the forests on this earth would exist if they were not capable of recovering from complete and utter destruction over wide areas of their range. This is, of course, a relative statement. If every lodgepole pine seed on earth were destroyed by some means, that would be the end of lodgepole pine. If every tree seed were destroyed there would be no trees until they evolved again over millions of years, and then they would all be different species. But these are very unlikely scenarios. What *has* occurred in recent times is that vast areas of forest lands have been converted by humans into farmland and to a lesser extent, cities. If we removed the grazing animals, left the farmland fallow, and abandoned our cities, the forest would move back in quickly wherever it could grow. It would be just as if the ice had receded leaving the land ready for seed again.

There is little likelihood that humans will abandon this earth. Our numbers are predicted to grow even larger in the near future. The biggest threat to forests, particularly in the tropics, stems from the increasing need for food, firewood, and shelter for billions of people living on the edge of survival. This is another subject in another part of the world, but we all have a stake in this future and we should do what we can to assist the developing world in managing population growth -- and adopting sustainable agriculture and forestry.

Coming back to the Pacific Northwest, there is no immediate threat in this region of widespread conversion of the remaining forest land to non-forest use. We have seen from the example of the ice ages that even total destruction over most of the region does not result in permanent loss of forest. Why is it then that clearcutting much smaller areas and letting the forest grow back causes such concern about the creation of biological deserts and permanent loss of species? Are not the growth of urbanization and agriculture the worthiest objects of this concern, and are not most of the people with such concerns living in those cities surrounded by those farms?

The glaciers of the ice ages teach us that deforestation, even where the soil is completely destroyed, is not irreversible. As long as the ice remains the forest cannot return. When it is gone the forest will always return. The same holds true of our own destruction of forests. If we were to remove the condition that is preventing reforestation, whether it is goats or eight lanes of traffic, the trees would hurry back to reclaim their territory.

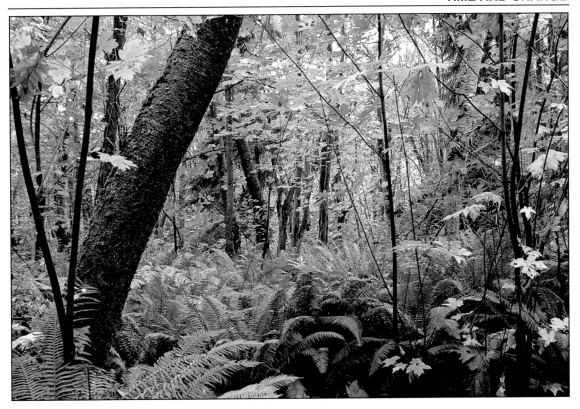

Three scenes from Pacific Spirit Park demonstrate how the same site can support very different types of forest. One (opposite page) is Douglas-fir and western hemlock, another (above) is bigleaf maple and cherry, and another (below) is western red cedar with vine maple. All three are on similar sites and have resulted from different histories of disturbance and renewal rather than any major differences in the sites themselves.

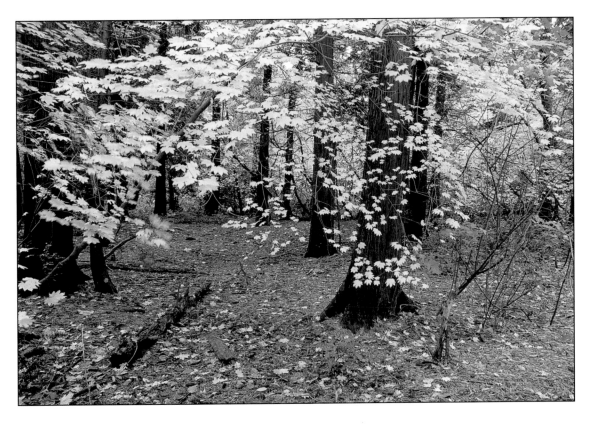

From Hard Rocks to Soft Rocks

The sequence of events that begins with barren rock and becomes a forest is called ecological succession. This refers to the succession of plant and animal species that leads from lifelessness to the profusion of a rainforest or to the relative simplicity of a Ponderosa pine savanna. Forests don't just suddenly appear, they evolve at the end of a long, complex process of change.

Living things have been referred to as "soft rocks" because when reduced to their basic elements they are found to be made entirely of water, air, and the minerals found in rocks. These are the minerals that form the ash in your fireplace after burning a cord of wood. They are the remains of cremation that we scatter in honor of loved ones passed on. All these minerals in all living things were originally derived from the stone that covers the earth's surface. All of them were incorporated into the tissues of plants that grew on soil derived from that stone, and then into the tissue of birds and animals that ate the plants. Because of this, soil scientists refer to the underlying geology as the "parent material". Essential nutrients such as potassium, iron, phosphorous, calcium, zinc and copper are all derived from the weathering of solid stone.

Often the first species to colonize otherwise bare rocks are the blue-green algae and lichens. Blue-green algae, really a type of photosynthetic bacteria, were among the earliest forms of life to evolve. Lichens, on the other hand, are a more recent development. The secret of their ability to live in such harsh conditions is that they are actually two species living together: a combination of fungus and green algae which by helping each other can live where neither could survive alone.

These first pioneer species get the nutrients they need from the weathering of the rock and from rainwater. They grow slowly but surely, and most important, they prepare the ground for the next succession of plants, the mosses and ferns. They do this by beginning the process of creating soil. Bits of dead lichen collect in cracks and depressions in the rock where they are invaded by bacteria and microscopic fungi. This organic matter is literally composted, becoming ideal sites for the spores of a hardy species of moss or fern to germinate. It might take a few years but before long what was bare rock is a thriving community of plant life. It is hard to imagine a situation where species like fungi, mosses, and ferns would have difficulty colonizing a new area. They seed by spores that are microscopic and carried on the lightest wind. Just as the spores that cause mold on bread are nearly everywhere, so are the spores of most forest species of fungi, lichens, mosses, and ferns.

A tuft of moss has colonized this bare rock and will now accelerate the weathering process, releasing nutrients and contributing to the build-up of new soil.

The mosses and ferns then begin to build the soil in earnest. Each new season more dead plant material is added to the rock's surface and the process of chemical weathering of the rocks is well underway. Chemical weathering occurs as a result of chemicals, usually acidic, that are produced by the plants themselves and that accelerate the release of minerals from the rock. At this stage, a wide range of flowering plants and shrubs are introduced, the particular species depending on the surrounding vegetation and available seed sources. Plants such as fireweed whose seeds drift for miles on the wind tend to be earlier arrivals than plants that need birds and squirrels to help distribute their seeds. But by one ingenious method or another a myriad of plant species eventually creates what can only be described as a new ecosystem in the making.

Juniper haircap moss and rag lichens are the pioneers on this roadside area that was bare gravel only a few years earlier. It won't be long before tree seedlings take root and a new forest begins to grow.

It does not take long for tree seeds to settle, germinate, and take root in the growing soil. The actual order in which tree species become established and the eventual composition of the forest depends to a large degree on circumstance. Factors affecting this are the composition of the surrounding forest, the mobility of seed, and whether or not seed is produced in a given year.

In the past, forest ecologists had a rather idealized model for the succession of the various trees and other plant species in a given ecosystem. They envisioned an orderly progression from the pioneer species, through intermediate species, and finally to the "climax" species, which were believed to be a final stage that then came into long-term equilibrium. The current view is less rigid than this and allows for a more varied succession of species. In some forests, where the frequency of major disturbance is very low, there are examples of ecosystems that have remained relatively stable for hundreds and even thousands of years. This is the case in some coastal rainforest where it is too wet to burn and is protected from windstorms. In the majority of forests major disturbance occurs at a frequent enough interval that no successional stage lasts long enough to reach equilibrium. In these forests the climax species are no longer seen as an end point of succession but rather as one phase of a cyclical process that is continually changing.

In the same way that no two human families or communities are ever identical, no two forest communities are ever identical. Every time a forest grows back to replace the one before it, it is different, even though it occupies the same piece of land.

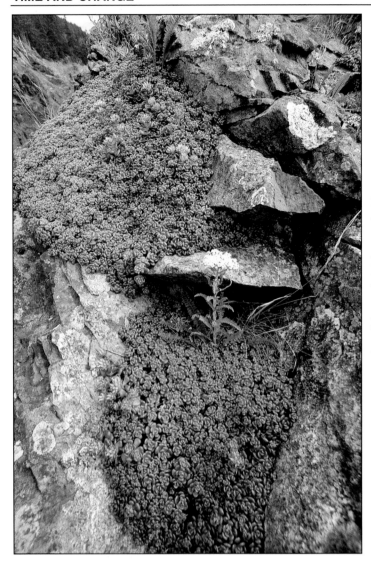

Crusty white lichens, yellow-flowering stonecrop and white-flowering yarrow grow in an exposed rocky area along the outer Pacific coast. The salt spray makes it too harsh for trees to grow here so this area will remain at an early successional stage indefinitely.

In many forests east of the Cascades, lodgepole pine is the first species to occupy a new site. As the pine trees mature, Engelmann spruce tends to seed in under them. It can grow in the shade of the pines whereas the pine cannot grow in its own shade. When the pine matures at 120-150 years it begins to die out, leaving the spruce with more sun. The forest then gradually becomes dominated by spruce, which creates a closer and therefore darker canopy than the pine. This makes it difficult for spruce to grow in its own shade but now the conditions are right for sub-alpine fir to seed in under the spruce. As the spruce reaches maturity at 200-300 years it dies and is then replaced by a forest dominated by sub-alpine fir. The sub-alpine fir makes the forest even darker so very little vegetation and no other tree species can grow up under it. When the sub-alpine fir reaches maturity and begins to die the forest gradually goes into a state of decline. This stage may last for hundreds of years.

This pattern of succession involving pine, spruce, and fir raises some intricate questions for foresters. Which of the three species should be planted on the site after logging? Is it acceptable to plant all three species at the same time even though this might not occur without human assistance? Would it be more "natural" to plant the species that dominated the site at the time of harvest or to plant lodgepole pine because it is the usual pioneer species? These questions cannot be answered by referring to a text on forest ecology. As stated earlier there is no perfect ecosystem for a given site and many sites are capable of sustaining a number of types of forest over a period of time. The answer to these questions is often reduced to finding out what works and what doesn't, in other words trial and error based on careful observation.

Another example that demonstrates the variability of succession can be found in the coastal forests where Douglas-fir and red alder often compete to be the pioneer species. If the soil has been badly disturbed by a landslide it is likely that alder will be first to grow as it can survive on very poor soil. If the soil is not badly damaged, Douglas-fir is able to establish itself and form the pioneer forest. But alder is also capable of germinating on good soil, and being opportunistic, is sometimes able to beat Douglas-fir to the site. In some years Douglas-fir doesn't produce seed whereas alder produces seed every year. Alder seed is smaller and is therefore carried further on

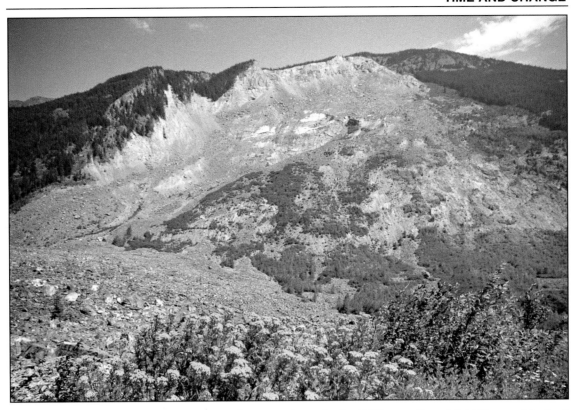

The Hope Slide was triggered by a minor earthquake in 1965, sending 1.6 billion cubic feet (46 million cubic meters) of rock and snow into the valley below causing loss of life and total destruction of the forest. Thirty years later the site is beginning to heal as pioneer species colonize rock that was left entirely barren after the landslide.

the wind. The pattern of alder and Douglas-fir distribution in the surrounding area will also influence which species arrives first at a recently cleared site.

On most sites in the Pacific Northwest neither red alder nor Douglas-fir are capable of growing in their own or in the other's shade. Therefore the one that gets established first can eliminate the other's chances. As red alder lives only 60-70 years it is soon replaced by shade-tolerant species such as western hemlock and red cedar that grow up under it. Douglas-fir, on the other hand, can live to 500 years or more so it remains the dominant species on the site for much longer than red alder. Eventually even Douglas-fir will die and be replaced by western hemlock and red cedar. If there is a wildfire that kills the Douglas-fir there is always a chance that red alder will come in and cut Douglas-fir out of the next cycle. If there is no fire or other major disturbance, as is often the case in the wettest rainforest, both alder and fir can be supplanted by hemlock and cedar which can become the dominant species for hundreds of years without interruption.

Two sites close to each other may have very different histories of successional change and may at any given time be occupied by different tree species. Whether or not, and how hot, a fire burns in these forests depends on many factors including drought, wind, and whether the site faces north or south. A south-facing site high on a hillside will be much more susceptible to catastrophic fire than a north-facing site near a valley bottom. A dry site may never get past the lodgepole pine stage of succession, burning every 50-100 years. A very wet site may not have burned for 500 years. In between are forests that might burn after 50 years but then not burn again for hundreds.

These examples present a simplified explanation of a highly complex subject. They illustrate two important points: first, that over time forests can recover on their own from catastrophic events such as ice ages and fire, and second, that the pattern of recovery and the resulting forest composition depends on a multitude of factors.

Old Growth

What are we missing in trying to read this world by the inappropriate scale of our small bodies and minuscule lifetimes?

Stephen Jay Gould - A Wonderful Life

The fate of old growth forests is second only to clearcutting as a flash point for environmental campaigns to preserve wilderness. When the two come together the confrontation between environmental and economic interests has become as intensely emotional as a clash between competing religions.

As with so many forest issues, it is a bit of a confused conflict. There is, for starters, no precise, universally accepted definition of an old growth forest. As a popular term, old growth is often used to describe forests containing trees that are simply big and old, usually over 200 years old. As a scientific term it refers to a forest containing trees that have reached the age of maturity for the particular species. From this perspective the size of the trees is largely irrelevant and designation of old growth depends on the species of tree, not on what we consider old in years.

Strictly speaking, a forest of alder or birch would be classed as old growth at about 50 years of age as these species live for only 60-80 years. In practice the term is reserved for longer-lived tree species. In the Pacific Northwest this excludes most of the hardwood species except madrone (arbutus) and Oregon oak (Garry oak), both of which are relatively small and limited in their range.

The consensus in much discussion of the subject is that old growth refers to forests 150-250 years and older, depending on the forest type and location.[5] The range in ages reflects the fact that some forests tend to survive to an older age due to the longer-lived species they contain and the lower frequency of destructive wildfires. But these definitions are arbitrary. Serious students of the subject believe that the presence -- or absence -- of defining characteristics of old growth is more important than the age of the individual trees. These characteristics include such things as standing dead trees large enough for cavity-nesting birds, fallen dead trees as habitat for insects, fungi, and small animals, and a fully developed diversity of plants, shrubs, and trees on a given site.

In many types of forest it does not take 150-250 years to develop these defining features of old growth. In coastal Douglas-fir forests on good sites these features begin to appear after 70 years of growth and are often highly developed in 100 years. Environmental activists, in campaigning to preserve old growth forests, commonly state that it will take 500-1,000 years for an old growth forest to develop after clearcutting. While it is certain that it will take 500 years for a tree to become 500 years old this does not mean it takes that long for old growth features to develop in a new forest.

Environmentalists have further confused the issue by also using the term "ancient forest" in their campaign to preserve old growth forests. This is clearly intended to heighten the emotional appeal of old trees and to allow old growth to be redefined. Whereas old growth refers to all forests composed of old trees, regardless of their size or commercial value, ancient forest was defined as "commercially valuable low-elevation to mid-elevation old growth forest."[6] This definition excludes the vast areas of old growth that are not valuable for timber, particularly on the outer coast of Alaska and British Columbia and in higher elevations throughout the Pacific Northwest region. The term is confusing because it uses the word ancient even though the environmentalist definition excludes a great deal of old forest, some of which is older than the so-called "ancient forest." This rather deceptive use of language has enabled environmentalists to state that all unprotected ancient forest will soon disappear at the hands of the forest companies. All this really means is that commercially valuable old growth that is not protected in wilderness areas and has been designated for timber production will eventually be logged and converted to new forest. Obviously the forest that has been specifically dedicated for harvest will eventually be logged. The real issue is whether or not sufficient old growth is protected, either formally as wilderness or because it is not economically useful for timber.

In a rather bizarre twist, Greenpeace has recently re-defined "ancient forest" so that it now includes the vast boreal forests of Canada and Russia and the Amazon rainforest. The trees in these areas are seldom old growth and are often very young, growing back from fire. Greenpeace explains that "Ancient forests are forest areas that are relatively undisturbed by human activity. The term refers to the ecosystem as a whole, rather than to the individual trees within them."[7] In other words, a forest with 25 year-old trees can be an ancient forest but if humans disturb a forest with 500 year-old trees it is no longer "ancient." In this case, "ancient" is apparently being used as a synonym for "sacred", and "human disturbance" for "sacrilege and desecration." This is a classic example of treating humans as if they are not a legitimate part of nature.

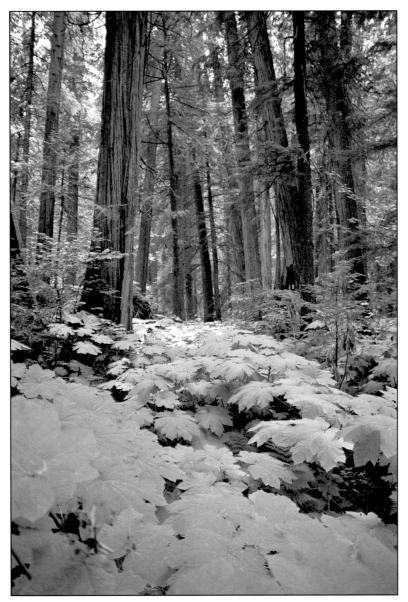

This grove of huge 500 year-old cedars in the Lardeau Valley in the West Kootenay of British Columbia is typical of the beautiful, very productive forest that most people associate with the term "old growth." This area has been protected as a prime example of old growth habitat.

Unfortunately, these heated debates have more often clouded than clarified public understanding of forestry. In the news media, the choices available to society have been presented in polarized terms as between the preservation of pristine beauty or its destruction. The old growth forest has been idealized by images of the most photogenic trees in the best light contrasted with the worst possible portrayal of barren clearcut devastation. Environmentalists have publicized the view that all old growth forests are composed of majestic, perfectly formed specimens that if protected from the chainsaw will remain that way forever. They portray all clearcut logging as total destruction with no chance of recovery.

In fact, a more accurate portrayal of old growth forests must include the tremendous variety of forest types including many that are not all that photogenic and truly are in a state of decline. It's even more important to convey the understanding of the process of forest renewal and succession that begins after the clearcut and goes on for tens or hundreds of years. If people are shown only two pictures, one of beautiful old growth and the other of apparent destruction, they will pick beauty every time. If they are told that the only way to "save" a forest is to prevent logging they will be against logging. But if they are shown a new forest that was cut down 50 years ago and is now full of beautiful young trees they may well chose it for "saving" over the old growth it replaced. To be complete, the information must cover the 100 or so years of forest renewal that comes after the clearcut and before the old growth. The process of forest development is cyclical, not a one-way street that leads either to the perfect forest or to permanent destruction.

When a forest is destroyed by whatever cause it seems like a loss when you look at it and remember what was there before. But forests have been repeatedly destroyed over hundreds of millions of years and have repeatedly recovered, often evolving into more beautiful and diverse ecosystems than the ones that went before. What would happen to a forest that was never destroyed and continued undisturbed by fire or wind or disease? You might think it would just get more beautiful as it aged. In the coniferous forests of the Pacific Northwest and British Columbia this is not always the case.

One of the more interesting and enlightening examples of forest growth and development can be found in the wettest west coast rainforest. This coastal fringe is so wet that it will not burn even in the driest summer. Where it is sheltered from the wind it never blows down in the frequent hurricanes that roar in from the Pacific. Because red cedar is so predominant in these forests there is little chance of disease as cedar is immune to most fungi and insects. As a result, large areas of coastal rainforest have remained relatively undisturbed for thousands of years as individual trees have grown and died. Composed almost entirely of red cedar and western hemlock, this type of forest occurs from around Juneau on the Alaska Panhandle south to Tofino on the west coast of Vancouver Island. Today, the western hemlock is stunted and heavily infected with mistletoe while the red cedar is gnarled and dying back from the top. Locals refer to these forests as "cedar spike-top country" or "cedar-hemlock scrub." Much of it is so full of rot that it is not worth cutting for timber. The ground is usually choked with a thick layer of salal.

Until recently it was assumed that there must be something wrong with the soil on these sites, perhaps a calcium deficiency, or perhaps it is too wet for good growth. Clearly the cedars were once green to the top and are now in a state of decline, what foresters call over-mature. It is now believed that these forests are in decline because they are too old. Extensive research has shown that the deficient nutrient is nitrogen, an element that is derived from the atmosphere with the help of soil bacteria. As these forests grow older, the nitrogen in the soil is lost to deeper layers below the tree roots. What is left is taken up by salal, a shrub that acts as a parasite on the roots of the trees. As time goes on the health of the forest gradually declines and reaches a state of long-term decay.

In these same wet coastal areas on the northern BC and Alaskan coast there is another type of forest that is characterized by relatively young and highly productive stands of western hemlock and amabilis fir. These very fast-growing forests are often right next to the decadent cedar spike-top forests, almost as if someone drew a line between them. Upon investigation, it has been found that the highly productive, younger forests are in areas that are subject to periodic blowdown from the violent hurricanes that come in from the Pacific. They are therefore constantly renewed and recycled, making them healthier and richer in the ingredients required for fast growth and tall, straight timber.

Why would periodic disturbance make a forest healthier? First, it tends to break the cycles of disease such as mistletoe and fungal root rot, and infestation by insects like bark beetles. Second, it allows new young trees to become established, replacing trees that have gone into decline due to old age. Third, it helps recycle nutrients from the old trees so they are more available to the new trees. It is almost as if forests have come to "need" disturbance (like humans need a certain level of stress) because they have always experienced it. They are sometimes better adapted to survive disturbance than old age.

This forest of old growth subalpine fir is typical of mid-elevation sites in the interior of British Columbia and the Pacific Northwest. The trees are dying as fast or faster than they are growing. Compare the ground in the interior of this forest with the recent clearcut in the same area shown on page 18.

There is no denying that many old growth forests are very beautiful, provide important habitat, and in areas where fires are infrequent, live to be centuries old. There is also no doubt that young forests of every age can be beautiful, provide important habitat, and contribute to our material needs. The choice between the two is not an absolute choice between good and evil. There are actually many choices, and in many of those a balance among the positive features of both old and new forests can be found.

We are most fortunate in the Pacific Northwest and British Columbia to have benefited from past experience in other parts of the world. More recently the knowledge we have gained from the science of ecology and the values of environmentalism have combined to make our society more willing to give up some material pursuits in favour of ecosystems that are not entirely dominated by people.

Progress has been made in resolving controversies over the preservation of old growth forest. Governments have enacted initiatives to greatly increase protection in the National Forests in the US Pacific Northwest and to double the land designated for parks and wilderness in British Columbia. At the same time, areas set aside for timber production are being more clearly defined and subject to stronger, more ecologically-responsible management codes. It's unfortunate that some environmentalists have not yet accepted these new policies and continue to make demands that are both unreasonable and unrealistic.

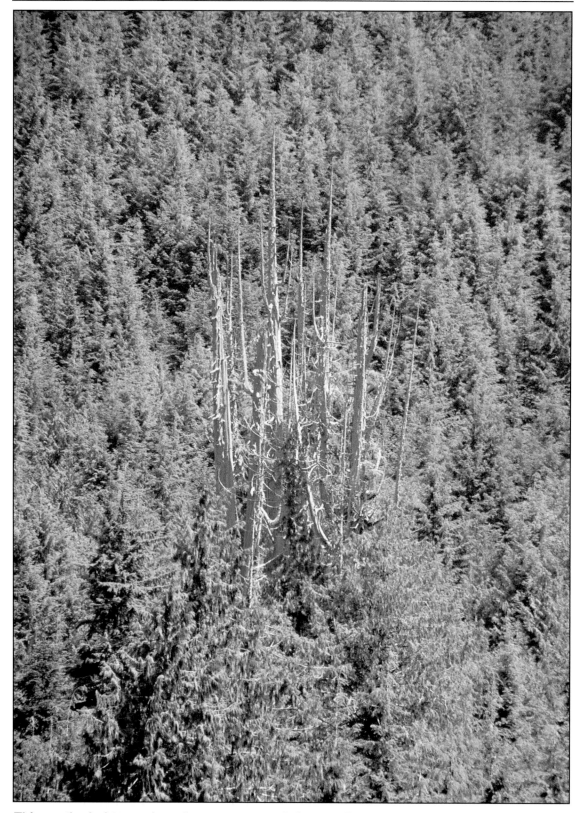

This cathedral-topped cedar snag was left standing when my father logged the surrounding forest in 1945. It may have been dead for over 100 years when the forest was cut and was over 1000 years old when it died. When it finally topples over, it will take over 1000 years to decay, as cedar is very resistant to rot. Such ancient structures will not be re-produced in managed forests. This highlights the need to protect areas of old growth forest to conserve their unique features.

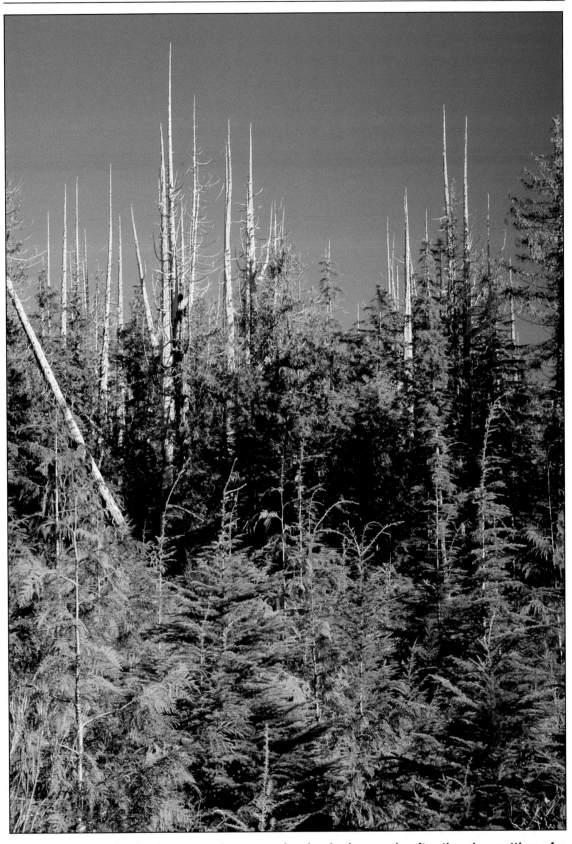

The young trees in the foreground are growing back vigorously after the clearcutting of a forest that was in decline due to old age. The original forest, seen in the background, is dying and very few new trees are taking their place. In some coastal rainforests like this one, the disturbance caused by logging can help restore the land to a more productive state.

Fire in the Mountains

While the changes caused by ice are as slow as glaciers, the destruction caused by fire is instantaneous by comparison. A lightning strike or a careless camper can burn an entire hillside or valley in a matter of hours. The worst fires last for weeks, destroying new areas each time the wind picks up to fan the flames. Forest fires spark fear in humans and animals alike. If you find yourself in the wrong place at the wrong time the flames cannot be outrun.

Public attitudes towards forest fires have always been strong. Fear, fascination, and anxiety over environmental and economic devastation have combined to generate powerful opinions. People who live in communities surrounded by forest want to be able to control fires so their towns don't get burned to the ground. Foresters view fire as sometimes beneficial and sometimes harmful, depending on a wide range of factors. Many environmental activists take the view that since fires are natural occurrences they are therefore good and should generally not be controlled.

Little can be gained by arguing about whether forest fires in general are good or bad. First, forest fires come in a great variety of sizes and intensities. Some fires burn a small area and kill only the shrubs and ground-cover, leaving the trees alive. Other fires kill virtually everything over vast areas including the seeds and soil, leaving the site sterile and subject to erosion. Second, while forest fires are often "good" as a way of temporarily increasing forage for wild grazing animals they are just as often "bad" for soil, trees, fish, birds, and humans. We tend to think worse of wildfires the larger the insurance claim when there is loss of human life and property. This may seem reasonable to us but it has little to do with the health of forest ecosystems.

For the sake of discussion forest fires can be placed in one of three groups: those started by lightning, those started by humans through carelessness or accident, and those caused by humans on purpose, often called "prescribed burning." Wherever forests are valued for timber, recreation, and wildlife, efforts are taken to control wildfires to protect these values. In 1924 the US Congress passed the Clarke-McNary Act, an agreement among forest land owners, the western States, and the Federal government to cooperate in controlling fires. A monument at Snoqualmie Falls in Washington State commemorates the historical meeting where the agreement was reached. Since that time fighting fire has become a sophisticated enterprise employing satellite surveillance, helicopters, fire-retardant chemicals and water bombers, in addition to the traditional fire-spotters in mountaintop watchtowers. Each year thousands of fires are reported and most of them are controlled before they spread very far. Some of them get away and do a lot of damage before they are contained.

In British Columbia, fire control is the responsibility of the provincial government. In an average year some 2,500 wildfires are reported, of which about half are caused by lightning and half by people. In addition, hundreds of fires are ignited on purpose for a number of reasons including brush control, preparation of harvested areas for planting, and improving grazing land for wildlife and cattle.

Forest fire control has had a significant impact on the "natural" cycle of forest disturbance and renewal that occurred prior to the advent of modern forest management. Areas severely burned were particularly large during periods of drought. Even today, in the far northern boreal forest of Alaska, Yukon, and the Northwest Territories, where there is little incentive to control fires, vast areas are burned by lightning strikes nearly every year. When these fires spread without any intervention they have sometimes wiped out whole mountainsides and valleys. If the soil is badly burned it can take decades for the forest to recover on exposed rock. These periods of catastrophic burning were followed by periods of re-growth and a new succession of forests that were burned again when conditions were right. Today, in areas where forests are commercially valuable, most potentially devastating fires are put out before they get out of control but there are still many fires that defy early attempts at control and burn large areas.

Some species of plants and trees are specially adapted to survive forest fires. Trees such as Douglas-fir, western larch, and longleaf pine have thick bark that protects them from ground fires. The seeds of some trees are adapted to survive all but the hottest blaze and some of their cones actually require heat from fire to trigger the release of seeds. The nutrients in the ashes from fires, so long as they are not washed away by heavy rains, provide a basis for rapid growth of new plants on the site.

Foresters realize that in some areas small frequent ground fires play an important role in reducing the potential for eventual catastrophic fires. The ground fires can clear away the accumulation of dead wood and brush before the fuel load becomes large enough to support a fire that kills the trees. While this might lead one to think that fires should therefore be allowed to burn whenever they start it is not that simple. It is often difficult to tell in advance if a particular fire is the kind you want or if it might develop into an inferno that wipes out a whole forest. When there are towns nearby the decision becomes even more difficult. This is a good example of a real-life situation that requires judgment based on experience and knowledge. The answer cannot be found in a rule or regulation and even the wisest person will get it wrong sometimes. It's instructive to consider two examples of situations where judgments were questioned and where there has never been a resolution on the subject of whether a wildfire should have been put out or not.

The Penticton fire of July 1994. When the forest is dry enough the fire burns in the crown and often kills all the trees over a wide area. Sometimes the flames are so hot that the soil is sterilized, killing all the plants, including their roots and seeds.

In the summer of 1994 there was a large forest fire near Penticton in the Okanagan Valley of British Columbia. The fire started in rugged hills south of the town in timber not considered valuable. Initially, winds were light and blowing away from the town so forestry and environment officials decided to let it burn as a way of clearing off the fuel load and improving grazing for wild mountain sheep. This worked fine until a few days later when the wind came in strong from the south and fanned the flames in the direction of the town of 35,000. I watched as the pines exploded in flame and the blaze leapt from tree to tree. Whole suburbs were evacuated, 18 homes were burned down, and the town's electrical supply was threatened. Water bombers were called in from Vancouver Island and as far away as Ontario to combat the blaze and save the town. Luckily the combined efforts of forestry firefighters, water bombers, and the Penticton Fire Department kept the damage confined to the outskirts. Needless to say, government officials came under severe public criticism for not doing more to extinguish the fire. Even so, environmentalists and wildlife advocates declared that the fire would result in improved wildlife grazing habitat.

After the Penticton fire (above) the land is devoid of life and even the seeds have been incinerated in the soil. Only two years later the very same area was entirely changed (below). Seeds of grasses, fireweed and other plants have blown in on the wind and covered the land with new life and beauty.

A much larger fire began in July of 1988 during a hot dry summer in Yellowstone National Park.[8] At first the officials in charge decided to let the fires burn as part of the natural cycle. As the summer progressed the fires became more numerous and spread throughout the park. Local environmentalists strongly opposed controlling the fires even though they were spreading outside the park into commercially valuable forest. Loggers, ranchers, and residents of nearby communities wanted the fires stopped. By September the main lodge at Old Faithful was threatened with destruction and the decision on action was passed all the way up to the White House. By the time President George Bush ordered the National Guard in as firefighters, a massive effort was required to subdue the blazes, ultimately costing over $120 million. In the aftermath those in favor of controlling such fires before they get out of control felt they had been right all along. The environmentalists disagreed, stating that even though it had been finally judged necessary to put the fires out that they had been beneficial to the ecosystem. They believed the forest would recover quickly from this "natural" event.

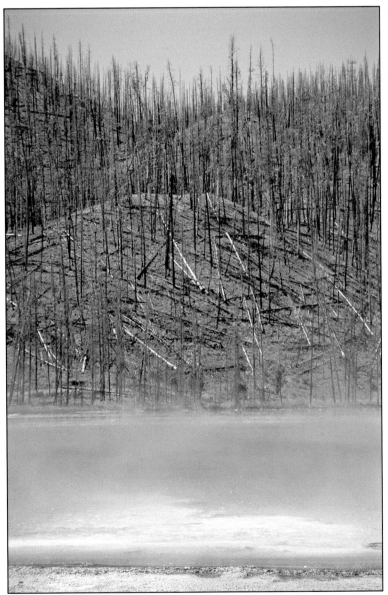

The great Yellowstone fires of 1988 killed trees in over a million acres of the park. Eight years later the hills behind the Grand Prismatic Basin were only beginning to recover. It will be many more years before a forest returns to this area.

Eight years later I visited Yellowstone, and made extensive observations on the effects of the fire, which in the end affected over a million acres (400,000 hectares), nearly 50 percent of the area of the park. There are huge areas of forest where all the trees and plants were killed and there are other vast stretches where the forest was partially burned. It soon became clear to me that depending on where one looked, a case could be made for both positions regarding the impact on the ecosystem. In some areas, where the fire had not been severe, new lodgepole pine seedlings have grown back so thick they look like a green carpet. These sites will recover fairly quickly. But in other extensive areas, such as the Lewis River canyon, all the trees are dead and very few new trees have grown back. These areas were so hot that the seeds were burned and the phosphorous in the soil was vaporized. The only vegetation after eight years is from seeds like fireweed and cottonwood that have blown in on the wind. The soil has

These two photos show contrasting situations six years after fire swept through over a million acres (400,000 hectares) in Yellowstone National Park in 1988. In the area above the seeds were burned and no young trees have emerged. In the area below even though all the trees were killed the seeds survived in a moist seepage area and there is already a thick carpet of new pines beginning to renew the forest. Seeds from these trees will eventually spread to the areas where the seeds were killed and the forest will be renewed.

been heavily eroded in places and it will take many decades before a healthy new forest becomes established.

It is one thing to debate the merits of forest destruction by fire in a park and quite another when commercially valuable timber is at stake. It is even more problematic when a fire starts in a park and then spreads outside the park into areas designated for forestry. The two land uses, parks and timber production, are managed according to different values. In the park we care about aesthetics, recreation, and an environment not dominated by the material needs of people. On commercial forest lands we care about wood production, wildlife, and recreation. Fire is not aware of these distinctions and does not respect the boundaries between them.

I don't believe there is an absolute right or wrong answer to the question of whether a particular fire should burn or not. Wildfires in forests, whether caused by lightning or people, remind us that we are not always in control of the outcome of events. The only rational approach is the combined use of experience, careful judgment, and common sense. It is just as foolish to reject efforts to control forest fires as it is to think they should always be put out. The most reasonable approach must balance forest health, timber supply, human safety, and property protection. Such a complex mix of factors, each depending on circumstance, cannot be reduced to a simple formula.

In many of the areas where it is practiced, logging has replaced fire as the major cause of change in the forest. To some extent clearcutting and other forms of harvesting can "mimic" the impact of fire in the evolution and successional development of the forest. This is discussed later in this chapter.

No matter how severe the fire or other disturbance the land eventually recovers. During the early stages of renewal there is abundant forage for grazing wildlife such as this elk feeding in Yellowstone where the trees were killed by the fires of 1988.

Volcanoes: Back to Basics

 At 8:35 on the Sunday morning of May 18, 1980, I was brushing my teeth at home in Vancouver, BC, when I heard an explosion that sounded like something serious had happened nearby. When I turned on the news a few minutes later to hear of the volcanic eruption of Mount St. Helens in southern Washington, I was amazed sound could travel over 200 miles. As the day went on the story came in: 57 dead, rivers overflowing with mud, forests flattened like match-sticks, half a mountain blown into the air and dust raining for hundreds of miles around.

When the skies finally cleared weeks later an awesome sight greeted those on the scene. The power of the inner earth had come calling to the surface, reminding us that a very thin crust of cool stone separates us from molten rock. Near the new crater there was not a sign of life where fine forests had once sheltered the earth. Further afield huge trees were sheared off at their stumps and those still standing were stripped of tops and branches. The heat of the volcanic gases killed nearly every living thing in the immediate vicinity and then buried them in rock and ash. In terms of ecological succession much of the surrounding area was back to the beginning.

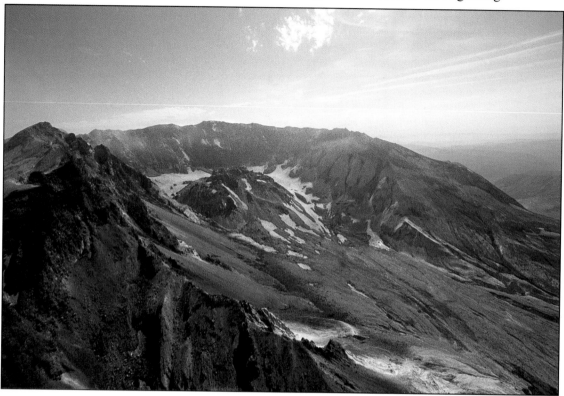

Mount Saint Helens as it looks fifteen years after the volcanic eruption that destroyed forests over a wide area of the blast zone. Today this region provides a fascinating study of the renewal of nature, both unaided and aided by human intervention.

There is not much good about such destructive events except the excitement they provide for those not directly affected. In the case of Mount St. Helens, though, some powerful lessons in forest ecology were about to unfold in the aftermath of the eruption. Before the blast the land around the mountain was mostly forested, some areas with old growth and some with second-growth after logging. Part of the land was in the Gifford Pinchot National Forest managed by the federal government and part was privately owned, the largest owner being the Weyerhaeuser Company. The volcano damaged 15 percent of Weyerhaeuser's forests and an even higher portion of the federal forest. As a result of this division of ownership a unique experiment was made possible.

Weyerhaeuser's immediate reaction was to salvage as much of the dead timber as possible before it was made worthless by insects and fungi. During the following two years they removed enough timber to build the equivalent of 85,000 three-bedroom homes. By 1987 the company had planted more than 18 million noble fir and Douglas-fir seedlings in the damaged areas.

The US federal government took an entirely different course of action. In 1982 they designated their lands within the blast zone as the Mount St. Helens National Volcanic Monument. The purpose of the monument is to allow ecological processes to proceed unaided by humans and to open the area for public viewing and scientific study.

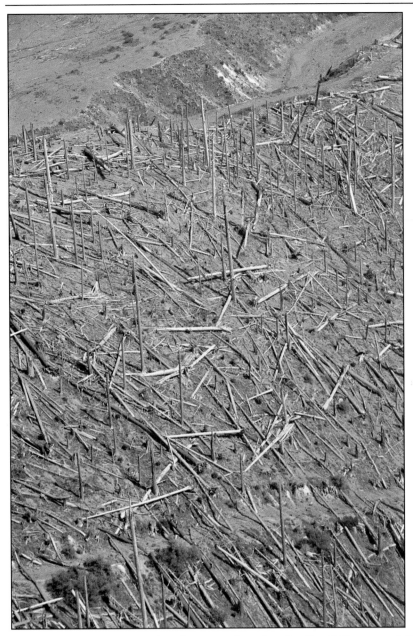

After the 1880 eruption, the Mount Saint Helens National Volcanic Monument was created to provide scientists with an opportunity to observe natural recovery from an environmental disaster, unaided by human activity. Fifteen years later the land is still mostly barren as the thick layer of volcanic ash is relatively sterile and will require many years to form a new soil. It will be a long time before there is a new forest here but the area will eventually provide good grazing for deer and elk.

The two approaches have produced radically different and fascinating results. Whereas much of the Volcanic Monument today is barely beginning to recover after 20 years, the Weyerhaeuser lands support a thriving young forest that will produce commercial timber in the year 2026. It is clear to any one visiting the two sites that human intervention has greatly accelerated the healing process. There are a number of reasons for this difference in the rate of recovery.

In the Volcanic Monument the thick layer of volcanic dust covering the land made it difficult for new plants to establish themselves even when their seeds were blown in. The dust is quite sterile as it is entirely lacking in nitrogen so only alders and other nitrogen-fixing plants can find nourishment there. Where the dust is not too thick, plants that were already rooted in the soil before the blast have pushed up through the ash and survived. Few coniferous trees have returned to the site and it will be many decades before healthy forests are re-established.

Over much of the Weyerhaeuser land the salvage operation resulted in considerable disturbance as trees were felled, bucked to length, and hauled away. The original soil was exposed to the surface where the ash was gouged, thus providing a fertile seed bed for flowers and shrubs. In addition, the tree-planters poked through the ash in order to implant the roots of the fir seedlings in good soil. Even where the firs were planted directly in the ash the roots found their way down to fertile ground. The trees have grown as if the ash layer did not exist. Now that the forest is established it provides a moist, shady environment that allows other plant and animal species to re-colonize the site.

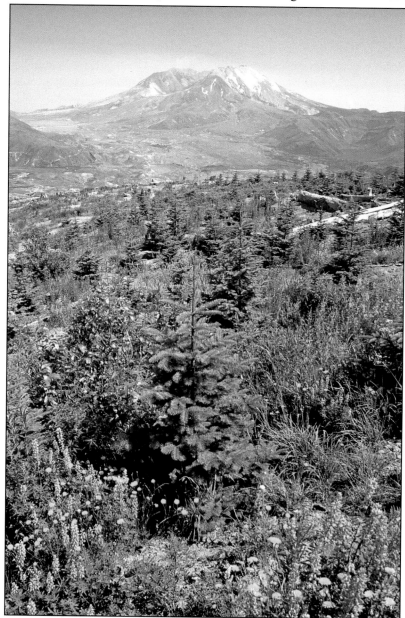

On their forest lands that were destroyed by the volcano Weyerhaeuser salvaged the timber and planted new fir seedlings. This shows the dramatic difference that can be achieved by human intervention in the process of healing and forest renewal after destruction by nature.

Which of the two approaches is best? They both have their purpose. The lands in the Volcanic Monument will remain at the "temporary meadow" stage for much longer than the reforested areas. They will provide valuable grazing land for the large elk herds that returned to the area the year after the eruption. But there is no doubt that the Mount St. Helens experiment proves that human intervention in forest management can be beneficial for forests and wildlife as well as people. There is a real win/win for all species when biological diversity is returned and material needs are provided at the same time.

The story of Mount St. Helens also gives some insight into how difficult it is to communicate anything positive about forestry to the general public. One day while writing this book I was cruising the Internet and came across a bulletin on the "Preservation of Natural Diversity" by Alexander Cockburn.[9] The story was broadcast into the global network by Ecological Enterprises at the University of Wisconsin. Among other questionable claims the article states that, "After the eruption of Mount Saint Helens in the Gifford Pinchot National Forest in Oregon (sic) in 1980, the half that was salvaged is coming back at a far slower rate than the half that was left alone." It is disheartening to realize that many people who are unable to see the area themselves will believe this false statement.

But for those who wish to see the land with their own eyes it is now possible to get there via a new highway built through the rubble of the blast zone. Anyone who makes the effort will discover in Mount St. Helens a fascinating study in natural history, with plenty to keep a person thinking about time and the evolution of forests. There is no substitute for first hand observation of forest renewal.

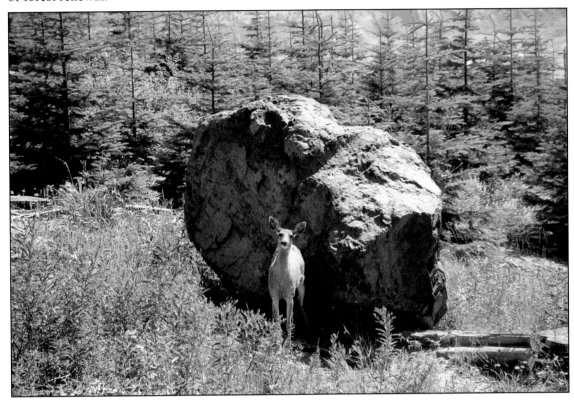

15 years after salvage logging and planting, a new forest is providing habitat for many plants and animals. There will be a commercial harvest of timber on this site in 2026.

Wind in the Hemlocks

In the driest season in the wettest coastal rainforest of Alaska and British Columbia it is virtually impossible to start a fire, the forest is so soggy. It is on some of the more fertile sites in this region, as I noted in the section on fire, where the oldest forests have developed, with cedars over 1,000 years old and 16 feet (5 meters) in diameter. But many of these forests, also characterized by a proliferation of dying cedar spike-tops, are over-mature and in decline.

On other sites in this rainforest, the trees are relatively young and productive with some of the highest growth rates on the coast. These forests were recently renewed, not by fire but by wind.

Each winter the Pacific coasts of Oregon and Washington, the west coast of Vancouver Island, the Queen Charlotte Islands, and the northern mainland coast of British Columbia and Alaska are subjected to violent windstorms. Most of these are south-easterlies that originate in the Gulf of Alaska. Less frequently they come in from the direction of Hawaii to the south-west and are known as "The Pineapple Express." By far the majority are typical winter gales that cause little damage. But a few times each season they reach hurricane force with gusts over 80 miles per hour (130 kilometers per hour). Heavy rains often accompany these storms, some of which endure for five days or more, soaking the ground and flooding the creeks and rivers. On the "wet coast" it can rain as much in three or four days as it does in drier forests over the entire year.

Occasionally there is a storm that brings unusually high winds as well as unusually high rainfall. The rain soaks the soil and turns it semi-liquid while the wind strains exposed trees to the breaking point. On steep ground this can result in landslides as the trees topple, roots and all, cascading down the slope taking lower trees with them. All along the coast on exposed mountain slopes there is a history of these slides. In 1961 a severe November storm resulted in numerous such landslides on the north end of Vancouver Island. One of the slides crossed my father's logging road and cut off the community of Winter Harbour from the logging equipment on the other side. It took two months of digging through mud and debris to open the road. These slides began high in the mountains where no logging or development of any kind had occurred.

Landslides uncover mineral soil and rock, setting forest succession back to the beginning. Subsequently, slide areas are often colonized first by red alder, which eventually gives way to hemlock and amabilis fir. These new forests are usually more productive than surrounding older forests that have not been disturbed. The new trees are healthy because the mistletoe and root rot that attack older trees have been removed by the landslides.

While landslides caused by wind and rain occur quite frequently on steep ground, once every 100-250 years there are more extreme forest blowdowns in areas exposed to high winds. Characteristically, these events are the result of extremely violent storms that devastate tall forests of fast-growing hemlock and fir. These forests are usually the result of rapid re-growth from previous blowdown events. Areas of forest that are protected from the wind escape this fate and eventually become dominated by slower-growing red cedar and hemlock.

90 years after blowing down in a hurricane this new, naturally regenerated forest of hemlock and amabilis fir is healthy and very productive. The periodic destruction of some areas of coastal rainforest by wind helps to control disease and recycles nutrients.

A classic historical case of blowdown occurred on the north end of Vancouver Island as a result of storms that swept through between 1904 and 1906. During this period, 30,000 hectares (75,000 acres) of prime hemlock and fir forest were blown down in huge swaths across the landscape. The amount of timber lost was equivalent to what would be logged over a 15-year period at today's cutting rate. This blowdown occurred before the advent of industrial forestry in the area. Eyewitness accounts refer to total devastation with entire valleys laid flat.

Today the forests that were knocked down in these storms are among the healthiest and fastest growing on northern Vancouver Island. Those that are in parks and protected from logging will continue to grow rapidly and will more than likely be knocked down again by extreme hurricane winds. Those that are within the area where logging is permitted will be harvested and either regenerated naturally or replanted with hemlock or a combination of hemlock and cedar.

It is not really possible to control blowdown in the same way as we can control fire. Some forests are exposed to the wind by virtue of topography and if the wind blows hard enough the trees will go over. When forests blow down they are essentially recycled on the spot as the new forest uses the nutrients from the rotting trees. Hemlock is a species that will germinate and thrive on wood, as it doesn't really need soil to grow. The fallen trees therefore act as a seed-bed for the new forest, which grows on, over, and around them. Eventually the roots of the new trees reach the ground where they spread out and provide stability. This pattern of growth results in a built-in vulnerability to future blowdown. As the fallen trees rot away they leave hollows among the new tree's roots. This makes the trees less stable and more vulnerable to wind than if they had rooted directly into the ground initially.

Many areas of coastal forest are subject to landslide and blowdown from high winds in the fall and winter. These areas are generally more productive compared with nearby forests that are not exposed to periodic blowdown. This is another example of how catastrophic disturbance can contribute to forest health and productivity.

Trees Get Sick Too

From the moment a tree seed germinates it becomes a target for a wide range of fungi, bacteria, predatory insects, grazing animals, and parasitic plants. Like most other living things, trees are most susceptible to disease when they are young, and again when they are old. During the hardier middle years they can still be subject to sickness, especially when stressed by extreme conditions such as drought and injury.

Some people might say that diseases are a natural part of the forest so they must be good for trees in the long run. Species of beetles that chew the life out of pine trees are, after all, part of the biological diversity of the forest. Why should we refer to them as a "disease" when they have just as much right to live as the trees?

This is about the same as saying that smallpox and the HIV virus are good for humans. Disease may well play a positive role in evolution but this is hardly going to convince us to let epidemics run wild with no effort at prevention or cure. The same is true for domesticated plants and animals. When confronted with a disease that threatens to destroy or damage crops our reaction is to find a control for the disease, not to welcome it as part of biological diversity. It is a bit fanciful to expect otherwise.

Foresters who concern themselves with forest health are no different in this respect than medical doctors, veterinarians, and plant pathologists. They prefer healthy, productive forests that are not infested with fungi and insects that damage or kill trees. They have developed a whole range of strategies to reduce the incidence of disease in trees and many of these have resulted in dramatic improvements in growth and survival. Some pests, like bark beetles, must be accepted as a fact of life and the best approach is to "manage around" them. Whatever tactics are used, the knowledge of and treatment of tree diseases is an integral part of forest science. The desire to cure disease is at least as natural as the disease itself.

Concern for forest health in managed forests is one more powerful argument for the protection of some forests as wilderness. There is good reason to make sure that the full range of species, including the disease species, survive to some extent. There is a possibility that some deadly tree parasite will turn out to produce a wonder drug that cures a disease in humans.

Some of the most interesting studies in the interaction between people and forests involve tree diseases. I will explain this with two examples, one that is common in interior forests east of the Cascades and the Coast Range, and another that occurs along the forests of the Pacific coast.

In the interior forests of British Columbia and the Pacific Northwest there is no more fascinating and controversial subject in forestry than the bark beetle. Some types of beetle, such as the ambrosia beetle, prefer dead trees. But there are two particular species of this prolific bug that prefer living trees: the pine bark beetle and the spruce bark beetle. They are not as fussy as their names imply as both will occasionally attack a number of other tree species.

The bark beetles lay their eggs under the bark of the tree after burrowing through to the sapwood. The adults carry the spores of a fungus that germinates and feeds on the nutrients and sugars traveling up and down the stem. When the eggs hatch the larvae take up residence in the sapwood and survive by eating the fungus. Between the beetles boring and the fungi plugging up the trees plumbing it doesn't take long before the tree starts to die. Bark beetles are parasites and they are quite content to kill their host. The beetles remain in the tree as larvae for one or two

years, after which they emerge as adults and the whole process begins anew.

When a forest is attacked by bark beetles the results can be dramatic. Within two years most of the trees can turn red and die. Then if lightning strikes the whole thing goes up in an inferno, often causing damage to soils and setting forest succession back by many decades. The relationship between trees, fire, and beetles is a complex one. Where fires are frequent and burn the forests down before they reach maturity the beetles can't get established. Where fires are less frequent or where they are controlled by firefighters the trees get older and more susceptible to bark beetle attack. Then the trees die, dry out and are much easier to burn.

The early stage of a bark beetle infestation in a forest dominated by lodgepole pine in the Wildhorse region of the East Kootenay in southeastern British Columbia. The red trees are recently killed by the beetles that burrow under the bark and destroy the trees' circulatory system.

The control of wildfire has been so successful in the interior that these forests are older on average now than before logging began. This has made them more susceptible to beetle attack than they were when fire swept through more often. Some people believe that because fire is natural it should be allowed to burn. They argue that the beetle epidemics are the fault of the people who are controlling the fires. Then when the beetles attack they are pronounced as natural and therefore should be allowed to run their course and kill the trees. If this in turn results in a conflagration caused by lightning, that is also natural and should be welcomed even if it takes 100 years for the soil to rebuild. People who make their living cutting trees find this line of reasoning hard to accept.

The story of what happened when bark beetles infested the Bowron River valley, southeast of Prince George, BC, illustrates the issues involved in this debate. The country is total wilderness with forests of spruce, pine, and fir. Set in its midst is the Bowron Lakes Provincial Park, a canoer's paradise where lakes form a circle with easy portages between them. In the 1970s bark beetles invaded the forest inside the park boundary and began killing trees. As this was a natural phenomenon the authorities decided to let it run its course. An alternate opinion was offered that the beetles should be controlled by a "surgical harvest" of the infected trees but this was rejected as interfering with nature's way in a park.

A few years later the beetles began to spread across the park boundary into the Bowron River valley. This area was designated for commercial forestry and the trees there were in the prime of life. The beetles threatened to destroy the value of the forest and much discussion ensued as to the course of action to take. In the end it was decided that the forest companies should harvest the trees as they died, thus providing employment and producing lumber and chips rather than letting the forest rot or burn.

The later stage of bark beetle attack in the Yaak Valley in northern Montana. Most of the trees are dead and drying out in the sun. If lightening strikes the forest will go up in an inferno killing the trees, other plants, and wildlife.

At the time, no one could have predicted the eventual extent of the area to be devastated by the beetle. For the next 15 years the loggers "chased beetles" as they followed the outbreak and harvested the trees after they succumbed to attack. By the time the beetle population began to dwindle, more than 20,000 hectares (50,000 acres) of forest had been cleared. This is probably the largest progressive clearcut in Canada. The original forest was mainly a spruce monoculture that had grown in after wildfire wiped out the whole valley over 100 years earlier. This had made it more susceptible to attack as the trees were all the same species and all the same age.

In the wake of the loggers, teams of tree planters reforested the entire area. They sometimes planted a more diverse combination of trees than had been in the valley before the beetle outbreak. All the trees planted were native to the area. It is hoped that the new forest growing up will contain a more diverse mix of species and be less susceptible to massive infestation in the future.

Told in this factual way the story of the vast clearcut in the Bowron Valley seems reasonable enough. Unfortunately, most people who have heard of this clearcut have been told a different story. It is a good demonstration of what can happen when an interest group's agenda and the media's need for sensation coincide. Environmentalists have spread the message around the world that British Columbia is home to "the world's largest clearcut, so vast it can be seen from outer space." People were told that this was a result of a conspiracy of corporate greed and political corruption that allowed such wanton destruction of the temperate forest to occur. The impression was given that clearcuts of this size were routine and acceptable practice throughout British Columbia. In many accounts, such as in the Sierra Club's widely-distributed book, "Clearcut: The Tragedy of Industrial Forestry", the bark beetle was not even mentioned.[10] When the beetle attack was mentioned in other accounts it was either blamed on poor forest management or it was argued that because the infestation was a natural occurrence it should have run its course without human intervention. In the environmentalists' presentations it was consistently assumed that the "natural" pattern of death followed by conflagration is better for the ecosystem than salvaging the trees for lumber and then replanting with new trees. I cannot accept such an argument that consistently puts tree-killing beetles ahead of human welfare and forest management.

On the Pacific coast there is another widespread tree disease that causes tremendous damage. This is the dwarf mistletoe, a close relative of the European species of mistletoe that is hung in doorways at Christmas. The mistletoes are parasitic plants that prey on the growing tips of tree branches. They intercept nutrients and sugars meant for the growth of the tree and in doing so cause gross deformities in the branches' structure. These deformities are called "witch's broom" owing to the way in which the mistletoe causes the limbs to branch out. Western hemlock, the most abundant tree on the coast, is severely affected by this parasite. In older stands every hemlock tree can be infected, resulting in stagnation of growth and deformity to the stem as well as the branches. Mistletoe spreads from one branch to another and from tree to tree by shooting out tiny seeds that land lower in the canopy. The only effective way to remove the infection is by killing their hosts.

In drier areas fire can sweep through and effectively sanitize the forest of mistletoe infection. In wetter areas landslides and blowdowns are the only means of forest renewal and where they occur the mistletoe is usually controlled. The new trees growing up from seed often remain healthy for over 100 years, producing a fast growing, straight, and tall forest. Eventually the mistletoe re-invades as the trees reach maturity. In very old forests that have not burned or been blown down the hemlocks are usually badly infected with dwarf mistletoe.

The dwarf mistletoe problem in western hemlock illustrates the kinds of considerations that must be made when deciding how to manage a forest. Say, for example, a forest owner decided to use selection logging rather than clearcutting in a stand of old growth western hemlock. We will assume that selection cutting is technically feasible and that because hemlock is shade-tolerant that it will be possible to get new trees to grow up under the old ones left standing. The problem with this scenario is that the new trees would be subjected to a rain of mistletoe seeds from the big trees growing over them. They will be infected at an early age and will not get a good start in life. What seemed like a good idea to avoid clearcutting, would produce a forest of deformed, slow-growing trees. This is not good for the trees or for the owners trying to make a living and pay their taxes.

To follow another scenario, if an old growth stand of hemlock was clearcut, the new trees coming in, whether planted or by natural regeneration, would be healthy from the beginning. Any trees that became infected could be thinned out as the forest grows and reaches the optimum size for harvest. If at this stage there was no serious mistletoe infection the decision to employ selective cutting might be a good one. Perhaps it would then be possible to continue with selection cutting for more than one generation of trees. If the mistletoe eventually returned it might be necessary to clearcut once more to control its spread.

The subject of tree disease is complex. Many foresters dedicate their entire careers to the subject and much has been learned about controlling and managing serious pests. The most important lesson is that trees do get old and sick just like humans and sometimes this makes forest management a lot more complicated. We cannot simply accept disease as "natural" and do nothing, but there are also limitations on how we can combat it. The public in the Pacific Northwest will never accept the idea of large-scale aerial spraying of insecticides. In addition, few foresters believe this is an effective, long-term solution to insect infestations. The best solutions involve gaining a thorough knowledge of the pest species and developing clever strategies to manage the threat they pose.

This huge clearcut in the Matthew River valley in the Cariboo near Bowren Lake is the result of salvaging timber killed by bark beetles. Under normal circumstances clearcuts of this size would not be permitted. Where beetles kill the trees the choice is between salvaging the timber or letting it rot or burn in a lightening fire.

What About the Dirt?

Are forest soils being destroyed by today's forest practices, especially clearcutting? Many environmentalists argue that this is indeed occurring. They have widely publicized their claim that repeated harvests of trees impoverishes soils and that clearcutting by its nature causes soils to erode away. While there is some basis to these concerns the situation is not as bleak as it is usually portrayed.

In the recent past some logging practices have led to serious incidents of soil erosion. The main cause has been the improper construction of logging roads in steep terrain, particularly in coastal rainforests. Design and engineering standards were often too low, and maintenance neglected. Many mid-slope roads had too few culverts and inadequate ditches to carry run-off from heavy rains. What ditches and culverts there were often plugged up with debris causing water to back up and break through the road, resulting in mudslides, landslides, and severe soil erosion in gullies. In too many cases, the eroding debris ended up in salmon streams, damaging spawning grounds.

Invariably these roads have been built to access areas that have been clearcut. Environmentalists have been quick to blame clearcutting itself for the erosion when poor road building caused the damage. If these areas had been logged by cable systems or helicopters, eliminating the need for mid-slope roads, little erosion would have occurred. Still, where soil has sloughed away it is often difficult to stabilize the slope and establish new vegetation or trees. This can result in long-term loss of productivity in areas that were productive before they were logged.

In recent years the regulations governing logging road construction have been greatly improved. Surveys of soil and geology are required on steep slopes before roads are built.[11] Better ditching and more and larger culverts are required. Many temporary roads are now removed by digging them up and re-contouring the soil to its original slope so trees can be planted there. More cable and helicopter logging is employed to avoid building some roads in steep terrain.

Landslides caused by inadequate construction of logging roads in many cases remain eyesores for decades. Photographs of logging-related slides have been used effectively to support criticism of the forest industry. A few such photos can give the impression that soil loss from landslides in coastal mountains is widespread when if one were to calculate the total area affected it would be very small (less than 1 percent of the total area logged). Even so, there is no good excuse for the extent of the damage caused over the years.

Along the outer coast rainforest, naturally occurring landslides play an important role in forest renewal. Where the forest is too wet to burn, blowdowns and landslides are the only ways old forests are replaced with new growth. The scars caused by natural landslides often take a long time to heal but when they do they usually support highly productive stands of trees.

Another commonly held belief about forest soils is that if the trees are regularly cut, say every 40 years, that after a few rotations (crops) the soil will lose its fertility. It is easy to see why this impression could be gained as the timber removed is of considerable volume. There is also the obvious comparison with agricultural crops that have been known to cause loss of soil fertility. In the extreme version, environmentalists conjure up the image of deserts replacing rainforests for a willing media to report.

The idea that timber harvesting will result in permanent soil damage has been given credibility by a few isolated examples where forestry did cause loss of soil fertility. The two most notable examples occurred in Germany and Australia.[12] In both cases, the areas were not only characterized by poor, sandy soils, but by gleaners and firewood-gatherers who removed every

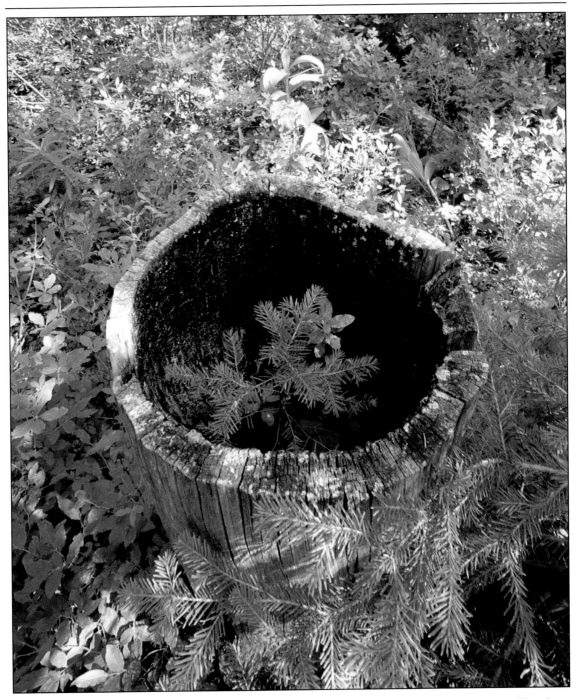

Stumps are often seen as raw wounds in the aftermath of logging. Later in life they perform many important functions; habitat for insects which in turn are food for birds and bears; fertilizer for other plants and trees that sprout on them. This subalpine fir stump which was rotten in the center when it was cut now provides a natural planter for a new fir seedling.

last twig after the timber had been cut. Under such extreme conditions on poor soils it is possible to reduce fertility over time, but these are exceptional cases.

The fact is, the trees themselves make most of the soil in forests. Rather than depleting the soil of its nutrients, each generation of trees adds to the build-up of soil. If there were no trees or plants to drop their leaves each year, to compost on the forest floor, there would be no organic soil. It is therefore incorrect to think of trees as a kind of sponge that simply soak up the soil, and then when the logs are removed from the site they take the soil's fertility with them. Part of this misconception has to do with the difference between biomass, or the bulk of the tree, and nutrients, or the essential elements that are necessary for soil fertility. The woody stems of trees are high in biomass and low in nutrients, whereas the needles, leaves and roots are high in nutrients and relatively low in biomass.

Fully 50 percent of wood is carbon, derived from carbon dioxide in the atmosphere. Hydrogen and oxygen from water from rainfall make up about 49% of the rest of the composition of wood. Only about 1% that remains as ash when wood is burned is derived from the soil. Most of the nutrients drawn from the soil are held in the roots, needles, and fine branches of the tree. These parts usually remain after logging to decompose and contribute to the soil. This is unlike agricultural crops where the most nutrient-rich parts of the plant are removed for food, usually on an annual basis. In forestry, the least nutrient-rich part of the plant is removed and then only once every 7-200 years, depending on the site and species. Because of these fundamental differences, growing trees will nearly always result in the continual building of soil as new minerals are weathered from the rocks and added to the living material. In the final analysis, sustainability of forest soils means that minerals are added by weathering of the underlying geology as fast or faster than they are removed by harvesting or soil erosion.

It's ironic that another common criticism of logging is that too much wood is left behind on the ground and wasted. Many people prefer to see a nice clean forest floor left after logging as it looks neater and tidier than a jumble of woody debris. But this contradicts the other widespread concern that logging will eventually result in soil depletion through repeated removal of trees. The forest industry has had to get used to being criticized for both taking too much wood and for leaving too much wood behind at the same time.

This is a classic case of confusing economic efficiency with ecological sustainability. The concern that wood should be used and not left to rot is an economic concern. It is indeed inefficient to cut down a forest and leave valuable wood behind to rot. But it is also inefficient to remove wood that has no economic value, or in other words would cost more to remove than it is worth in the market. Where the line should be drawn between economic and non-economic wood involves a constantly changing array of factors (demand, tree species, distance to market, labour costs, and so on). As world demand for wood increases there will be a tendency to remove a larger percentage of the wood from a given area.

From an ecological perspective the "waste" that is left behind by loggers is not waste at all. Many species of fungi, insects, plants and animals make their homes in woody debris and use it as a food source. It is valuable fertilizer that will decompose to form part of the soil for the next generation of trees. If too much wood and other parts of the trees are removed too frequently, particularly on naturally poor soils, reduction of soil fertility could take place. For this reason it is important to leave some woody material behind, even though it might look unsightly and wasteful for a time.

We are fortunate in the Pacific Northwest that the amount of wood left behind is nearly always more than enough to satisfy the ecological need for soil nutrition. In old growth coastal forests, in particular, there is often a great deal of rotten and broken wood left behind. As wood becomes more valuable it will be important to make sure that enough is left behind to ensure healthy soil. It may be necessary, on some sites, to leave wood that could be harvested at a profit. Whereas in the past governments have often over-reacted to public concern by insisting that non-economic wood was removed, in future they may be charged with making sure more is left behind.

Deforestation: A Two-Stage Process

It is not surprising that many people associate deforestation and destruction of forests with logging. After all, the first stage of deforestation is the removal of the trees. But deforestation is a two-stage process and the second stage is by far the most critical in determining the fate of the forest. The second stage involves human activity directed at making sure the forest is not allowed to grow back after it has been cut.

The subject is all the more confused by forestry critics who use the terms deforestation and clearcutting as if they were identical. Colleen McCrory of the Valhalla Wilderness Society in British Columbia, for example, flatly states that "Clearcutting is deforestation regardless of whether new trees are planted."[13] Greenpeace Germany tells their members that after clearcutting "what remains is an ecological desert ... never again will the Forest return: it has been destroyed forever ... many species of plants and animals are being eliminated."[14] The issue is more than mere semantics. These critics give the impression that an area that is clearcut, and therefore "deforested," will remain forever damaged regardless of subsequent events. It is a disservice to the public's understanding of forests to misinform them in this way. If real deforestation is to be halted the public must have a clear grasp of the difference between logging followed by reforestation and logging followed by conversion to agriculture, urbanization, and industry. The first stage of deforestation, clearing the land, is only the most dramatic. It is the second stage, the permanent conversion of land to another use, that really causes the damage and results in a state of deforestation.

There are three main categories of activity resulting in deforestation, the permanent removal of forest cover. The most widespread cause of deforestation is agriculture, including food and fiber crops, and animal husbandry. Most food and fiber crops are grown on land once occupied by forest. The only major exceptions to this are native grasslands (prairie) and irrigated lands otherwise too arid to naturally support trees or agriculture. It is not usual to refer to farm fields and pastures as "deforested land" but this is an accurate description. We tend to think of deforestation as something that happens in other countries when in truth most of us live in and are surrounded by areas where forests once thrived but are now occupied by cities and farms.

Scotland provides a good example of the ability of domestic animals to influence deforestation. When settlers cut the original forests over 500 years ago they put sheep on the land to graze on the plants that grew in after clearing. The sheep ate everything, including any seedling pine or spruce coming up in an effort to establish a new forest. Over the centuries the clearing was so extensive that the source of tree seeds was virtually eliminated, thus making it impossible for a new forest to grow even if the sheep were removed from the land. This same pattern has occurred in many areas. Goats have been a major factor in deforestation in the Middle East and the Mediterranean. Cattle are the primary agents preventing forest renewal in many tropical countries such as Costa Rica. In many areas it is not so much the people as it is their animals that are the basic cause of permanent loss of forests.

The second major cause of deforestation is urbanization, the cities and towns that are home to the vast majority of the 6 billion people now inhabiting the earth. In this process, even the soil is largely covered or destroyed as concrete and asphalt eliminate virtually every living thing beneath them. In our cities we pride ourselves in lining the streets with trees from distant lands and planting our gardens with flowers and shrubs, both exotic and highly bred. It's almost as if we were consciously determined to eliminate the natural ecology forever, so complete is the alteration caused by our habitation.

Deforestation by urbanization provides a graphic example of the fact that aesthetics has little to do with ecological health. In terms of biological diversity it makes no difference whether the land is occupied by the Sistine Chapel in Rome or an eight-lane freeway in Los Angeles. Concrete and stone are concrete and stone no matter how beautiful their expression of our cultural and historical values. The obliteration of living species is as complete by art as it is by asphalt.

The third cause of deforestation is industrial development such as mining, quarrying, and all manner of mills, factories, and warehouses. These do not occupy the same vast areas as agriculture but their destruction of native ecosystems is usually more profound. It is hard to imagine that lush forests once grew in the industrial heartland of the Ruhr valley or among the vast oil refineries outside Philadelphia.

It is important to remember that the initial clearing of land is not sufficient in itself to cause deforestation. Left alone, land that was forested will eventually return to forest after it is cut down. It is only by determined and continuous effort that our farms, cities, and industrial areas are prevented from returning to a forest similar to the one that was removed. Forests are as capable of recovering from human disturbance as they are from other natural disturbances.

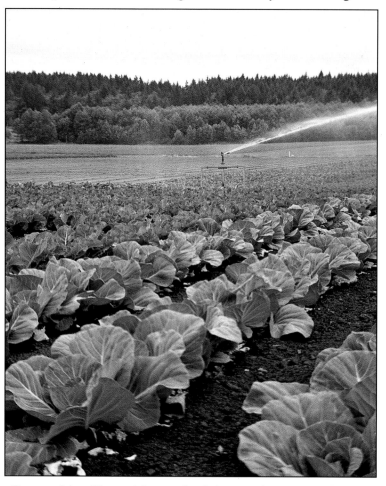

Rows of healthy cabbages look better than tree stumps but they are a prime example of deforestation for monoculture farming. They occupy land that was once covered in native forest. We must grow food to survive but every acre that is cleared for farming is one less acre of forest.

Over human history about one-third of the earth's forest cover has been lost due to clearing for other uses.[15] Forest destruction has been going on since the dawn of civilization, beginning in the Middle East, spreading to Asia, Africa, Europe, and the Americas. Everywhere the process followed a similar pattern. First the forest was cut for timber, the wood being used for everything from building ships for naval conquest to firewood for heating wooden homes. From antiquity to the modern age entire forests have been cut to smelt copper and iron and to melt sand in glassworks.[16] There has never been any shortage of ideas for the use of wood, whether for the manufacture of material goods or supplying energy for a multitude of purposes.

Sometimes the forest was left to recover in which case it could be exploited for timber again. More often than not expanding human populations eventually converted the forests to pastures, farms, and towns. New forests then fell to the ax and the pattern of development began

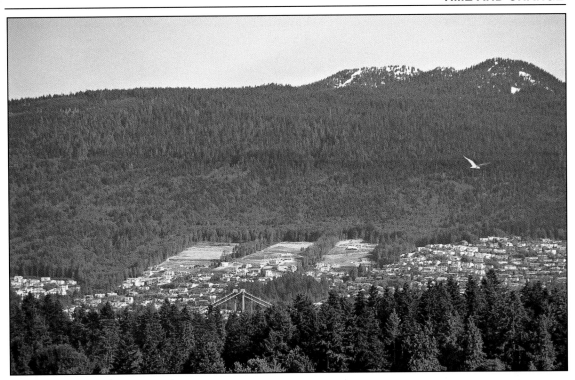

These clearcuts on the slope of Mt. Hollyburn in West Vancouver will not be reforested. They represent the conversion of forest land to urbanization and the relatively permanent destruction of the native ecology.

again. So long as there was new forest to exploit there was no need to be concerned about the conversion of some of it to growing food and housing people. In some regions the destruction of forest was so complete that civilizations fell into decline partly due to lack of wood supply.[17] It is hard to imagine in an age of fossil fuels that until 150 years ago wood was the major source of energy for cooking, heating and industry throughout the world.

Despite the displacement of wood by fossil fuels for energy in industrial countries the demand for wood has continued to increase. In the last 40 years alone, world wood consumption has doubled in keeping with the doubling of population.[18] It is almost certain the demand will continue to increase as more than 80 million people are added to the global population each year.

It is often suggested in environmentalist literature that deforestation could be halted if only the people in industrial countries would reduce their consumption of paper products. Greenpeace Germany informs its members, "Because of our paper consumption the forests in Canada and Sweden are dying."[19] Unfortunately, the situation is not that simple. Worse still, this focus on paper diverts the public's attention from the real causes of deforestation and from an understanding of the more fundamental changes required to save the world's forests. Some basic statistics about the use of wood illustrate this point.

Each day every person on earth consumes an average of 3.5 pounds (1.6 kilograms) of wood. Multiplied by the 6 billion population this adds up to a total of about 3.85 billion tons (3.5 billion tonnes) of wood extracted from the world's forests every year. North Americans consume about four times the global average. A family of four in the US or Canada consumes about 35 pounds (15 kilograms) of wood every day of the year. This seems like a tremendous amount and it makes sense to many people that if we reduced our wood consumption this would be good for the environment, as it would save forests from destruction. A closer look at our patterns of consumption reveals a very different picture.

About 55 percent of global wood consumption is used as fuel for cooking and heating, primarily in the tropical developing countries. About 2.5 billion people depend on wood for their

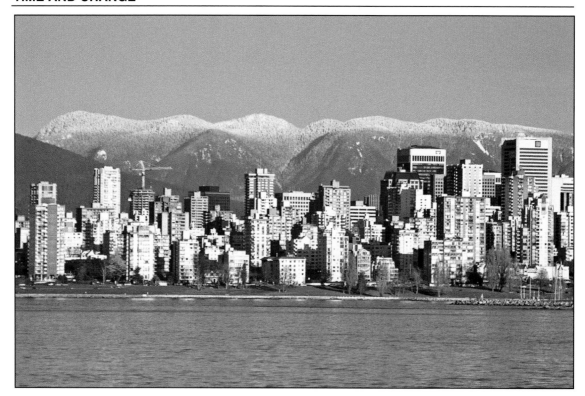

Skylines like Vancouver's form the heart of the urban areas in which the majority of people live, work and play. The forest that occupied this site until 100 years ago was as tall as these buildings. It was growing there for about 10,000 years.

primary source of energy. There is no substitute for most of this wood, as the people who need it for basic survival cannot afford to purchase alternative fuels. The main alternatives to wood for energy are coal, oil, and natural gas, all non-renewable fossil fuels. Fossil fuels are the main contributors to greenhouse gas emissions and the threat of climate change. Under the Climate Change Convention the industrial nations have agreed to reduce greenhouse gas emissions. This would not be possible if 2.5 billion people in the developing countries started burning fossil fuels instead of renewable wood.

The demand for fuelwood has reached unsustainable levels in many tropical countries. Exploitive fuelwood gathering with no replanting contributes to deforestation in parts of Africa, Asia, and Latin America. The solution to this problem is the establishment of sustainable fuelwood plantations, not switching to expensive, non-renewable fossil fuels.

About 15 percent of global wood consumption is utilized for solid wood products such as lumber, plywood, and particle board. Most of this is used for construction and furniture. The difficulty with reducing lumber consumption is not due to a lack of potential substitutes. Cement, steel, plastic and brick are readily available alternatives. The problem is the alternatives are all non-renewable, involve severe environmental impacts of their own, and require vast amounts more energy to produce than wood. More energy invariably results in more fossil fuel consumption and increased greenhouse gas emissions.

The reason that substitutes for wood require more energy to produce is the very reason that wood is the most sustainable of all construction materials. Most of the energy that goes into making wood products is solar energy. Wood is produced through photosynthesis, combining carbon dioxide from the air, water and nutrients from the soil, and energy from the sun. Wood's naturally renewable quality is its strongest asset from an environmental perspective. It can be accurately stated that wood is the material embodiment of solar energy.

The remaining 30 percent of wood consumed is manufactured into pulp and paper products for printing, packaging, and sanitary uses. Half of this fiber is waste wood obtained from

94

the sawmills that produce lumber. Most of the balance comes from pulpwood plantations or tree farms. A small percentage comes directly from natural forests, such as the aspen forests of northern Canada. Nowhere is permanent deforestation occurring specifically to make paper products.

Viewed in this light it becomes obvious that there is no simple solution to the increasing demand for wood or the problem of deforestation in the tropics. But most important, it is clear that using wood results in reduced consumption of fossil fuels and greenhouse gas emissions. This highlights the importance of looking at these issues in the broadest context, in order to understand the connections among the many resources we use for energy and materials.

Another source of misunderstanding comes from the fact that many people think the terms logging and forestry mean the same thing. They don't and the difference is important. Logging refers to the harvesting of trees; forestry refers to the science and practice of cultivating forests. Logging has been practiced for thousands of years; forestry is a much more recent development.

In the same way that hunting and gathering for food was gradually replaced by agriculture thousands of years ago, the transition from simply logging the forest to managing it is now underway. In earlier times it seemed there were always new forest lands beyond those already cleared for cities and farms. By the mid-18th century, civilization began to experience the limits of the forests' natural ability to satisfy wood requirements. People realized that the forests needed tending and renewal, and this led to the development of forestry (more formally known as silviculture), the art and science of growing trees.

Today, an increasing proportion of the world's wood supply comes from forests that have been managed for that purpose. During the past century deforestation has been effectively halted in the temperate regions as some lands formerly cleared for farming have been reforested for

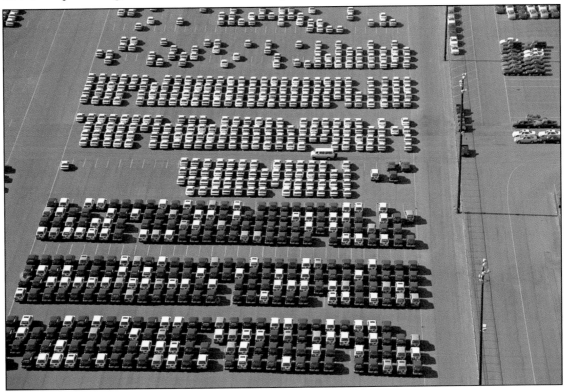

The ultimate in deforestation. Asphalt, a toxic waste from petroleum refining, covers the earth, killing every living thing so cars can move freely over the land. This was once an old growth forest near the mouth of the Columbia River in Washington State.

timber production.[20] Between 1980 and 1990 the forested area of temperate regions increased by 64 million acres (26 million hectares) for an increase of 2 percent in the total forested area. The most dramatic example of this trend is in the eastern US where early settlers cleared vast tracts for farming. Much of this has now returned to forest cover and is managed for trees rather than food crops. A similar pattern of forest recovery is occurring in Sweden, South Africa, and New Zealand.

The popular belief that forestry is responsible for deforestation is therefore very misleading. Nearly all the deforestation presently taking place is in tropical and subtropical forests. Between 1980 and 1990 deforestation resulted in the loss of 380 million acres (154 million hectares) or 8 percent of total tropical forest area. Clearing for agriculture and urbanization were the main causes.[21] To be sure, logging for timber caused a small percentage of this deforestation, largely due to a failure to follow good forestry practices.

A report from the Food and Agriculture Organization of the United Nations (FAO), "State of the World's Forests – 1999" indicates some grounds for optimism. During the first five years of the 1990s, deforestation in the tropics declined to a level of 0.65% per year, down from 0.8% per year in the previous decade. In addition, the forested area of the temperate regions increased by 50 million acres (20 million hectares) over the same time period, increasing to a level of 0.3% per year from 0.2% per year in the previous decade.

While deforestation appears to be slowing it is inevitable that more land will be cleared to provide food for a growing population. The FOA estimates that 220 million acres (90 million hectares) of new land will be required for farming by 2010, half of it from forests.[22]

The challenge of communicating the real causes of deforestation is often made more difficult by inaccuracy and sensationalism on the part of the news media. The German newsmagazine, Der Spiegel, wrongly informed its millions of readers that "Only 10 percent of the denuded areas of British Columbia are reforested -- with a few species of genetically manipulated seedlings, most of which soon die."[23] The fact is the law in British Columbia requires that 100 percent of logged areas must be reforested. The survival rate of the 250 million seedlings planted each year is about 85 percent.[24] The 15 percent mortality rate is compensated for by planting more seedlings than will be required in the new forest. Forest renewal is very successful in British Columbia and yet the opposite is repeatedly told to millions of people who live too far away from the province to see the truth for themselves.

In the United States there are about 750,000 acres (300,000 hectares) of forest lost each year.[25] How many Americans, if asked what they thought was the cause of this loss, would answer "logging" or "timber harvesting"? In fact, nearly all this forest loss is caused by urban expansion as over 200 cities sprawl out over the land.

It is somewhat ironic that the three most effective actions we can take to stop deforestation have nothing to do with forests or forestry. These are:

- **Population management.** So long as the human population continues to grow there will be a need for increased food production. The FAO estimates that world food production will increase by 1.8% per year until the year 2010 and beyond. It is no coincidence that this is similar to the current 1.5% per year population growth rate. In order to grow this additional food it will be necessary to clear more forest.

- **Intensive agriculture.** Since 1960, US farmers have more than doubled the amount of food grown on the same acreage of land.[26] This has been possible due to genetically improved seed, the use of chemicals and fertilizers, and technology. Unfortunately, much of the agriculture in the developing world is low-intensity subsistence farming that uses far more land per person than intensive agriculture.

- **Urban densification.** Urban sprawl often covers up the best farmland around cities. This makes it necessary to clear more forest in order to make up for lost agricultural production.

Urban densification requires building cities up rather than out. This not only saves land for farms and forests but also results in a more efficient infrastructure that requires less energy and maintenance.

In conclusion, it is essential that the public understands that forestry results in reforestation, while deforestation is caused by the conversion of forests to cities, farms and industrial sites.

Sustainable Forestry

It is a boy's statement, and does not imply much wisdom, to discover that "little strokes fall great oaks," for the sound of the ax invites our attention to such a catastrophe. We can easily count each stroke as it is given, and all the neighborhood is informed by a loud crash when the deed is consummated; but there are few who consider what little strokes, of a different kind and often repeated, raise great oaks or pines. Scarcely a traveler hears these or turns aside to communicate with that Nature which is steadily dealing them.

Henry David Thoreau - Faith in a Seed.

The advent of the modern environmental movement in the late 1960s stimulated an increasing concern for the ecology of forests as a whole. This concern is expressed in two fundamentally different ways.

First, there is a strong movement to protect and preserve remaining first-growth forests as wilderness areas, not to be disturbed by logging or other industrial development. So long as these areas are large enough it is possible to provide relatively intact ecosystems in which all species dependent on forest cover can flourish. The extent of the area required to sustain the larger predators such as grizzly bears and big cats is still a subject of some debate.[27]

Second, where forests are managed for wood production, there is growing pressure to do so in a manner that protects as many features of the original forest as possible. This is best accomplished by planting native tree species and by retaining and enhancing critical elements of the forest such as standing dead trees required by cavity-nesting birds. This approach to forestry has been called "ecologically-based forestry" or "New Forestry."[28] This is the direction in which most forestry activity is moving in North America. The challenge is to provide habitat for as many species as possible in managed forests while at the same time maintaining an economically viable forest industry.

Through the art and science of forestry it has been possible to understand a great deal about trees and the environments that support their growth. Many of the lessons learned over the long history of agriculture are applicable to forestry, particularly regarding soil science, nutrition, and disease control. Over the last century forestry has also benefited from advances in our knowledge of genetics, physiology, and ecology.

Until recently foresters were concerned primarily with commercial species of trees and with those wildlife species such as deer and elk that have economic importance. Little consideration was given to non-commercial species such as frogs, mice, woodpeckers, ferns, mosses, and fungi. It was just assumed that if a new forest was established that these species would recover as the trees grew back. In some parts of the world where non-native tree species were used to replace the original forest this was not always case.[29]

The most common term associated with improvements in forest management is "sustainable forestry." This is derived from the general concept of sustainable development[30] or "sustainability" as it is now often expressed. Sustainable forestry means adding the environmental issues to the social and economic issues and balancing all three. This is no small task.

On one level, sustainability is an ideal state in which the actions of today's generation have no adverse impact on the opportunities of future generations. On another level, it is a pragmatic, rational approach to changing our behavior in order to conserve rather than squander our natural resources so future generations have more choices. There is no perfect state of sustainability. It is a relative concept that requires a high level of strategic planning and consideration of details.

Before we can determine what sustainable forestry means for a given area of forest land we must first decide what it is we wish to sustain. Sustainable forestry, at its simplest, means a commitment to retain trees on the site. But which species of trees? It may be possible to cut down a native coniferous forest and replace it with non-native hardwoods such as maple and oak and still have a sustainable forest. But some of the other species that lived in the coniferous forest may not survive in a hardwood forest. In that sense they would not be sustained even though the hardwoods themselves could be sustained over a hundred generations. Some other plant and animal species would prefer the hardwoods to the original conifers and hence could be more sustainable in a new environment created by human management.

The key to understanding sustainability is to realize that it is entirely about planning for the future. Sustainable forestry is not concerned with what has happened to forests in the past, but what will happen to the land during coming generations. It is not legitimate to declare that a particular piece of wood came from a sustainable forest unless we know that forest will continue to be maintained in a healthy, productive state into the future. Therefore the most important factors underlying sustainability are the institutional arrangements that ensure the land will be properly tended and will not be converted to other uses such as agriculture or urban development. Such things as the nature of ownership, management agreements, laws requiring government approval before forest land can be converted to shopping malls; these are the real guarantees of sustainability. No amount of details about forest practice, environmental protection, or public participation can produce sustainable forestry if there are no trees left to cut and nowhere left to grow them.

Once we have decided what it is we wish to sustain; timber production, native tree species, and recreation for example, it is necessary to consider the time frame in which we are operating. No state of affairs is sustainable eternally. Climate will change, ice ages may return, eventually the sun itself will burn out. We need not think in these geological time frames to fashion a practical approach to sustainability. Even so, it is important to set goals for sustainability that take into account the needs of several future generations. In forestry this means looking forward at least 100, and preferably 200, years. This is what sets sustainability theory apart from traditional economic thinking which seldom attempts to forecast more than 5 or 10 years ahead. Despite the long life span of many tree species it has been unusual, even in forestry, to think in such long periods of time.

The third point that must be considered is the area of land over which sustainable forestry is to be practiced. Some land is not suitable for growing trees so it would be pointless trying to carry out sustainable forestry there. Other land is already designated for cities, factories and farms making it difficult to convert back to forest. Still more land is protected in wilderness preserves and parks where society has decided not to cut trees for wood. This leaves a limited area of land that is both suitable for forestry and not designated for some other purpose.

Much of the conflict over land use stems from the fact that one piece of land, such as a fertile river delta, may be excellent for many uses while another, such as a steep alpine slope, is unsuitable for any economic purpose. The river delta would be well suited for industry, housing, farming, forestry, and/or wilderness. The decision on the use for which a given piece of land is designated depends on the complex interplay of economic, environmental, and political factors. As we have seen too often in recent years, conflicts over land use are not easily resolved without serious strife, even in our democratic societies. Not all interests can be accommodated by the decisions that determine land use and ownership. Someone will always be disappointed. Commitment to the practice of sustainable forestry can provide a basis in our communities for achieving consensual agreement to resolve forest land-use conflicts. Readers interested in the use of consensus process at the community level to achieve plans for sustainable forestry will be interested in the Quincy Library Group, based in the Sierra and Plumas Counties in northern California.[31]

A 60 year old stand of Douglas-fir that has grown back from logging in the Koksilah River valley on southern Vancouver Island. This forest is a natural tree monoculture but is rich in other species that grow beneath the canopy. It will soon be ready for a second harvest when it will once again be regenerated with native species of trees.

It is not possible here to give an exhaustive definition of sustainable forestry. In the Pacific Northwest States and British Columbia alone there are hundreds of statutes, regulations, and guidelines governing forest practices, many of which are aimed at ensuring sustainability. Such issues as road building standards, old growth protection, wildlife preservation, fisheries, biological diversity, and forest renewal each require volumes of description and elaboration. Sustainable forestry is a very complex subject. But it is generally agreed that sustainable forestry must take into account the full range of values found on the land. These include non-material issues such as spiritual and cultural values as well as material concerns. There are special places in forests where natural features combine to encourage contemplation and wonder. There are places of deep cultural and historical significance where commercial activity must be curtailed. The material values range from the vast number of insect species to the growing of wood for human use to the protection of clean water and air. The discussion of each of these issues will no doubt continue for centuries to come.

The following listing of major subject areas, based on the Principles of Sustainable Forestry, developed by the Forest Alliance of B.C., will give the reader a feel for the complexity of sustainable forestry. While these principles were written for application on public forest land, most of them apply to the management of private forest land as well.

Environment

• The most fundamental aspect of sustainable forestry is the protection and conservation of soil. Forest roads and skid-trails, especially on steep slopes, have the most potential to damage soil. Roads should not be built where there is a risk of severe soil erosion. Where roads are built they must be up to standards that will ensure long term erosion control. Temporary roads should be removed to provide more space for growing trees. Harvesting methods such as skyline cable systems and helicopter logging that reduce the area disturbed by roads should be used wherever practical.

• Logging operations must be planned on the basis of watersheds. The clearing of excessive areas within a given watershed can lead to flooding, soil erosion and damage to fish bearing streams and rivers.

• Fish habitat must be protected through careful planning along waterways. Buffer strips of forest should be maintained on major streams and rivers to maintain stream bank stability, provide shade, and maintain water quality.

• Wildlife habitat must be protected by ensuring that critical features such as deer winter range, bird nesting trees, and woody debris are provided.

• Biological diversity in its totality must be protected by ensuring that representative areas of all successional stages, including old growth or original forest, are present in each forest ecosystem.

• The forest industry's contribution to greenhouse gas emissions, and hence to the potential for climate change, should be minimized through energy efficiency, wildfire control, soil conservation, and rapid reforestation of harvested land.

Forestry

• Government and industry must ensure there are up-to-date and accurate inventories of all forest resources on which to base forest management plans and to determine sustainable harvest levels.

• Care must be taken to use harvesting practices and equipment that minimize soil disturbance and damage to the remaining vegetation and wildlife habitat.

• Where some form of clearcutting is determined to be an appropriate harvesting practice it must be done in a manner that satisfies all the other Principles of Sustainable Forestry. Other harvesting systems, such as selection and partial cutting should be used where they are appropriate from a silvicultural perspective.

• All commercially valuable wood that is cut during logging operations should be utilized to avoid economic waste. This must be balanced with the need to leave sufficient woody debris and organic matter to provide wildlife habitat and nutrients for the next generation of trees.

• All logged areas should be rapidly reforested either by natural regeneration or by planting with appropriate species. (Throughout North America this usually means native species). Forest practices such as brushing and thinning should be employed to ensure the survival of the new forest and to improve the quality of wood production.

• The use of conventional chemical pesticides must be minimized by employing alternative methods of pest and weed control wherever practical and environmentally sound.

• Burning must be carefully prescribed and used only where it is necessary to ensure reforestation, prevent wildfires, and improve wildlife habitat.

Other Commercial Values

• Other commercial uses of the forest must be protected and taken into account when planning logging operations. These values include tourism, livestock grazing, hunting, fishing, trapping, honey production, and berry, mushroom and foliage picking.

Public Involvement and Recreation

• Local communities must be directly involved in decisions that effect their stability, employment, economic viability, and quality of life.

• Communities and individuals have a right to access information, to be involved in forest planning and to monitor industrial performance.

• Forests should be managed with concern for recreational use by the public. This includes the appearance of roadsides and harvested areas and assistance in providing campsites, picnic areas, boat ramps and trails.

• Visual impact should be taken into consideration when planning logging operations near communities, recreation areas and along major travel corridors.

• Environmentally appropriate practices such as recycling, waste oil recovery, solid waste reduction and management, energy efficiency, pollution control, the appearance of industrial sites and a positive attitude towards environmental programs must be incorporated in all forest industry operations.

Research and Monitoring

• Research and development programs must be undertaken to increase knowledge of forest management, to generate more value-added products, and to protect the environment.

• There must be an independent forest practices monitoring system that reports its findings to industry and the public.

All of these principles should be enshrined in appropriate legislation and must be properly enforced. They must be interpreted for the particular ecological, cultural and economic conditions of the region. In the Pacific Northwest and British Columbia this is resulting in a trend towards much smaller clearcuts that are placed more carefully in the landscape. Protection of rivers, fish and wildlife, and public involvement in decision-making are now a routine part of the planning process. Last, but not least, forestry must be carried out efficiently so as to provide the greatest possible contribution to human wealth while meeting the legislated level of compliance with each of the principles outlined above.

A number of references are provided for the reader interested in further pursuing the technical aspects of sustainable forestry.[32]

Forests and Climate Change

Much mention is made in the environmental literature of the potential for clearcutting in particular, and forestry in general, to contribute negatively to the potential for climate change. It is argued that by converting old growth forests to second growth forests there will be a significant release of carbon dioxide (CO_2) into the atmosphere, thus contributing to the build-up of greenhouse gases.[33]

To counter this, foresters point out that fast-growing trees in healthy second growth forests take up carbon dioxide rapidly whereas

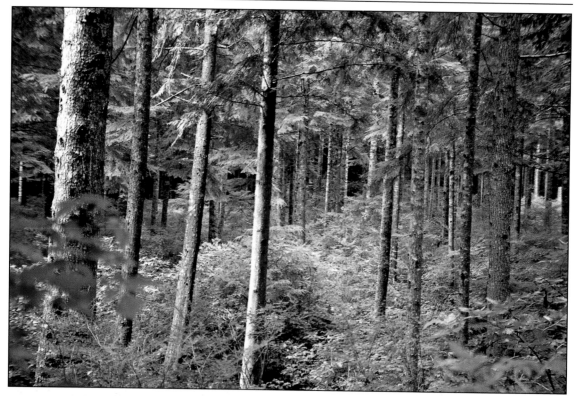

A 35 year-old forest growing back in a clearcut in Clayoquot Sound on the west coast of Vancouver Island. Amid accusations of "ecological collapse" and "species extinction" the forest quietly returns, providing a home for all who dwell there.

old growth is in a state of near equilibrium, releasing as much CO_2 as they are absorbing.[34] In some cases old growth forests are even in decline, thus contributing to a net release of carbon dioxide. Unfortunately for the understanding of the interested public, there are merits to both arguments and the truth is somewhere in the middle.

The subject of greenhouse gases and climate change, as they relate to forests, is one of those many aspects of forestry that can fill volumes and even then is not fully understood. Simplistic statements are not to be believed from either side of the debate and a great deal of skepticism and open-mindedness is in order. In general, some aspects of forestry contribute to greenhouse gas emissions while others have a positive result by absorbing greenhouse gases.

The relationship between trees and greenhouse gases is simple enough on the surface. Trees grow by taking carbon dioxide from the atmosphere and, by photosynthesis, converting it into sugars. The sugars are then used as energy and material to build the cellulose and lignin that are the main constituents of wood. When a tree rots or burns the carbon contained in the wood is released back to the atmosphere as carbon dioxide and the cycle is complete.

Carbon dioxide is the most important greenhouse gas. During the past century, as a result of increasing fossil fuel combustion and deforestation, carbon dioxide has been building up in the atmosphere. Fossil fuel use is responsible for most of this trend. Fossil fuels are the oldest of all forests, conserved as organic remains in an altered state beneath the surface for hundreds of millions of years. Now we are using the remains of these ancient trees to fuel industrial growth around the world.

Carbon, the common currency of all living things, occurs in only two forms as far as the discussion of climate change is concerned. It is either in the form of carbon dioxide, a greenhouse gas that now constitutes about one-third of one per cent of the atmosphere; or it is in the form of "fixed carbon" in plants and animals, soil, fossil fuels, dissolved in seawater, and as calcium carbonate deposits, otherwise known as chalk, limestone and marble. Calcium carbonate deposits are the remains of shells, mostly from microscopic plankton but also from mollusks.

Carbon becomes fixed when carbon dioxide is converted either to sugars by photosynthesis in growing plants or to calcium carbonate by metabolism in creatures with shells. Processes that result in carbon fixation are called "sinks". Carbon is converted back to carbon dioxide when plants and animals rot, when wood is burned, when fossil fuels are burned, and when limestone is converted from calcium carbonate to calcium oxide in cement production. These processes are called "sources". Carbon is in a constant state of flux between the fixed forms and the atmospheric form. During the past century, and particularly during the past fifty years, there has been an imbalance in the flux. More carbon dioxide is now added to the atmosphere each year than is removed by conversion to non-atmospheric forms.

One of the more confusing aspects of the "carbon cycle" involves the difference between the rate of change of carbon from one type to another versus the total amount of carbon in a particular form. Using a financial metaphor, this is similar to the difference between a statement of cash flow and a balance sheet. One is a measure of change over time while the other is a snapshot at a given time. Old growth forests often have a large "balance" of carbon that has built up over time in wood and soil. They are not adding much new carbon because they are decaying at about the same rate as they are growing. In financial terms, this is like a company that has a lot of assets but is operating on a break-even basis. Young forests have a smaller balance of carbon compared to old forests but they are accumulating carbon at a rapid rate. In that sense they are like an emerging company that has few assets but is very profitable and growing rapidly.

This is why the seemingly opposite points made by environmentalists and foresters are both true to some extent. Old forests do contain more carbon than young forests and young forests are absorbing carbon faster than old forests. Beyond these fairly simple truths, however, the carbon story becomes much more complicated. Every forest type has a different carbon budget both in terms of quantities in various forms and the time for change to occur. Forest products such as wood and paper continue to hold carbon in a fixed state for varying lengths of time. A piece of furniture made in the Elizabethan era still holds the carbon fixed hundreds of years ago. A newspaper used to light an inviting fire releases its carbon back to the atmosphere within days of manufacture.

It has only been in the last ten years, as concern about climate change escalated, that scientists have begun to pay close attention to the role of forests in the global carbon cycle. A number of general statements can be derived from their work:

• Deforestation, primarily in tropical forests, is responsible for about 20% of global carbon dioxide emissions.[35] This is occurring where forests are permanently cleared and converted to agriculture and urban settlement. There is seldom as much carbon stored in crops or settled land as in the original forest so there is a net loss of carbon that is not replaced. Deforestation is by far the most significant net contributor to greenhouse gas emissions associated with forests.

• In many countries with temperate forests there has been an increase in carbon stored in trees in recent years. This includes New Zealand, the United States, Sweden and Canada. In Canada, for example, an average of 200 million tonnes* per year was added to carbon stored in forests between 1920 and 1989.[36] This highlights the fundamental difference between deforestation and reforestation. In some countries where land is remaining in, and being returned to, forest cover there is a net uptake of carbon from the atmosphere. Unfortunately this nowhere near offsets the carbon released from deforestation in the tropics.

---

* **In this section, I use the metric system throughout, as this is the standard adopted by the international community for the discussion of climate change.**

• In some old growth forests, such as the outer coast rainforests of the Pacific Northwest, there may be less carbon stored in managed forests than in the original forests. Depending on the fate of the products produced from the trees, this can result in a net release of carbon from the forest to the atmosphere when the forest is converted from old growth to managed forest. In other forests, such as the interior dry forests of the Pacific Northwest, managed forests tend to have more carbon on average than the original forests. This is mainly due to the control of fire, resulting in forests that are older than if natural fire from lightning were to periodically sweep through. In total, forest management in itself does not have a significant net effect on the carbon cycle. The most important factors are deforestation on the negative side, and the use of wood, grown sustainably, as a substitute for non-renewable materials and fuels on the positive side.

When considering the broader impact of forest management on the carbon cycle it is most important to determine whether or not the wood is being used as a luxury or as a substitute for some other material. For example, it may be argued that excessive wooden trim in the interior of a house is a luxury while a kitchen table made of wood is not. In the case of the table it would be necessary to substitute some other material in order to avoid the use of wood. As mentioned previously, every wood substitute, including steel, plastic, and cement, requires far more energy to produce. More energy usually translates into more greenhouse gases in the form of fossil fuel consumption or cement production. Most wood consumption is for necessity rather than luxury, such as the lumber used for building houses. Granted, we could live in smaller and smaller houses but even to this there is a limit. In general, wood is preferable to all other structural materials if we are trying to reduce the emissions of greenhouse gases.

At the United Nations "Earth Summit", held in Rio de Janeiro in 1992, the Climate Change Convention was adopted with the goal of first stabilizing and then reducing greenhouse gas emissions worldwide. The signatories to the Convention met in Kyoto, Japan, in December 1997 where they passed the Kyoto Protocol which recognizes the important role of forests and forestry in the carbon cycle. Along with emissions from fossil fuel combustion, countries are instructed to include "net changes in greenhouse gas emissions from sources and removals by sinks resulting from direct human-induced land use changes and forestry activities."[37] This means that countries must include emissions caused by deforestation and that they can include net removals of carbon dioxide resulting from the reforestation of previously cleared land. Thus, the Climate Change Convention may have a powerful influence on the expansion of the world's forests and the use of renewable wood as a substitute for non-renewable fuels and materials.

It might be expected that the environmental movement would unanimously embrace the idea of using forests to reduce greenhouse gas emissions, but this is not the case. Some environmental groups, notably the Nature Conservancy, the Environmental Defense Fund, and the World Resources Institute, have taken a positive stance towards using forestry projects to offset emissions from fossil fuels. Many other groups, including Greenpeace, the World Wildlife Fund, and Friends of the Earth, have taken a hard line against the inclusion of forests in national carbon budgets. To date, they refuse to concede the positive role forestry could play in both reducing carbon dioxide emissions and increasing forest cover. Hopefully they will eventually realize, that despite their legitimate concerns about bad logging practices, forestry promises to lead the way in the supply of renewable energy and materials, in the reduction of greenhouse gas emissions, and in the expansion of forest habitat with positive impacts for soils, water quality and biodiversity.

Rather than being portrayed as part of the problem of climate change, forestry and the growing of trees must be adopted as part of the solution. It is generally agreed that it is not possible to completely offset the present fossil fuel consumption by planting more trees. Just the same, reforesting areas previously cleared for farming could have a significant positive impact on carbon storage.[38] The sustainable use of the wood grown in these forests could substitute for fossil fuels directly as firewood and for steel and cement as construction materials. The solution is to use more wood, not less, and this means growing more trees.

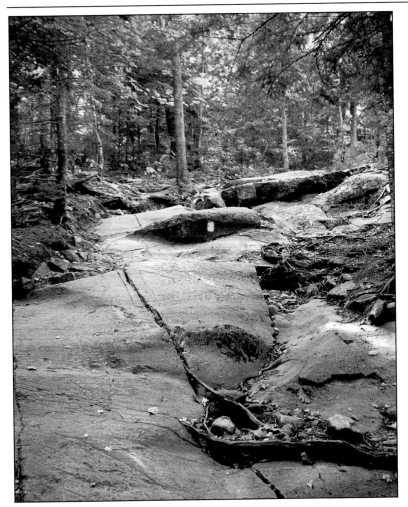

This exposed rock in a creek bed in near Cambden, Maine was scoured smooth by glaciers thousands of years ago. The climate was colder then, and nearly all of Canada and northern parts of the United States were covered by ice up to a mile thick. What will this place look like 500 years from now? What about 5,000 years from now? Will there be palm trees here or will the ice return?

It is instructive to consider some of the numbers involved in the carbon cycle. The global atmosphere contains about 750 Gigatons (750,000,000,000 tonnes) of carbon in the form of carbon dioxide. The Earth's living vegetation contains about 600 Gigatons of carbon, of which about 500 Gigatons is in forests. Each year about 60 Gigatons of carbon is absorbed by vegetation and then re-emitted to the atmosphere as a result of the annual growth in the Spring and Summer and decay in the Fall and Winter. This compares with a total of 6 Gigatons of carbon emitted annually by the use of fossil fuels and about 2 Gigatons emitted due to deforestation. From this it can be seen that a relatively small change in global vegetation, forest cover in particular, could have a significant impact on the carbon cycle.

Trees are the most powerful concentrators of carbon on Earth. The atmosphere contains 360 parts per million of carbon dioxide, or 0.177 grams of carbon per cubic meter. Through photosynthesis, trees concentrate carbon by 1.4 million times, producing wood that contains about 250 kilograms of carbon per cubic meter. This means that a hectare of forest, growing at the rate of 10 cubic meters per hectare per year, will absorb the carbon from a column of air 1.4 kilometres high above that hectare *every year*. Over the forest's growth cycle, it can absorb the carbon from a volume of air over 1,000 times the volume taken up by the forest itself.

By growing more trees, and then using the wood as a substitute for fossil fuels and non-renewable materials, we could reduce greenhouse gas emissions substantially. First, the increased biomass of trees results in a reduction in atmospheric carbon. Second, the substitution of wood for fossil fuels and materials that require fossil fuels for their manufacture, results in reduced emissions of carbon dioxide from fossil fuel combustion.

Annual wood consumption is now 3.5 Gigatons per year, representing about 1.75 Gigatons of carbon. If we could halt continued deforestation in the tropics, and gradually increase wood production to double the present consumption, we would make a significant contribution to the reduction of CO_2 emissions.

While forest management could have a positive impact on potential climate change, climate change itself could have a devastating effect on forests. If the climate changes as rapidly as some scientists predict it may be impossible for some tree species to migrate quickly enough to become established in cooler regions. Forest fires may become more frequent in many types of forest leading to forest destruction, a disruption in harvesting rates, and shortages in wood supply. This is all the more reason to plant more trees and make the earth as green as possible. Reforestation projects can be effective in urban and agricultural areas as well as in rural regions. It is hard to imagine a more all-purpose, environmentally friendly act than that of contributing to the number and variety of trees growing in all environments that will support them. In the age of climate change, Johnny Appleseed takes on a new meaning.[39]

Clearcutting: Defending the Seemingly Indefensible

Clearcutting is the focal point. Opposition to it is the rallying cry of a wide range of environmental critics. They broadly condemn clearcutting as causing deforestation, extinction of species, loss of soil, and permanent destruction of ecosystems. Timber harvesters who employ this method of cutting trees are portrayed as greedy, short-sighted, and ignorant. The elimination of clearcutting is seen as central to the practice of enlightened forestry where forests are preserved forever while at the same time providing timber through selective cutting.

The public debate on this issue has become thoroughly clouded with emotional rhetoric and misunderstanding. Many have suggested that the problem is the word "clearcut" itself, it has become too negative a term and we should give it a new name so the public will think the practice has been stopped. Swedish foresters have invented the term "select area felling", complete with the acronym SAFE. What this means is that first you select an area and then you cut all the trees down in it; in other words, clearcutting. In the pine forests of the US Southeast the term "regeneration harvest" has been adopted as a way of focussing on reforestation after clearcut logging. Most recently MacMillan Bloedel has adopted the term "variable retention harvest" where the focus is on the trees that are retained in the landscape rather than those that are cut (cleared). This approach, which may help industry get beyond the debate over clearcutting, will be discussed in more detail later in the chapter.

In fact there is no sanitized answer to the controversy over a complex issue like clearcutting. The word has become so laden with emotional connotations that these get in the way of any rational discussion. Perhaps the first point to make is the need to separate the technical definitions from the political and emotional ones. As a technical word, "clearcut" simply means that all the trees are cut in a given area of land. The area cleared could be one acre or it could be 100 acres or more. It could be done in a way that damages soil and ruins fish habitat or it could be done carefully with no lasting damage and good reforestation. As a political and emotional term, "clearcut" means something like "total destruction of the ecosystem for the sake of corporate greed." Clearly these are two very different meanings of the same word. Understanding forest practices requires getting beyond the emotional and focussing on the technical.

There are some very real reasons for the negative impressions of clearcutting. In the not-too-distant past, there were few rules governing the conduct of logging operations, and this is still the case in some parts of the world. In North America, forests were cleared for timber and the land was converted to farms and pastures. Huge areas "fell to the axe" with little regard for wildlife or fish streams. Gravel was dredged from salmon spawning rivers and used for road construction with no regard for environmental impacts. Certainly there was no one paying much attention to the needs of woodpeckers and owls, never mind frogs and salamanders. It is easy to see how the public could confuse the issue of how the logging was done with the issue of clearcutting itself. The fact that stumps and recently logged areas don't look nice even when the most stringent regulations are followed adds to the negative impression.

It is easy to see why clearcutting is portrayed as permanent destruction when a recently logged area such as this is presented as evidence. The stark landscape of woody debris looks ruined but beneath this broken organic matter lie the living roots and seeds of countless plants waiting for the rain and sun to begin the process of renewal. In the meantime, the woody debris provides habitat for numerous species of birds, animals, plants and insects. Eventually, as the wood decays, it provides soil and nutrition for a new generation of trees.

Even the leading environmental organizations have been unable to come up with a uniform policy on clearcutting. Greenpeace, and several other groups, are strongly committed to an abolitionist approach and are calling for a global ban on clearcutting.[40] Groups that base their policies more on science, such as the World Wildlife Fund, haven't joined the ban and, up to now, have been unable to decide on a clear position. Perhaps they don't want to reveal signs of division within the movement or, more importantly, give their average donor the impression that WWF is in favour of clearcutting. In correspondence, the World Wildlife Fund Canada stated that, "While we are not supporting Greenpeace's call for a ban on clearcuts, that does not mean that WWF thinks clearcuts are great, or necessary." Muddying the waters further, they went on to say "our consistent message is one of extreme caution if not unequivocal opposition."[41] If WWF doesn't think clearcuts are necessary, what is preventing them from agreeing with Greenpeace? Clearly they realize, by virtue of their more scientific approach to issues, that clearcutting is appropriate under certain circumstances. This was recognized in a WWF brief to the British Columbia government in which they stated, "We think clearcutting does have a place in some Canadian forests, but only when it is shown to be the best harvesting and regeneration system for a specific forest ecosystem and stand condition from the perspective of maintaining forest quality."[42] This is a reasonable position and leaves a lot of room for interpretation of which forests are best harvested by clearing all the trees in a given area.

The fuzziness about this issue begins with the basic question: what is a clearcut? The answer may seem obvious, but it is not enough to simply say: "a clearcut is an area where all the trees are cut down." How large an area and how many trees must be cut to constitute a clearcut? There is no definitive answer because the word clearcut is a concept rather than a unit of measure such as "acre" or "hectare". But most foresters do agree that the size of area that constitutes a clearcut depends on many factors such as: the type of forest, the species of trees, the height of the trees, the slope of the land, and the latitude of the site.

Foresters who have tried to find a workable definition of clearcutting have recognized that the most important factor is the change in the environment at the earth's surface.[43] When a small area of trees is cut down the surrounding trees still have a dominant influence on the patch of bare ground. In particular they provide shade from the sun and shelter from wind. The taller the trees the farther into the clearing their effect extends. The higher the latitude the lower the sun is in the sky, so the trees surrounding a bare patch of ground in Alaska offer more shade and shelter than the same size trees in northern Florida.

Many environmentalists argue that clearcutting should be replaced everywhere by single-tree selection logging. It is often assumed that given the choice, selective methods are always preferable to clearcutting. In the idealized version of selection logging the old growth forest remains intact while new-age loggers manage to extract a few individual trees each year, preferably with horses rather than machines. In reality this is only practical in very limited circumstances. Let's look at the choice between clearcutting and selection logging from a practical viewpoint.

First it is necessary to distinguish between "selective" cutting and "selection" cutting. Even though the words are nearly identical, they describe very different methods of harvesting. Selective cutting means taking only those trees that are desirable for the tree-cutters' purposes. This could mean that in a forest of five tree species only two species are cut and then only when they are of a certain size. This type of logging is commonly called "high-grading" or "taking the best and leaving the rest." It is often the most economical method in the short-term as it maximizes the benefit to the logger who wastes no time or money on the less desirable trees in the forest. With selective cutting the short-term gain is offset by a longer-term degradation of the forest as desirable trees are harvested and less desirable species are left to take over. Before long there are no valuable trees and the forest is reduced to a state of no economic value. It is also very different ecologically from the forest that was there before any logging took place.

For example, an original forest may be composed primarily of two species of trees, one which is valued for timber and one which is not. If a sawmiller takes only the valuable trees and leaves the undesirable ones standing, the undesirable species will tend to seed in where the valuable trees were cut. If this pattern is repeated three or four times over the course of 100 years, the forest is gradually converted to one that is dominated by the undesirable species and it has little or no commercial value. If, on the other hand, both species are removed during logging the new forest that grows back will often be similar to the original forest, as seeds and seedlings of both species will have a chance to regenerate.

Few people realize that selective logging has caused far more degradation of the quality of forests than clearcutting. All around the world where sawmilling industries were established, forests were high-graded for saw-logs. In Australia, Scandinavia, and the US South the story is the same. Forests that were originally full of high-value timber trees were reduced to scrubby remnants with little economic value. The only way to return these forests to a semblance of their original state is to clear them and begin anew with natural regeneration or seedlings. The pulp and paper industry, with its ability to use wood chips as a raw material, is able to use trees that cannot be used for lumber. This has made it economical to clear many degraded areas and to establish a new forest of more desirable tree species. In many cases, these new forests established after clearcutting are more similar to the original forests than the degraded forest they replaced.

Selection logging, on the other hand, means carefully selecting the trees that are cut on the basis of the ecology of the forest. The first consideration is whether or not the forest in question has a history that lends itself to this type of harvesting. The second is whether the forest will renew itself successfully after some trees are removed.

In North America there are a number of forest types that are best managed by selection logging. Many forests that are dominated by hardwood species, such as those found in the US Northeast and southern Quebec and Ontario, are best managed by single-tree selection or small group selection. In the Pacific Northwest there are some coniferous forests that lend themselves to various selection techniques. In general, they tend to be drier and higher (colder) forests that are marginal in terms of having sufficient water and warmth for survival. In dry forests, where a lack of water limits growth, clearcutting often makes it difficult to renew the forest. If all the trees in an area are cut the soil becomes even drier because the shade of the trees is gone. New trees may fail to germinate and when they do may die from lack of moisture. The area will become a grassy meadow, waiting for a series of unusually wet years before trees can become re-established.

In high-elevation forests the trees shelter the ground from severe frost at night. If these forests are clearcut new trees are often killed by the cold and the site reverts to an alpine meadow. It can take decades for the forest to come back, which is no surprise as it took a long time for trees to colonize these marginal habitats in the first place. In these areas selection logging makes it possible to protect new trees from killing frost while they get established. In the most extreme regions it is probably wise to refrain from cutting altogether. This is particularly true for extremely dry and extremely cold regions. In these areas it is as difficult to renew a forest as it was for the forest to establish itself in the first place. The main point is, if trees are cut in these marginal areas, selection cutting is often the best method.

One of the better examples of an area where selection cutting is the preferred method is the region called the "dry-belt Douglas-fir" that ranges from east of the Cascades in Washington and Oregon north to Williams Lake in British Columbia. Here the forest that has evolved is dominated by two species, lodgepole pine and Douglas-fir. The lodgepole pine is a pioneer species with a relatively short life span while the Douglas-fir can survive to an age of 500 years or more. These areas are so dry that lightning fires regularly sweep through, sometimes killing the lodgepole pine. The thick bark of the Douglas-fir often protects it from these fires so it survives to preside over generation after generation of new lodgepole pine and new Douglas-fir growing back from fire. This produces a forest that has an even-aged component of lodgepole pine and an uneven-aged component of Douglas-fir that has survived numerous fires. Moose are particularly fond of grazing under old growth Douglas-fir.

If the forests in the dry-belt Douglas-fir area are clearcut the fir has a difficult time coming back. The result is usually a monoculture lodgepole pine forest with little Douglas-fir. This is not good for moose and definitely not good for Douglas-fir. It is as if a catastrophic fire had killed all the trees. This is certainly possible on occasion but it would not be the usual circumstance. A fire that kills most of the lodgepole pine usually leaves many of the Douglas-firs alive. By using selection cutting, a pattern of forest renewal that is closer to natural conditions can be attained. The typical method of selection cutting in these forests involves cutting all the lodgepole pine and about 50 percent of the Douglas-fir. The Douglas-fir left standing includes all age-classes thus emulating the effect of wildfire. This type of logging has proven effective in reproducing a forest more like the original than if clearcutting was used.

Even though it is impossible to provide a precise definition of a clearcut, there comes a point at which nearly everyone would agree that a clearcut has been made. This might be defined by area, say, greater than one hectare (2.5 acres), or by relation to tree height such as an area that is four tree lengths in diameter. Whatever definition is adopted it is bound to be an arbitrary one.

The same is true of the issue of how large a clearcut should be allowed by regulations. No one wants to make a 50,000 acre (20,000 hectare) clearcut but if fire or insects kill that much forest that is what you end up with if you harvest the dead trees. At one time it was common to clearcut areas in excess of 500 acres (200 hectares). This is now considered unacceptable for a variety of reasons including watershed management, wildlife habitat, and visual aesthetics. Most jurisdictions now restrict clearcut size to less than 100 acres (40 hectares) unless there are reasons like beetle kill, fire or blowdown to make them larger. This restriction on the upper limit to the size of clearcuts is a judgment based on many biological and ecological factors as well as common sense and an appreciation of public concerns.

Because they look ugly, scenes like this one from the karri eucalyptus forests of Western Australia have become very effective tools for the anti-forestry movement there. Ironically, the best way to ensure rapid reforestation and growth of karri trees after logging is to severely burn and disturb the site. Many forest species are highly adapted to fire and soil disturbance. Some species require disturbance for their survival.

It is popular to promote the use of forest practices that can be described as "close to nature" or "ecologically-based." Like the word clearcut, these terms have become confused to the point that they mean completely different things depending on who is talking. For some people "close to nature" means carefully selecting one tree at a time and retaining old growth trees at all times. For others "close to nature" means clearcutting relatively large areas in a pattern similar to that produced by naturally occurring fire, insect, and wind conditions. It all depends on which aspects of "nature" one chooses to emphasize. Not even the most zealous environmentalist would recommend copying the natural impact of a volcano or a huge fire-storm as an ecological way to manage a forest, even though these very destructive events are perfectly "natural".

Foresters often make the point that some form of clearcutting is the best way to "mimic" the way nature periodically disturbs and renews forests. Critics dispute this, claiming that clearcutting is fundamentally different from natural fires and blowdowns because it removes the trees from the site while with fire and blowdown the trees remain there. On this point, both foresters and their critics are right in their own way. When foresters use the word mimic, they do not mean that it is an exact copy of natural forest processes. No kind of forestry ever can be. Even the most careful single tree selection harvesting results in removal of trees. To better express their concept, foresters should probably say their approach is "taking advantage of our knowledge of how this forest functions under many different natural scenarios and, in light of that knowledge, employing forest practices that will result in the renewal of the forest and the survival of the many species living in it."

It is important to recognize that logging, whether by clearcutting or selection, is different from other forms of disturbance. But it is also true that other types of disturbance are different from each other. The disturbance caused by fire is different from the disturbance caused by a volcano which is in turn different from that caused by an ice age. In fact, no two fires are ever identical and fire can result in a wide range of impacts, from minimal to severe. The important common factor is the forest's innate ability to recover from even the most extreme disturbance, whether caused by humans or insects or some other means. Forests are equally capable of natural recovery from any kind of disturbance, so long as the factors causing the disturbance have ended. So long as the fire goes out, the volcano stops erupting, the ice retreats or the loggers go back down the road, the forest will immediately begin the process of recovery. The only generality that can be made is that the more severe the disturbance, in terms of species loss and soil damage, the longer it will take for the forest to recover.

So why use clearcutting at all? The reasons have as much to do with biology as with economics and technology. In setting out the rationale for using some form of clearcutting (or not) it makes sense to frame the subject in terms of the theory of sustainability. This requires analysis of all factors related to the environment, the economy, and the community (social issues). Let's start with the social issues.

There are two key social issues associated with the decision to use clearcutting or not. The larger public issue has to do with the aesthetics of the forest, a subject that was discussed fully in the chapter on Beauty. Foresters sometimes have difficulty accepting limitations based on visual aesthetics but there is simply no choice in the matter, particularly on public lands. Their reaction has been to design clearcuts that are smaller and take advantage of natural contours to make them less visible and less offensive to the eye.

The other social factor of importance is the occupational safety of forest workers. Logging is a dangerous activity at the best of times, particularly in old growth forests where the trees are large and many of them are partly rotten. In these types of forest the usual practice is to make an opening carefully and then to fall the remaining trees into the opening and away from the standing timber. This is far safer than trying to fall big timber in among other trees as would be required if single-tree selection logging were used. There are too many rotten tops and limbs, known as "widow-makers" to forest workers, to risk this type of harvesting. Armchair theoreticians who recommend cutting every second tree and leaving the rest are not taking this life-and-death issue into account.

From an economic perspective there is no doubt that some form of clearcutting is usually more efficient than selection logging. This is due to a number of factors, the most significant being the logistics of removing felled trees from among standing trees. With clearcutting there are far fewer obstacles to getting the logs to roadside whereas with selection logging it is necessary to take a machine to each log or to use quite complicated cable systems that are slower than those used with clearcutting. This is not to say that it is always uneconomic to use selection logging where this is determined to be the most appropriate method. There are many regions where selection harvests of one form or other are used routinely. In general, though, it costs more per volume of wood obtained to employ selection methods. This means that if all other things are equal, from an economic perspective the most efficient method of harvesting will usually be some form of clearcutting.

The environmental factors involved in deciding what form of cutting to use are far more complicated than the social and economic factors and require balancing or synthesizing a large number of issues. One way of expressing the overall objective of forest management from the environmental perspective is "to harvest the forest in such a way that it can be perpetually renewed to continue producing timber of a desirable quality as well as other specified values." The other specified values could include everything from wildlife to recreational opportunities to clean water. But the most important point is the renewal of the forest itself. As long as the trees grow back, by whatever method they are cut, the ecosystem can eventually provide the habitats and opportunities for other species that depend on it. If a type of cutting is used that results in long-term loss of forest cover or a severely degraded forest then some species will not do well.

This pioneer forest of Douglas-fir and western hemlock has come in thick and tall after clearcutting on this site in the Seymour River watershed in North Vancouver. Shade tolerant saplings of red cedar and western hemlock have grown in beneath the canopy but there are no young Douglas-fir as they will not grow in the shade in this part of their range.

The single biggest environmental reason for clearcutting has to do with the ability or inability of different tree species to tolerate shade. Many species of trees simply will not germinate and grow in the shade of other trees, even when the other trees are of the same species. This is a common characteristic of pioneer tree species that are particularly adapted to growing in areas that have been recently cleared. In the Pacific Northwest about 60 percent of all forests are composed of species that are shade intolerant to one degree or another. Tree species are not categorically either shade tolerant or shade intolerant. Rather, they display a continuum of shade tolerance from very intolerant to very tolerant with many species in between. Some species, such as Douglas-fir, are shade intolerant in the wetter part of their range and yet are shade tolerant in drier regions.

The best example of shade intolerance is provided by lodgepole pine. It is the main coniferous pioneer species east of the coast mountains in the Pacific Northwest. Lodgepole pine will only grow in full sunlight in areas that have been cleared by fire or logging. It will not grow in its own shade so it grows up as an even-aged forest, in many cases as a monoculture. Foresters believe that tree species requiring sunlight for growth are best managed by some type of clearcut system. Other species that fall into this category are Douglas-fir, spruce, aspen, most of the other pine species, red alder, and western larch.

Western hemlock and red cedar are good examples of trees that are tolerant of shade. They will grow in their own shade as well as in the shade of other species such as Douglas-fir. With these species it is biologically possible to use selection cutting and still get new trees to grow beneath the others. The problem is that most shade tolerant trees grow much slower in shade than they do in full sunlight where photosynthesis is more efficient. Most shade tolerant tree species do not require shade, they are simply capable of surviving in it. Foresters usually prefer to grow red cedar and western hemlock in cleared areas where they grow much faster than they do in the shade.

In these areas near Moyie Lake in the East Kootenay many of the western larch have been retained for seed trees as this is the most effective way of natural regeneration with this species. This method mimics the effect of natural fire which sweeps through, killing all the lodgepole pine and leaving some of the more fire-resistant, longer-lived larch alive.

Everyone who has studied forestry knows the history of how Swedish forests were degraded by selective cutting until many of them were of no economic value. Over the centuries the continual removal of high-value pine and spruce trees with no thought to forest renewal resulted in a forest dominated by species of undesirable trees and shrubs. They shaded the ground thus making it impossible for pine and spruce to become re-established. The solution to this situation was to clear and burn the forests and to plant new trees of the type that had grown there before exploitation. A law was passed requiring forest owners to use clearcutting followed by planting in all Swedish forests. In typical fashion the pendulum swung a bit too far and recently the forest laws have been relaxed to allow for more selection cutting where it is the best method. Clearcutting is still the predominant method of harvesting in all coniferous forest areas in Scandinavia.

The prevalence of pests and diseases is another reason for deciding to use clearcutting rather than selection harvesting. We have discussed the cases of bark beetles and dwarf mistletoe as examples where clearcutting is sometimes the only real option or is the preferred option. This is also the case for the class of fungal diseases known as root rot. Root rots not only attack roots but also the stem of the tree. They are often the reason why trees are hollow or rotten in the butt (the bottom end of the stem). These fungi spread from one tree to the next through their intertwined root systems and once a forest is heavily infected it is difficult to get out. Douglas-fir is particularly susceptible, even at an early age which can result in the commercial failure of the forest. The best way to eradicate or control root rot is to clearcut, sometimes pulling the roots out and burning them, and replanting with a tree species that is less affected by the fungi.

In support of their position against clearcutting, environmental critics often point out that Austria and Switzerland have both banned clearcutting in the Alps. As the Alps are somewhat similar in terrain to the mountain ranges in the Pacific Northwest and British Columbia, environmentalists suggest that we should follow the example set by these two countries. There are some elements of reason to this argument and there are some that do not apply to our situation.

Clearcutting was banned in the Alps after public outcry against excessive, unregulated clearcutting, mainly to obtain fuel wood for industry. Whole mountains were stripped of forest causing severe erosion, mudslides, and damage to roads and towns. It was made illegal to clear an area larger than 2.5 acres (one hectare) without specific government approval. (Again, it comes down to an arbitrary definition, a 2.5 acre clearing could be called a small clearcut)

Over the years the loggers in the Alps have developed a skyline cable system that allows logs to be lifted to roadside from many small clearings made along its length. This system is known as "small group selection" and essentially amounts to a series of small clearcuts rather than one large one. It works well in the second-growth forest of relatively small trees that have been established throughout the Alps. It is no coincidence that a similar type of selection harvesting is widely used in southeastern British Columbia, Idaho, and Montana along the western slope of the Rocky Mountains. The trees in that region are much smaller and younger than in the coastal rainforest and there is much less danger to workers from rotten limbs and snags. These are the main reasons the Alpine system is not as practical in old growth coastal forests.

Europe has never had forests to compare in size to the redwoods, firs, and cedars of the Pacific Northwest. It is almost certain that when it comes time to harvest the second-growth forests along the Pacific coast that much more selection logging will be used. The trees will be smaller and healthier and therefore much easier to manage. One forester put it bluntly: "It's about impossible to manage an old growth forest. The best thing to do is either leave it alone or clearcut it and start at the beginning with a new forest that can be managed."[44]

Selection harvesting, as mentioned earlier, is often the best method for certain types of forest. It is important, however, to recognize that selection logging has its own negative aspects. One of the most obvious is that selection logging requires a higher concentration of access roads and trails than are required for clearcut logging. In many ways, roads have a more negative environmental impact than the logging itself. They often result in soil erosion and they remove a portion of the land from timber production. It is therefore desirable to minimize the number of roads, especially permanent roads, in commercial forest landscapes. Selection harvesting nearly always requires more roads than some form of clearcutting.

The most serious drawback of selection logging has to do with the effect on the trees left standing. When trees are felled in among other trees there is always damage caused to the trees left standing. Branches are torn off and bark is scraped away by falling trees. This opens the remaining trees to infection by fungi and insects which can cause deformity, stunted growth, and death. Even more damaging is the process of removing the felled trees from the forest. It is difficult to avoid causing injury to the trunks of growing trees when logs are dragged out of the forest around them. Logs being hauled by cables along the forest floor often get hung-up behind stumps, standing trees, and other obstacles, with inevitable damage to the surrounding forest environment.

An aerial view near Cranbrook in the East Kootenay shows the pattern in the soil caused by ploughing after logging. This is done to expose underlying mineral soil as a seed bed for western larch and lodgepole pine. This is similar to the effect of wildfire that burns off the surface organic material and exposes the mineral soil, providing a good medium for germination and growth.

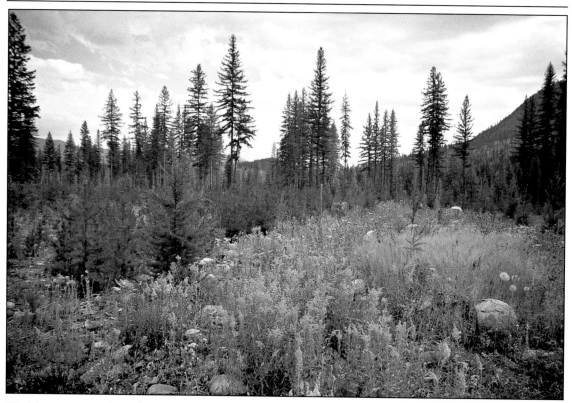

The temporary meadow stage, a few years after harvesting, in an area where western larch trees have been retained as seed trees. When the ground is opened to direct sunlight a profusion of flowers and grasses grows in.

About ten years after harvesting, lodgepole pine has grown back by natural regeneration among the western larch seed trees. The lodgepole pine seeds were either in the soil prior to harvesting, or were deposited during harvesting.

Despite a tremendous escalation of public opposition to the practice in recent years, foresters continue to use clearcut logging as the preferred method of cutting in most coniferous forests and some hardwood forests. Is this because they are controlled by greedy capitalists or is it because they are making good professional decisions?

Two in-depth studies on forestry and clearcutting conducted by governments in Canada support the latter conclusion. During the spring and summer of 1994 the Canadian House of Commons Committee on Natural Resources conducted hearings on clearcutting in response to the threat of international boycotts of Canadian forest products. Environmental groups such as Greenpeace and the Sierra Club have been openly lobbying in Europe, the United States, and Japan for boycotts against pulp and paper derived from clearcutting. The campaign variously targets all of Canada, British Columbia, production from old growth forests and particular regions such as Clayoquot Sound on Vancouver Island, and certain forest companies such as Western Forest Products that are clearcutting old growth forest. Amazingly, other countries that also use clearcutting such as the United States, Sweden, Germany, and Japan seem to be exempted from the boycott campaign.

During the parliamentary committee hearings, Greenpeace presented the strongest environmentalist brief in which they called for a total ban on clearcutting. They based their position on a number of surprising statements. Clearcutting is unnatural, the committee was told, because "in natural forest ecosystems, severe disturbances tend to be very rare... A lightning strike can kill a single tree or a small group of trees. A wind downburst can snap branches and trunks over an area the size of an office building."[45] Whoever wrote this fairy-tale version of natural forest conditions has obviously never studied the subject. Instead, they have re-invented nature to fit their campaign objective with no regard for the truth. Severe disturbances are actually very common in natural forests and often kill all the trees over large areas. The bark beetle outbreak in the Bowron Valley discussed earlier killed the majority of trees over an area of 50,000 acres (20,000 hectares). This forest was growing back after fire had swept through the same area over 100 years earlier. Records show that the majority of forests in North America are regularly and severely disturbed under natural conditions.

The Greenpeace submission to the parliamentary committee went on to state that "virtually no disturbance is so severe over so large an area that nature regenerates even-aged stands. Virtually all even-aged stands result from human activities including clearcutting and planting." This statement is simply false. Naturally occurring, even-aged stands are widespread, particularly in the boreal forest and dry interior forests in British Columbia and the Pacific Northwest. Many of these forests are not only even-aged but are also dominated by a single tree species, that is they are naturally occurring monocultures. By denying the existence of naturally occurring even-aged monoculture forests Greenpeace shows a fundamental lack of knowledge on this subject.

In the end, the House of Commons Committee on Natural Resources, comprised of members from all major national parties, stated that "On balance, the Committee concludes that clearcutting is an ecologically appropriate silvicultural system for most forest types in Canada."[46] Not surprisingly this was rejected by the critics who accused the committee of a pro-industry bias. The environmentalists did not explain why a group of politicians would come out in favour of a politically unpopular practice unless there were compelling reasons to do so.

An even larger study of the issue was conducted by the Ministry of Natural Resources in the province of Ontario.[47] This was an exhaustive review of forest practices in the provincial forests and took nearly six years to complete. Again, every conceivable interest group was involved and again the report recognized that clearcutting was closer to the natural pattern of disturbance in many types of forests than any other form of harvesting. The report recommended a maximum clearcut size of 100 hectares (250 acres), not because of forestry considerations but because moose do better when openings are larger rather than smaller. This reflects the fact that normal wildfire disturbance affects large areas in the predominantly boreal forest type in Ontario. Similar conditions exist in the interior forests of the Pacific Northwest from California to Alaska.

The Society of American Foresters has also made a full review of the issues involved in the debate over clearcutting and has adopted a clear position:[48]

> *"The Society of American Foresters believes the scientifically-based practice known as clearcutting, properly used, has a role in forest management to create desired conditions in forests. It is an appropriate silvicultural method for regenerating species that are shade-intolerant and the optimum method to achieve other management objectives. However, as with any land management practice, it can have undesirable effects if not used correctly. Clearcutting should be retained as a forest management tool and applied only by trained and experienced professionals under appropriate conditions, and as may be constrained by economic and social factors. The Society emphasizes that clearcutting properly applied, though at times unsightly, does not cause or promote environmental degradation, and neither does clearcutting equate to "short rotation" forestry. The benefits of clearcutting, when properly applied, can far outweigh negatives."*

In early 1998, MacMillan Bloedel, a British Columbia based company with large operations both there and in the US Southeast, announced its Forest Project that would "phase out clearcutting old growth forest over a five year period."[49] Many people interpreted this to mean the company would stop cutting old growth forest altogether, but that is not what they actually said. What they did say is that old growth would be cut by methods other than clearcutting.

Because there is no old growth forest on their land in the US Southeast, MacMillan Bloedel stated that the program would not apply there and that they would continue to use clearcutting (often referred to as regeneration harvesting). In British Columbia, where 50% of the company's 2.7 million acres (1.1 million hectares) of forest land is old growth, they would replace clearcutting with "variable retention harvesting". Upon reading the description of "variable retention" it soon becomes clear that it is very similar to what many foresters call "clearcutting with reserves". This involves leaving patches of trees and individual trees throughout the landscape but it also involves clearings, or "openings" as the company now prefers to call them.

The statement that "clearcutting" will be phased out is made possible by adopting a new definition of the word. Under MacMillan Bloedel's Forest Project, an opening is not considered to be a clearcut so long as "more than 50% of the opening is under the influence of an edge". Further, "the influence of an edge" is defined as "within one tree-length of an edge". This means that if the trees are 165 feet (50 metres) tall it is possible to have a cleared area that is 650 feet (200 metres) across, in other words what most people would call a clearcut.

How legitimate is it to simply change the definition and invent a new term for harvesting relatively large areas of forest? I believe it is legitimate providing the logging is done in a way that eliminates the unacceptable practices that gave clearcutting a bad name in the first place. These include practices that damaged soil, streams, and biodiversity. The potential disadvantage of this approach is that people might be surprised when they see that the logging still looks like a clearcut even though it is called something else. But there is probably no way to avoid this potential Catch 22. While it is difficult for someone like myself who likes to see words used to make things clear rather than cloudy, there is no escaping the fact that some people use words as weapons in a war designed to win popular support. Communications is as much an art as it is a science. In the case of variable retention harvesting there is actually a lot of substance behind the sound-bites about phasing out clearcutting.

The document that lies behind MacMillan Bloedel's Forest Project was prepared, with the leadership of Professor Fred Bunnell, by the Centre for Applied Conservation Biology at the University of British Columbia.[50] Titled "An Ecological Rationale for Changing Forest Management on MacMillan Bloedel's Forest Tenure", it is perhaps the best work to date linking forest management with the protection of biodiversity. The manuscript provides details for the 215 vertebrate species found on MacMillan Bloedel's land. It highlights the fact that different species have evolved to take advantage of all possible conditions in a forest, from recent disturbance and clearing to old growth with no clearings. From this it is concluded that the first rule of species protection is "Don't do the same thing everywhere." In other words, the largest number of species will benefit from a landscape that has old growth, medium growth, young growth, *and* recently cleared areas. The arguments presented to support the Forest Project can be applied to any forest that is managed for timber. A number of other companies have announced their intention to adopt a similar approach. And even though they may not be calling it "variable retention", many forest companies have adopted a style of harvesting that closely fits the definition. This includes retaining forest along fish-bearing streams, establishing permanent reserves within the managed landscape, and protecting more old growth than in the past.

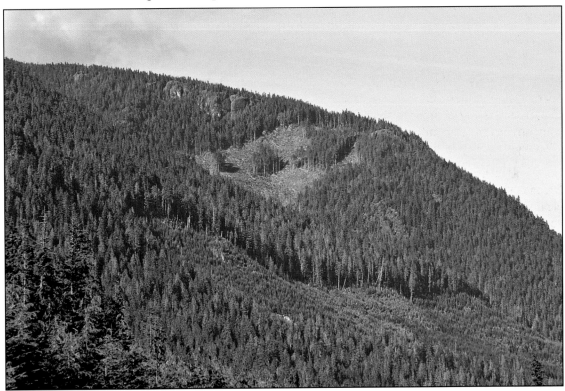

This variable retention harvesting on the upper slopes of a mountain near Sayward on Vancouver Island is very different from the wholesale clearcutting practiced in the past.

Variable retention harvesting is based on the premise that biodiversity is the most important value in the forest and that all species normally present should be maintained in the managed landscape. For practical purposes, it is assumed that vertebrate biodiversity (mammals, birds, fish, reptiles and amphibians) is a reasonable substitute for total biodiversity (which includes insects, plants, fungi, bacteria etc.). A detailed description of the habitat requirements, for breeding, feeding, hibernating etc., for each vertebrate species is developed. In MacMillan Bloedel's case, the forest is then divided into three management categories: old growth, habitat, and timber, with greater emphasis on those values within each category. While the variable retention system is too complex for a complete explanation here, the result is a style of harvesting that is designed for maximum protection of biodiversity while still extracting a large volume of timber. Although variable retention has been pioneered in coastal old growth forests, it is perfectly suitable for application in any forest where clearcutting has been the traditional method of harvesting.

In all this debate one thing has become clear. It is not logging or clearcutting per se that causes damage to the environment, but how, when, and where trees are cut. It is easy, through sloppy procedures, to cause soil erosion, damage fish streams, and reduce wildlife habitat. It is equally possible, given adequate knowledge, to design logging that protects soil, enhances salmon streams, and increases wildlife habitat. These are not simple formulas that can be communicated in 30-second news clips. An understanding of the place of clearcutting in modern forestry, by whatever name it goes, requires a great deal of knowledge and judgment. Emotionally charged presentations relying on photographs of messy landscapes are simply not adequate for determining the correct method of tree harvesting and forest renewal.

Certification – Telling It Like It Is

It is one thing for a forest company to satisfy itself that it is managing forests sustainably. It is quite another to convince a skeptical public, often told otherwise by environmental groups, that their forest management is sustainable. Most people who consume forest products live far away from the forests that produced those products, often in cities where they have never been directly involved in forestry. It is difficult for them to judge who is giving them the most accurate information and they will often perceive the industry to be biased towards its own interests. Therefore, by default, they often give more weight to environmental groups, even when the criticism is unfair or untrue.

This situation gives rise to the need for a system of independent verification of compliance with sustainable forest management, what has come to be called "certification". The idea of certification of sustainable forestry and forest products first came from the World Wildlife Fund (WWF). They realized that the issue of forest practices was very different from their traditional concern for endangered species preservation and the creation of parks and wilderness areas. WWF recruited some of the larger retail lumber suppliers in the UK, such as B&Q and Sainsbury's, to form a "buyers group" that pledged to buy and sell forest products that originated from sustainably managed forests. This led to the creation of the Forest Stewardship Council (FSC) in 1972, now with headquarters in Oaxaca, Mexico. The FSC has set itself up as a governing body to oversee a system of independent auditing of sustainable forestry under its 10 Principles and Criteria.[51] To date, over 200 forest operations in 30 countries, covering 40 million acres (16 million hectares) have been certified as sustainably managed under the FSC program. (65% of this is in two countries, Sweden and Poland)

The FSC has been widely accepted by the environmental movement as the only credible system for certification. It has not received such universal praise from the forest industry or from governments who regulate the industry. This is partly because the FSC is perceived as a very political organization, some of whose members, such as Greenpeace and the Sierra Club, seem more interested in preventing forestry than in helping to improve it. It was also unfortunate that there was no involvement of major forest companies or governments in the formation of the FSC. As a result, many companies rejected the FSC as too heavily biased towards preservation and most governments decided to take a wait-and-see approach. Lately the FSC has made progress by gaining the support of some of the large industrial forest companies in Sweden and by convincing large retailers such as The Home Depot that certified wood products should be favored over uncertified ones.

It is unlikely that the FSC will gain a global monopoly in the area of certification for sustainable forestry, and this is probably a good thing. Because the founding meeting of the FSC took place in Toronto, Canada in 1972, the Canadian forest industry became aware of, and concerned about the implications if being required to submit to a process in which they had no involvement. In 1993 the Canadian Pulp and Paper Association initiated a project to create a certification program under the Canadian Standards Association, the equivalent of the

Underwriters Laboratory in the US, affiliated with the International Standards Organization. Many Canadian forest companies signed up to this program and in April 1999 MacMillan Bloedel became the first Company to achieve certification on one of their operations on Vancouver Island.[52]

In 1995 Australia and Canada proposed that the International Standards Organization (ISO) establish a standard for sustainable forestry under the 14001 Environmental Management category. This resulted in the formation of the Forest Study Group, an international committee chaired by Ken Shirley, MP, of New Zealand. In 1998 the members of ISO voted unanimously in favor of the Technical Report on Forestry, making it possible for private and public forest owners around the world to have their operations registered as sustainably managed. In 1999 International Paper became the first company to have its forest lands registered under ISO 14001. Many other forestry operations around the world have received ISO registration and many more are in various stages of application.

In the United States the FSC has been largely rejected by private forest landowners both large and small. The large industrial forest companies, under the umbrella of the American Forest and Paper Association (AF&PA), developed the Sustainable Forestry Initiative (SFI).[53] They adopted a tough love approach to their member companies who were required to join the SFI program or leave the organization. During the first two years some companies did choose to leave rather than submit to outside scrutiny of their practices. Lately this trend has reversed and companies are joining the AF&PA in order to become involved in the SFI program. As of mid-1999 there were 55 million acres (22.3 million hectares) of private forest lands enrolled in the initiative. The SFI is monitored by an Independent Expert Review Panel composed of conservationists, foresters, academics, and other professionals. They make recommendations for continual improvement of the program. In the 1999 report, panel chairman Paul Hansen emphasized the need for independent verification of compliance and for more measurable standards.

Nearly 60% of the productive forest land in the US is owned by 9.3 million private citizens, and many of them harvest timber for income. 70,000 of those owners with 95 million acres (38.4 million hectares) have joined the American Tree Farm System under the sponsorship of the American Forest Foundation. Under the program they can become Certified Tree Farmers after developing a management plan that fulfills the program's requirements.

In Europe, where small private owners occupy the majority of forested land, they too have rejected the Forest Stewardship Council's program because it is too expensive and too political. In 1999 the Pan-European Forest Certification Scheme was launched by 15 countries representing millions of owners with 247 million acres (100 million hectares) of forest land. The program was developed first in Finland. In March 1999 the National Forest Certification Council was established in Helsinki with the ambition of certifying 30 million acres (12 million hectares) by the year 2000.[54] As this book goes to press there is news that B&Q, the equivalent to Home Depot in England and a strong supporter of the FSC, has accepted the Finnish system.

It is too early to tell at this writing what the outcome will be in the competition for control and credibility around the subject of certification. There is a lot of pressure on large retail outlets such as The Home Depot, Wal-Mart, and HomeBase to adopt FSC as the only acceptable program. At the same time, the other certification initiatives such as SFI and CSA are moving to independent auditing in order to be equivalent with FSC. But whatever the outcome, certification of sustainable forest management is here to stay and will gain even more influence over consumer choice in the future. We can look forward to a time when the public feels confident that forests are managed sustainably and when they feel good about using the many forest products that make our lives more livable.

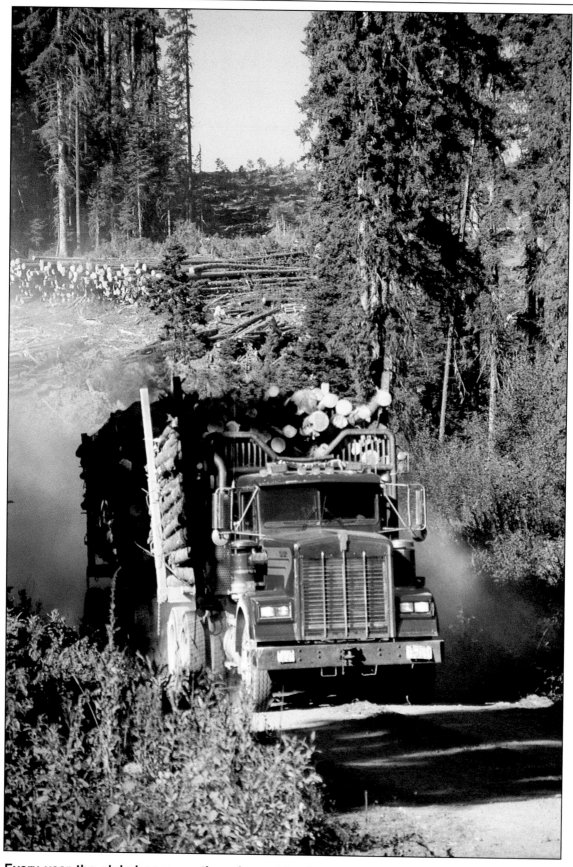

Every year the global consumption of wood is about 3.5 billion tons or about 70 million truckloads the size of this one.

REFERENCES

1 At the Ronning Farm, San Josef valley near Holberg on Vancouver Island there is a healthy 65 year old giant sequoia planted by trapper/horticulturist Bernt Ronning.

2 Ulrich Hecker, Baume und Straucher (Trees and Shrubs), BLV, 1991.

3 Stephen Jay Gould, Wonderful Life: The Burgess Shale and the Nature of History, W.W. Norton, New York, 1989.

4 James Gleick, Chaos: Making a New Science, Viking Penguin, 1988.

5 Towards an Old Growth Strategy, Public Review Draft, BC Ministry of Forests, January 1992.

6 Personal communication, Vicky Husband, Chair, Sierra Club of Western Canada, March 1994.

7 The Chain of Destruction, From Canada's Ancient Rainforests to the United States Market, Greenpeace, 1999

8 Micah Morrison, Fire in Paradise: The Yellowstone Fires and the Politics of Environmentalism, HarperCollins, New York, 1993.

Ross W. Simpson, The Fires of '88, American Geographic, Helena, Montana, 1989.

9 Alexander Cockburn, Smokey the Bear Is Wrong--Forests Burn Naturally, distributed by Ecological Enterprises, Madison, WI, 1994

10 Clearcut: The Tragedy of Industrial Forestry, p. 140.

11 BC Ministry of Forests, Timber Harvesting Branch, Forest road and logging trail engineering practices, July 1993.

12 Hamish Kimmins, personal communication, 1998

13 Colleen McCrory, The Valhalla Wilderness Society, information pamphlet, 1992

14 Cristoph Theis and Thomas Kunz, Greenpeace Germany fundraising brochure, March/April 1992.

15. State of the World: Worldwatch Institute Report on Progress Towards a Sustainable Society, Worldwatch Institute, New York, 1993.

16 John Perlin, A Forest Journey - The Role of Wood in the Development of Civilization, W.W. Norton, New York, 1989.

17 Ibid. pp. 43-68.

18 Wink Sutton, Are We Too Concerned About Wood Production? Institute News, New Zealand Forestry, November, 1991.

19 Christoph Theis and Thomas Kunz, Greenpeace Germany fundraising pamphlet, March/April 1992.

20 The Forest Resources of the Temperate Zones, FAO, Rome, 1993.

21 Forest Resources Assessment 1990, Tropical Countries, FAO, Rome, 1993.

22 FAO State of the World's Forests – 1999.

See: http://www.fao.org/waicent/faoinfo/forestry/FO/SOFO/SOFO99/sofo99-e.stm

23 Spiegel, "Pillagers of the North" Issue 46, November 15, 1993.

24 BC Ministry of Forests Annual Report, 1992-1993, and BC Ministry of Forests, Forest Renewal: Silviculture in BC, 1993.

25 Worldwide Fund for Nature, Forests For Life, 1996.

See: http://www.panda.org/forests4life/wwf1996ar.pdf

26 Archer Daniels Midland Company http://www.admworld.com/index2.shtml

27 Monte Hummel, Endangered Spaces: The Future for Canada's Wilderness, Key Porter Books, Toronto, 1989.

28 Doug Hopwood, Principles and Practices of New Forestry, A Guide for British Columbians, BC Ministry of Forests, February, 1991.

Dick Russell and Susan Reynolds, Old Growth Movers and Shakers, American Forests, Sept/Oct, 1991.

Jerry Franklin, Old growth Forest and the New Forestry, In Proc. Symp. on Forests - Wild and Managed: Differences and Consequences. A.F. Pearson and D.A. Challenger (eds.), Students for Forestry Awareness, U. of BC, Vancouver, January 19-20, 1990.

29 Kimmins, Balancing Act: Environmental Issues in Forestry, UBC Press, Vancouver, 1992.

30 Our Common Future, (The Brundtland Report), Oxford University Press, 1987.

31 Quincy Library Group, see: http://www.qlg.org/

32 Non-legally Binding Authoritative Statement of Principles for a Global Consensus on the Management, Conservation and Sustainable Development of All Types of Forests, United Nations Conference on Environment and Development, Rio de Janeiro, June, 1992.

National Forest Strategy, Sustainable Forests: A Canadian Commitment, Canadian Council of Forest Ministers, Ottawa, Ontario, May 1998. see: http://nfc.forest.ca/anglais/index.htm

Forest Practices Code of British Columbia, Standards with Revised Rules and Field Guide References, BC Ministry of Forests, 1994.

See: http://www.for.gov.bc.ca/tasb/legsregs/fpc/fpcact/contfpc.htm

Principles of Sustainable Forestry, Forest Alliance of BC, February 1992.

Forest Stewardship Council, Draft VI of the Principles and Criteria for Forest Management, October 15, 1992

The Scientific Panel for Sustainable Forest Practices in Clayoquot Sound, Sustainable Ecosystem Management in Clayoquot Sound: Planning and Practices, April, 1995

Sustainable Forestry Initiative, American Forest and Paper Association, Washington, DC. see: http://www.afandpa.org/Forestry/

33 Mark E. Harmon et al, Effects on Carbon Storage of Conversion of Old growth Forests to Young Forests. Science, Vol. 247, pp. 699-702, 9 February 1990.

34 C.D. Oliver et al, Effect of harvest of old growth Douglas-fir stands and subsequent management on carbon dioxide levels in the atmosphere. College of Forest Resources, University of Washington, Seattle, manuscript in progress, 1991.

35 Intergovernmental Panel on Climate Change, IPCC First Assessment Report Overview, August 1990.

36 W.A. Kurz et al, Twentieth century carbon budget of Canadian forests. Tellus 47B, 1995.

37 Kyoto Protocol to the United Nations Framework Convention on Climate Change, Article 3.3. December 10, 1998, http://www.unfccc.de/fccc/docs/cop3/l07a01.pdf

38 B. Schlamadinger and G. Marland, Net Effect of Forest Harvest on CO_2 emissions to the Atmosphere: A Sensitivity Analysis on the Influence of Time. Tellus B, 1999, in press.

39 See: http://johnnyappleseedfest.com/

40 Submission from Greenpeace to the Standing Committee on Natural Resources, Parliament of Canada, April 13, 1994.

41 Letter from Monte Hummel to Jack Munro, November 9, 1994.

42 World Wildlife Fund Canada, Making Choices, A Submission to the Government of British Columbia Regarding Protected Areas and Forest Land Use, November 1993.

43 R.J Keenan, and J.P. Kimmins, The Ecological Effects of Clear-cutting. Environ. Rev.. 1: 121-144. 1993. also see P.J. Burton, et al, The value of managing for biodiversity. For. Chron. 68: 225-237, 1992.

44 Personal communication, Jack Lavis, Professional Forester, MacMillan Bloedel Ltd. June, 1992.

45 Submission from Greenpeace to the Standing Committee on Natural Resources, Parliament of Canada, April 13, 1994.

46 Canada: A Model Forest Nation in the Making, Report of the Standing Committee on Natural Resources, House of Commons, Canada, June, 1994.

47 Class Environmental Assessment Act Approval for Timber Management on Crown Lands in Ontario, Ontario Ministry of Natural Resources, April, 1994.

48 See: http://www.safnet.org/archive/clearcut.htm

49 See: http://www.mbltd.com/enviro/forestproject/tfp_press.htm

50 Bunnell et al, An Ecological Rationale for Changing Forest Management on MacMillan Bloedel's Forest Tenure, Centre for Applied Conservation Biology, UBC, 1998.

51 Forest Stewardship Council, Principles and Criteria for Forest Management, January, 1999, see: http://www.fscoax.org/principle.htm

52 See http://www.sfms.com for a description of the Canadian Standards Association Sustainable Forest Management Standards.

53 American Forest and Paper Association, Sustainable Forestry Initiative (SFI) Program, 1999 4th Annual Progress Report. See also http://www.afandpa.org/Forestry/

54 See http://www.smy.fi/certification/eng/1.html

The Spirit of the Ancient Forest

There is a spirit in the woods

William Wordsworth, Nutting

Forests have always been viewed with a certain sense of awe. Dark and silent, they are places where people can feel small, alone, unsure of their way, and fearful of wild animals. But the beauty of towering trees and the lush undergrowth of colorful ferns, mosses, and flowers has also inspired poets and outdoor-loving people since time immemorial.

Many environmental activists believe that forests have a special spiritual dimension, above and beyond other types of environments. This is a major reason why the conflict between preservation and logging continues to defy logical resolution.

This belief has become central to the motivations and actions of many environmental campaigns. Contemporary environmental literature often employs the spiritual or sacred quality of forests as the bottom line argument against using the forest for timber production.[1] In the extreme case, the experience of forests is linked to shamanism, pantheism, and the neo-tribalism of new-age deep ecology.

In the Sierra Club's book, Clearcut: The Tragedy of Industrial Forestry, we are advised that: "Shamanic journeying helps to facilitate spontaneous encounters with the spiritual powers of Nature. That these encounters must be spontaneous is underscored by warnings against trying to capture a guardian spirit. A guardian spirit must choose to show itself to you three times before you can ask its help, for if it has shown itself three times, it has most likely chosen to help. If the quester, on a vision quest, tries to grab or control it, or flaunt it, it will be lost. It might even become an enemy."[2] I wonder if the board of directors of the Sierra Club had a chance to read these ramblings before their book was published. It really makes one wonder how one of the most respected environmental organizations in the United States could have fallen into using such material in the name of conservation.

The thinking is not all that clear these days even in more conventional circles. It has lately become the trend in government and corporate policy documents to acknowledge the spiritual dimension of forests in the preamble.[3] There is never much, if any, elaboration in the following text of what this means in terms of company policy or government regulation. Even among mainstream environmentalists it is not common to engage in discussion of just what this spiritual aspect of forests is or what it means other than we shouldn't cut the trees down. The unspoken message seems to be that if you have to ask you must be on "the other side" and probably wouldn't understand anyway.

When it comes to soul, however, not all forests are created equal. All manner of Biblical metaphors are used to give the impression that once a forest has been cut it is forever desecrated. Images of rape, pillage and plunder are employed to suggest loss of innocence and violence against nature. Now that the evil forest companies have come and destroyed the forest, God has left the land and will never return. Even if a new forest grows back on logged land, especially if people plant trees, it is portrayed as inferior in both material and spiritual qualities. The use of language that creates a sense of permanent loss is a powerful psychological tool.

126

Two phrases that are frequently used in environmental rhetoric help to cast some light on the subject. The first is "the spirit of the ancient forest," by which is meant that old trees have a special degree of spirituality. The second is "the ancient forest is like a cathedral," or metaphorically, "the ancient forest is a cathedral." This links forests directly with religion and suggests they are sacred places meant for worship of the Creator. The implication is that the destruction of an old growth forest is as unthinkable and immoral as the destruction of an ancient cathedral.

These are powerful and emotionally effective images that form a significant part of the preservationists' arsenal in the war of words over forest use. It is as much this emotional side of the debate, as opposed to the scientific and technical, that moves public opinion on the subject of trees.

There are many special places in the forest that should be left untouched by industry.

The Forest as a Cathedral

How valid is the metaphor of the forest and the cathedral? One obvious difference is that cathedrals don't grow back after they are destroyed or otherwise fall into ruin. They are human creations whereas the forest is self-created. This is a specific example of the tendency of urban dwellers to think of destruction in relation to human artifacts and to generalize this to include the "destruction" of nature. Once a building is destroyed that's the end of it unless people rebuild it themselves. People don't have to rebuild forests, they grow back very well without human interference and in many cases despite it.

Old forests and cathedrals do have one thing in common: tall columns capped with a "canopy." In the case of cathedrals the canopy is usually an arched ceiling atop stone pillars. It is probably more appropriate, therefore, to reverse the analogy and say "the cathedral is like an ancient forest" as the ancient forests existed long before cathedrals. Is it possible that ancient priests figured out that they could mimic the feeling of awe experienced in a tall forest by designing their cathedrals to feel like forests? The uplifting sensation, which we are told is caused by being nearer to God, may well be the same in both cases.

Is it reasonable to assume that God is closer to us in cathedrals and old forests than in any other location? Surely if there is a divine force it is everywhere all the time and not just in certain places like churches and old trees. Then what is this "spirit of the ancient forest" they speak about? Is it a special spirit or is it the same spirit that is everywhere?

There is no doubt that one gets a different feeling in a tall dark forest than, say, sitting in your car in rush hour. But I do not believe this is because you are closer to God in the forest. It is because the physical environment is different and causes a different mental state due to a combination of overwhelming size and a fear of the unknown. By calling this feeling "spiritual" we are confusing the real meaning of spiritual with an environmentally-induced state of mind caused by being in a forest -- as opposed to the different sensation we would have in another setting.

This means, to my mind, that the spirit of the ancient forest is embodied in the physical manifestation of the trees and other plants in the woods. What contains the essence of this physical pattern of living species? The answer is, "their seeds". Thoreau expressed this with his usual eloquence in his book, "Faith in a Seed":

"Though I do not believe that a plant will spring up where no seed has been, I have great faith in a seed. Convince me that you have a seed there, and I am prepared to expect wonders."[4]

So long as the seeds of the species that make up the forest survive and grow, especially the trees, the spirit of the forest is alive. If the seeds die and the species becomes extinct part of the spirit is lost. If a new species appears the spirit changes and grows. Looked at in this way it is possible to explain the spirit in the forest in terms of the living things that make it up rather than by some invisible, mysterious "spirit" that lurks behind the trees. The spirit of the ancient forest, I believe, is in the DNA of the spores, seeds, and fertilized eggs of the species living there. They represent the continuing evolution of the forest ecosystem that has proceeded through 400 million years of changing climates and occasional cataclysms caused by fires, volcanoes and meteor impacts. Without the species that make it up, there would be no forest, ancient or otherwise, and no spirit of the forest either. In the same way, the essence of the human spirit resides in our genes, which are passed on from generation to generation. This kind of "spirit" is not the same as the spiritual dimension of religion, something that is outside the material world and pervades everything, not just people and trees. One of the reasons I chose the name "Green Spirit" was to capture both of these meanings; on the one hand the spirit of life in the here and now, and on the other the spiritual belief in a God that is all-knowing and beyond our comprehension.

What is it then that makes us feel elated when deep in an old growth forest or in a cathedral? I have spent a lot of time walking alone deep in the rainforest and I think I know why I get a slightly elated feeling from time to time. It is due, first of all, to the beauty of the living trees and plants, and the silence, ruffled only by the wind. It is also due to the sense of being alone and aware that, at any moment, a large wild animal might appear from behind a tree, or worse still, from a limb over my head. This feeling of the unknown stays with the most experienced woodsman because if you are in real wilderness there is always the possibility that a cougar or grizzly is just around the next bend in the trail. This was once true in most forests of the world so it is a universal experience in our evolution. My belief is that the feeling of elation or slightly elevated anticipation is partly hormonal, adrenaline being the most likely cause. Could it be the same in a cathedral, that the feeling of wonder is actually a replica of how we react in a forest?

The Sacred Singing Cedars

The perceived spirituality of forests was highlighted by a controversy in the West Kootenay region of British Columbia. Local environmentalists had demanded that a grove of old growth cedars be protected because they were thought to be sacred.[5] Not only were they sacred but their defenders claimed that these particular cedars can sing and that the words of the song have been recorded. The environmentalists maintained that the trees were singing that they want to stay alive and asked the loggers to please go somewhere else. The "sacred singing cedars" issue resulted in a lively discussion of whether or not this was a valid reason to spare these trees from the chainsaw. In the end, it was generally agreed that the invocation of sacredness was not particularly helpful to reaching a decision.

The claim that certain trees are sacred and should therefore be preserved leads to a number of philosophical dilemmas. Surely if any trees, or any living things for that matter, are sacred then all trees and living things are sacred. Are some trees more sacred than others? Likely not. This leaves us with no guidance at all as the problem then becomes which of the sacred trees shall we cut and which of the sacred living things shall we kill and eat? We have no choice but to consume as we are animals that need food and if we are to continue living in northern climates we need shelter and fuel. The decision of which trees to cut and which to leave is therefore not made any easier when spiritual reasons are invoked for their protection. In the end we must make intelligent decisions based on a host of considerations to do with the more tangible issues of ecology, economy, and community.

After deliberating on the question of special spiritual status of forests, I wonder if this kind of issue was what led to the separation of church and state centuries ago, in the political developments leading to our present system of liberal representative democracy. It is simply not reasonable or practical to allow highly subjective and ill-defined ideologies to be the basis of deciding public policy. I feel strongly that public policy issues need to be determined by practical, defensible criteria rather than obscure matters of individual spiritual belief. I have no difficulty marveling at the beauty and even the spirituality of a tree and then cutting it down to build my house so long as I know a new tree will grow in its place. I don't like to see a forest cut down and covered with cement or turned into farmland where we have enough already. Perhaps this best sums up my personal philosophy, my appreciation of forests, and all they provide for our material and spiritual well-being.

Pacific Spirit Park

When I want assurance that the spirit of the forest can return from destruction I go for a walk in Pacific Spirit Park. Situated between the city of Vancouver and the University of British Columbia on Point Grey, the park encompasses 1,885 acres (763 hectares) of densely forested land that has grown back from clearcutting for lumber early in the century. After Point Grey had been cleared of forest, most of it was designated the University Endowment Lands, part of which was subsequently developed for the university campus, research institutes, and housing. In 1989, due to strong public opinion, the remaining 1,885 acres of undeveloped land were set aside as a regional park and named Pacific Spirit Park.

This is what Pacific Spirit Park looked like in 1914 after the original forest was clearcut to feed the sawmills that built Vancouver. Nothing was done to protect the environment and no trees were planted on the site after logging. But because most of the area was left alone and not developed, the forest returned naturally and today provides proof that even devastating clearcutting will heal in time.

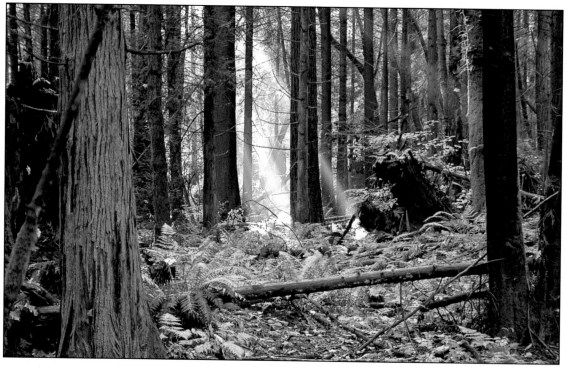

It would be easy to mistake this for a photo of pristine old growth in the wilderness of British Columbia. In fact, this forest is in the heart of Vancouver less than 300 yards from my city home. It looked just like the photo above about 90 years ago. Now called Pacific Spirit Park, the area has grown back from clearcutting at the turn of the century.

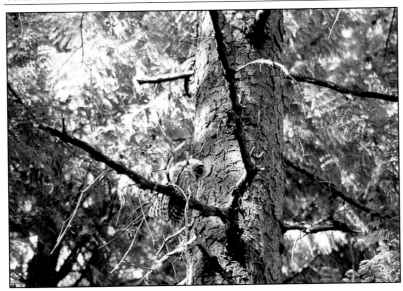

I surprised this barred owl (a close relative of the spotted owl) while it was feeding on a mouse it caught in Pacific Spirit Park. It flew up into this Sitka spruce and watched me while I fumbled for lenses before it disappeared into the forest.

Today, the only evidence that this land was laid waste to feed the sawmills that built Vancouver is the remains of huge cedar and Douglas-fir stumps among the lush new forest. Over much of the area the forest has regenerated with stands of Douglas-fir, western hemlock and red cedar mixed with other areas dominated by alder, maple and cherry. Majestic bigleaf maples are adorned with thick layers of moss in which licorice ferns find root. Vine maple forms a thicket of undergrowth beneath which a carpet of swordferns indicates a site rich in nutrients. In some areas the Douglas-fir have reached over 3 feet (1 metre) in diameter and 165 feet (50 metres) in height after only 80 to 100 years.

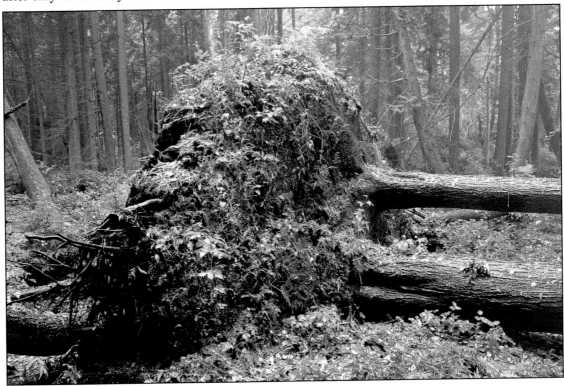

The new forest in Pacific Spirit Park is exposed to heavy winds that occasionally knock down healthy trees, sometimes in fairly large patches. This allows light to the ground where new plants and trees can thrive and give the forest a greater variety of species and tree ages.

There was absolutely no thought given to the reforestation or biological diversity of this area as it recovered from logging. Over large areas regular firewood cutting and speculative clearing made recovery difficult. Yet a new forest stands over the entire extent and there is nothing missing from it other than the large mammals. They have been more than replaced by the two-legged variety that arrive daily by the hundreds to stroll or jog along the network of trails that follow the old logging roads.

Pacific Spirit Park is as rich in species of trees, shrubs, flowers, ferns, mosses, and fungi as any old growth forest. The majesty of the Douglas-firs gives the same soaring feeling and the skunk cabbage swamps are as smelly and mucky as in the deepest wilderness. Ravens, jays, owls, and flickers thrive in the canopy, and squirrels leap from tree to tree in search of abundant seeds. Tall Douglas-firs toppled by high winds create new openings where berry bushes thrive. The new forest is so similar to the original that part of it has been set aside as an Ecological Reserve for scientific study. It is the only Ecological Reserve in British Columbia that is situated in a former clearcut.

A walk in Pacific Spirit Park on an early Saturday morning is a tonic for the soul. Every time of year is special as the seasons change and the rains feed the rich carpet of mosses and ferns growing beneath the towering canopy of Douglas-firs. It provides an opportunity to forget all the science, ecology, and intellectual analysis, and just enjoy the beauty of it all. The spirit of the forest is all around and I feel like I am back in the world of my youth, rambling in the forests of Winter Harbour. Deserts may be starkly beautiful and alpine meadows breathtaking in their colours, but there is nothing to compare with the smell and feel of the deep green of the deepest forest glen. In Pacific Spirit Park I can forget about pavement, computers, and the troubles of the world. I can find a timeless place and focus in on tiny tips of moss where dew drops contain a universe of their own. There is a place in life for this communion and without the forest there would be no place for me.

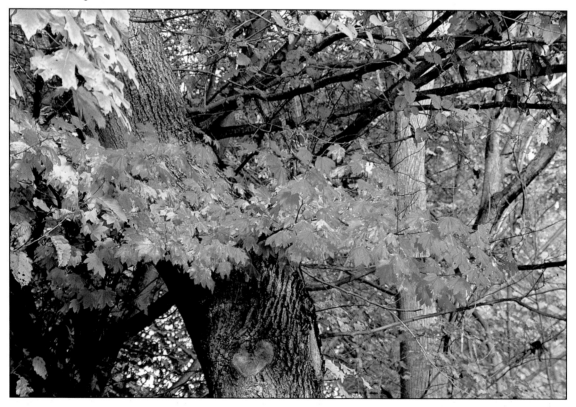

Where vine maple is exposed to direct sunlight it turns brilliant red in the fall, adding color that is often lacking in the deep green of the coastal coniferous forest.

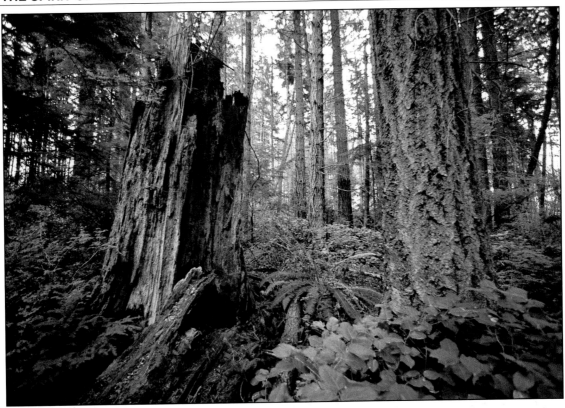

Throughout Pacific Spirit Park there are remnants of the old forest returning to the earth while new trees thrive on the fertile soil built by previous generations of trees.

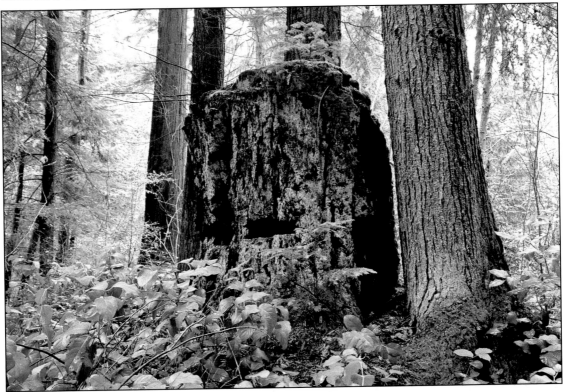

The springboard notch in this Douglas-fir stump is a reminder of the days when these huge trees were felled by hand with axes and crosscut saws. The 75 year-old western hemlock growing beside it is literally devouring the roots of the Douglas-fir and transforming them into new life.

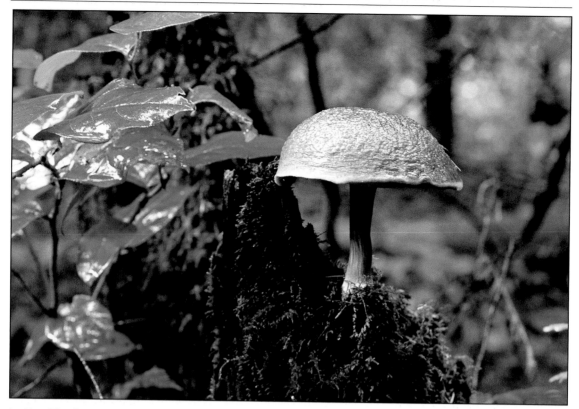

In Pacific Spirit Park there are hundreds of species of fungi, including the boletus above and the polypores below, dining on dead wood and turning it into soil for a new generation of trees. All the biodiversity of mosses, ferns and fungi has returned to the area even though it was completely clearcut decades ago. What will this forest look like 100 years from now?

Pacific Spirit Park offers proof that clearcutting is not deforestation. Given time to recover, the biodiversity has returned. The fungi, mosses, ferns and insects are once again abundant. There are ravens, eagles, pileated woodpeckers, owls, bluejays and even a large rookery of great blue herons nesting in the second growth cedar trees. Coyotes, skunks and raccoons skulk through the thickets in search of food. If the park were not in the middle of a large city it could also support deer, bear, wolf, and cougar as well as an old growth forest. Now that it has been protected as a park it will be able to recover to full old growth status. I wish I could live to see the size of those Douglas-firs 100 years from now. How fortunate for the people of Vancouver that they have a wilderness park right on their doorstep. What a miracle is the west coast rainforest that it can recover in full and total splendor from devastating ruin. Surely we must celebrate this new life at least as much as we mourn life lost elsewhere. The spirit has returned to Pacific Spirit Park as it has to most of the other areas logged for timber in the Pacific Northwest and British Columbia.

Pacific Spirit Park is truly a forest reborn; reborn from what is routinely described as the total and irreversible destruction of nature. I don't accept that description. I know that if forests can recover by themselves, without any help from people, that with our growing knowledge of forest science in genetics, biodiversity conservation, soils, silviculture etc., we can ensure that the forests of this word continue to provide an abundant, and hopefully growing, supply of renewable wood to help build and maintain our civilization. These same forests can also provide an abundant, and hopefully growing, supply of habitat for the thousands of other species that depend on the forest for their survival every day, just as much as we do. It is a fact that "a world without forests is as unthinkable as a day without wood". It's time that environmentalists, foresters, scientists, politicians, teachers, journalists and the public got that balance right, because we must get it right if we are going to achieve sustainability in the 21st Century.

REFERENCES

1 Alan Drengson, Remembering the Moral and Spiritual Dimensions of Forests, in Clearcut: The Tragedy of Industrial Forestry.

2 See above.

3 See Principles of Sustainable Forestry, Forest Alliance of BC, 1992 and Provincial Land Use Strategy, Volume 1, Land Use Charter, Commission on Resources and Environment, November, 1994.

4 Faith in a Seed, Henry D. Thoreau, Edited by Bradley P. Dean, Island Press/Shearwater Books, 1993

5 CTV - W5, Singing Trees, January 24, 1995.

Trees are the Answer

If trees are the answer, you might ask, what is the question? I believe that trees are the answer to a lot of questions about our future. These include: How can we advance to a more sustainable economy based on renewable fuels and materials? How can we improve literacy and sanitation in developing countries while reversing deforestation and protecting wildlife at the same time? How can we reduce the amount of greenhouse gases emitted to the atmosphere, carbon dioxide in particular? How can we increase the amount of land that will support a greater diversity of species? How can we help prevent soil erosion and provide clean air and water? How can we make this world more beautiful and green? The answer is, by growing more trees and then using more wood, both as a substitute for non-renewable fossil fuels and materials such as steel, concrete and plastic, and as paper products for printing, packaging and sanitation.

When the world's leaders met in Rio de Janeiro in 1992 at the Earth Summit they agreed that three issues are at the top of the international environmental agenda. These are; climate change, biodiversity, and forests. Of course there are many other important issues, including toxic chemicals and nuclear waste, but they are secondary compared to these "Big Three", all of which are global in nature. Unfortunately, most scientists, activists, and policy-makers have specialized in one or the other of these critical areas of concern, and have not focussed as strongly on the profound inter-relationships among them. This has resulted in a situation where most of the environmental movement has adopted a position on forests that is logically inconsistent with its positions on climate change and biodiversity. The risk of climate change is mainly due to fossil fuel consumption and the emission of CO^2. The risk to biodiversity is mainly due to the loss of forests caused by clearing for agriculture and cities. A large part of the solution to both these issues involves growing more trees and using more wood. The environmental movement has adopted a policy that is the opposite of this approach.

By considering forests in isolation from the other major issues, it may seem logical that we can save them by reducing wood consumption, that is, by cutting fewer trees. Greenpeace has appealed to the members of the United Nations to reduce wood consumption and use "environmentally appropriate alternatives" instead.[1] The Rainforest Action Network is campaigning for a 75% reduction in wood use in the United States through its "wood use reduction program."[2] The Sierra Club has adopted a formal policy called "zero cut" that would put an end to commercial forestry on federal public land.[3] All these campaigns can be summed up as "cut fewer trees – use less wood."

There are two problems with this approach. First, just because people stop using wood for fuel or building houses doesn't mean they will not need warmth or shelter. The fact that 6 billion humans wake up every morning with real needs for energy, food and materials must be taken into account. All the likely substitutes for wood: steel, concrete, plastic and fossil fuels, have far higher emissions of CO^2 associated with their production and use. Using less wood will automatically result in the use of more of these non-renewable resources. Second, much of the land that is used to grow trees could just as well be cleared and used for grazing, farming, and housing. If there is less demand for wood there will be less economic incentive to grow trees and retain forests. It is unrealistic to expect people to retain vast areas of the landscape in forests if they cannot use them. The best way to encourage people to retain and expand forests is to make the resources they provide, including wood, more valuable.

It is often stated that we could reduce our consumption of wood and other resources because we are "conspicuous consumers" who waste far too much with lavish lifestyles. While this may be the case for a minority of the world's people, it is important to recognize that nearly half the world's population lives at a material standard that we in the industrialized countries would not consider acceptable for a dignified life. The challenge, at least while the population continues to grow, is how to provide these people with more resources, not less. This cannot be solved by just taking from the rich and giving to the poor, although the question of global equity is a real and moral one. We must develop strategies to deliver more clean water, energy, food, and building materials while at the same time reducing the negative environmental impacts of doing so.

There is a common misconception, supported by some environmental leaders such as Paul Ehrlich, that per capita consumption of energy and resources is directly related to negative environmental impact. We are told that because the average American consumes 80 times as much as the average Bangladeshi they therefore cause 80 times as much damage to the environment.[4] This is not always the case in the real world. All one need do is travel to countries such as Bangladesh, Guatemala and Kenya to see the impact of poverty on the environment. Forests are stripped bare for subsistence farming, rivers are fouled for lack of sewage treatment, and wildlife is decimated by poachers for lack of enforcement. While it is often convenient to blame the rich and powerful for the world's wrongs, it is not that simple. Wealth often makes it possible to afford clean air and water, to enforce environmental laws, and to plant trees and tend them.

One thing we can't change is the past. While it is often useful to reflect upon past successes and failures, it is more fruitful to plan and work for a better future. I remind myself of this whenever I try to figure out who to blame for what's wrong with the world. Let's focus on what we can do to make it better in the future; at least we have a fighting chance to change things that haven't happened yet!

There is one thing about the future of North America, and for that matter the world, of which I am quite certain. One day when coal, oil, and natural gas are less abundant and minerals are scarcer, we will rely on trees as the basis of our wealth even more than we do today. They are by far the most abundant of all the world's renewable resources and with proper care they will continue to grow over much of the earth's surface indefinitely. In North America we are particularly blessed with vast areas that grow many desirable species of coniferous and broadleaf trees.

At present we are too caught up in the immediate issue of which forests to protect and which to manage to appreciate the long-term significance of forests to our economic well-being. The present abundance of non-renewable fuels and materials makes wood seem less important to the point where some predict that forestry is a "sunset industry" because technology will supposedly improve on wood products. This is far-fetched. It's extremely unlikely that there will be a man-made technology that will be as economical to produce, as abundant, as versatile, and as renewable as wood. The uniqueness and versatility of wood is illustrated by its use in the DC-X, an experimental rocket designed to prove the concept of a wholly reusable, one-part space shuttle. Balsa wood was found to be the lightest, least expensive, and most effective insulation material to keep the 1600 kilos (3500 pounds) of liquid hydrogen fuel at minus 423 Fahrenheit (minus 252 Celsius)[5]

It is not widely recognized how many human material needs can be met by trees. They have been used for fuel and timber for thousands of years and this remains the main reason for their consumption today. More recently, the byproducts from sawmilling and dedicated plantations have greatly increased the supply of pulp and paper for communications, packaging, and sanitary products. But trees provide the materials and chemicals for a host of other products and with the knowledge we have gained in working with petrochemicals they could provide many more. The cellulose that makes up about 50 percent of wood is used to make rayon and acetate as well as cellophane and explosives. But it is the lignin portion that makes up the other 50 percent of wood that has the most potential for new materials. Lignin is a complex mix of carbohydrates that could readily form the basis for a chemical industry in the same way that petroleum does today. The technology to extract lignin from wood in a form that is suitable for industrial purposes is well advanced -- and may be put into practice developing new products sooner than we think.

How many people have heard of the International Pine Chemical Association? Very few, and yet the chemicals derived from the sap of pine trees are indispensable for a wide range of industrial fields including dyes, food flavorings, synthetic rubber, adhesives, paints, and detergents. Pine trees have been tapped, in a manner much like maple trees are tapped for syrup, for thousands of years. The sap is distilled driving off the turpentine and leaving behind the rosin, or pine tar. Pine tar was so important as a wood preservative and, when combined with fiber, for caulking the seams in wooden ships that it became known as "naval stores". Pine rosin and pine chemicals are in everyday use in products such as Pine-Sol™, the rosin bag used by pitchers in baseball, and the rosin used on the bow of violins and other stringed instruments. Today, pine chemicals are still obtained from pine plantations tended for that purpose in China and other developing countries. In industrialized countries most pine chemicals are obtained as a by-product of pulping pine trees. Known as "tall oil", it is skimmed from the surface of pulp-mill vats and then refined in factories similar to oil refineries.[6] One US forest company, Westvaco Corporation, employs over 200 people in their Specialty Chemicals division, all working with chemicals from trees.

As the days grow shorter the aspens' fall colors make a sunset more beautiful in the richly diverse forests of the western slopes of the Rocky Mountains.

The greatest challenge for forests and foresters, which is becoming increasingly urgent, will be to provide for the rapidly growing demand for forest products while at the same time harvesting sustainable volumes of wood and maintaining protected areas as wilderness. In the past few years, it has become apparent to analysts of world timber supply that we are now coming up against the limits of forests to supply the demand for wood. It is likely that wood will become in critical short supply on a global basis long before food. Like food, demand for wood is strongly tied to population. As world population has doubled over the past 40 years so has the consumption of wood. Every year now about 95 million new people are added to the world population, thus creating about 25 billion board feet (60 million cubic meters) of new demand for wood each year. This represents about two-thirds of British Columbia's annual production and about twice that of the Pacific Northwest states of Washington, Oregon, and California combined. This means that during the decade of the 1990s the global demand for wood will increase by about six times the annual production in British Columbia and about 20 times that from the coastal states of the Pacific Northwest. No forester believes this to be sustainable forever.

It is the growth rate of our six billion-and-rising human population that is really unsustainable. To understand the implications of our steadily growing population more clearly, one has only to imagine what might happen if suddenly no more fossil fuels were available. Aside from puzzling over what to do with millions of cars and no gas, what would we use for heat, for running our industries, for firing the cement kilns? We would be forced to use wood. Within a very short time the world's forests would be decimated to provide for the desperate demand for energy. Soon the supply would end or at least dwindle to a trickle and hundreds of millions, if not billions, of people would perish. By all accounts we are not about to run out of fossil fuels in the near future. But one day we will run short of them. At that point, we may have to rely far more heavily on renewable forms of energy such as geothermal, solar, and wood. I just hope we get world population down to a more sustainable level before that day comes.

It is a surprise for most people to learn that wood supply may become critically short long before food supply. We don't get pangs of hunger for wood like we do for food, but wood is as necessary for survival (particularly in developing countries) as food. This shortage will result in greatly increased programs to reforest surplus agricultural land, to intensify silvicultural activity, and to get more use from a given volume of wood. This is the positive side of global wood shortage. The negative side is likely to be an inability to control deforestation, particularly in countries where economic conditions are most desperate. In a future time of shortage, one of the strongest arguments for maximizing production in North America would be that we have good forestry regulations and a strong tradition of abiding by democratic decisions

There is a great irony in the fact that many environmentalists have decided to focus on wood and paper when these are the most renewable and sustainable of all material resources. Even if it were possible to produce other renewable crops more "efficiently" they can never provide the habitat for other species that trees do. In the name of ecology the public is told to boycott forest products when there is no doubt that this would inevitably lead to the use of materials that cause far more damage to the environment. But the myth of forest destruction caused by logging is a powerful one that plays into the hands of media sensation and fundraising programs.

As this book goes to press the Coastal Rainforest Coalition, based in San Francisco and Washington, DC, is publishing full-page ads in the New York Times accusing British Columbia of threatening 50% of its wildlife species with extinction, drying up salmon streams, and destroying the last old-growth forest.[7] They are trying to convince movie producers to boycott British Columbia as a film location; as if there are other places that have a better record of protecting wilderness and improving forestry practices.[8] They are actively lobbying Fortune 500 companies such as IBM, Liz Claiborne, Levi Strauss, Nike, Bristol-Meyers Squibb and Hewlett-Packard, trying to convince them to boycott forest products from BC. They refuse to recognize any of the progress that has been made in creating scores of new parks, improving forestry practices, and maintaining healthy wildlife populations. They are misinforming millions of people who have never visited our vast province and who cannot see for themselves how beautiful it is. They show pictures of the worst damage ever done and give the impression that the forest will never grow back. They have nothing good to say about people in a region that is doing more to protect nature than any other region in North America. Many of their leaders have either never been to British Columbia or have very limited exposure to its vast geography

Among the more ridiculous proposals from this wrong-headed group is a demand for "tree-free paper." Many environmental groups argue that because it is wrong to kill trees to make paper we should make paper from something else. They suggest substituting hemp and kenaf. Hemp is the plant from which marijuana is derived. It was formerly used for making ropes (Manila hemp) and sacks before being replaced by petroleum-derived substances such as nylon and polypropylene. Kenaf is a member of the hibiscus family. Both hemp and kenaf originate from the far-eastern sub-tropics and contain excellent fibers that can be used to make fine paper and cloth. The advocates of this proposal believe that we should embark on a vast program to replace wood with these crops as our primary source of paper products.

A few years ago I attended a reception for Robert Kennedy Jr. in a small art gallery in a trendy part of New York City. He is on the staff of the Natural Resources Defense Council and has been a leader in campaigns against water pollution, hydroelectric development, and forestry. I found myself standing with a group of environmental activists who were having a lively conversation about the desirability of tree-free paper. A young woman reported that she was hoping to get tobacco farmers to grow kenaf instead of tobacco, with the apparent intention of earning double eco-points by simultaneously saving trees from death and people from lung cancer. "Wouldn't it be better," I offered, "to plant trees that are native to the area and use them to make paper? In that way the tobacco farms could be put back to something like the original Carolinian hardwood forest." To this came the quick reply, "People can't plant a forest, only nature can produce a forest. People can only plant trees." Surprised by this I tried again: "But surely it would be better to plant native trees than some exotic sub-tropical annual farm crop that needs pesticides and fertilizer. Birds and squirrels would like trees more than kenaf." This line of reasoning got nowhere. When I suggested that if all the paper derived from wood had to be replaced with wood-free paper we would end up deforesting vast areas of the continent to get enough land to grow hemp and kenaf, my listeners' eyes rolled back and I could see I was dismissed. It amazes me that some people can't understand that if you don't use trees to make paper and other forest products there is less reason to plant and grow trees. The next thing you know, there will be a campaign for "tree-free wood."

A large number of the younger generation have been convinced that it would be good if we stopped using trees to make paper and switched to crops like hemp and kenaf instead. I know this because I speak to high school and university audiences on a regular basis. When asked "Where would we grow all these new crops, on Mars?" they soon realize that we would have to grow them here on Earth on land that could otherwise be used to grow trees. Its not as if there is a huge surplus of spare land that is available for hemp farms, and most important, even if there was it would be better for biodiversity to grow trees than hemp. Give me an acre of land and ask me to grow something there that I could make paper from and that would also be best for biodiversity and I will plant trees every time, without exception. It is quite ridiculous for environmental groups, who say their main cause is to protect biodiversity, to advocate massive monocultures of exotic annual farm crops where we could be growing trees. Even the most simplified monoculture pine plantation provides more habitats for birds, insects and wildlife than any annual farm crop.

Back to the real future, it is reasonable to hope that more environmental activists will develop a more positive and enlightened stance on forestry issues. The present preoccupation with preservation and clearcutting must eventually be balanced with support for planting, growing, and using more trees. The recognition that forestry must be practiced with concern for worker safety and economy in mind will surely come as the debate matures. It is certain that foresters will be required to increase the productivity of forests and their ability to support a wide variety of native species and other values. One can only hope that environmentalists and foresters will increasingly accept the reasonable points in each other's agendas and work together for sustainability rather than being at odds with each other.

It is a testament to the complexity of forest issues that the Earth Summit in Rio de Janeiro in 1992 failed to achieve an international agreement on sustainable forestry. While world leaders did sign conventions on climate change and biodiversity, the wide divergence of opinion on forestry resulted in the adoption of a rather weak statement of non-binding principles. The main obstacle to agreement was whether the document should focus on preservation of forests or on their development. Forest-dependent nations such as Canada and the Scandinavian countries found themselves allied with developing countries such as Malaysia that wished to develop their forests for economic purposes. Other industrialized countries such as Germany and the United Kingdom wanted to stress the preservation of forests, particularly those in other countries such as Canada and Malaysia. This was clearly not a basis for a workable agreement.

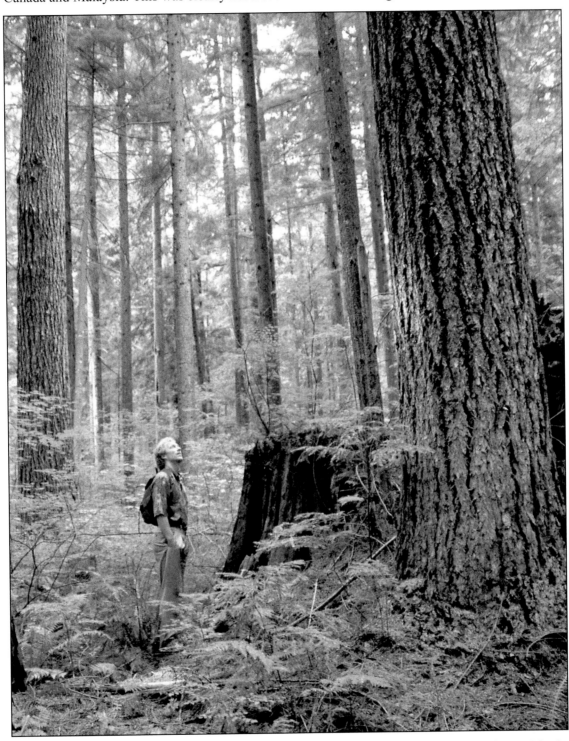

In the Seymour River watershed one of the oldest clearcuts in British Columbia is recovering its former majesty. Logged about 100 years ago during the early settlement of Vancouver the valley now provides tens of thousands of visitors with recreation and a demonstration of forestry at work.

Since 1992, many governments have continued discussions towards an international agreement on sustainable forestry. The 1995 meeting of the UN Commission on Sustainable Development agreed to establish an International Panel on Forests to work towards this goal. After two years of meetings in Geneva and New York, under the able chairmanship of Sir Martin Holdgate, former head of the International Union for the Conservation of Nature and Natural Resources, no agreement was reached. This was due in part to a policy reversal by most of the environmental movement. Whereas they had originally supported the idea, they suddenly changed and announced their opposition to an international agreement. This was largely because, as the discussions developed, it became clear that the agreement would have to focus on management and development. After all, even if 10-15% of the world's forests are set aside as parks and wilderness, the challenge is how to manage the remaining 85-90% for other purposes. Greenpeace referred to the potential agreement as the "Chainsaw Convention", thus indicating their true agenda, opposition to cutting trees. So long as this style of anti-forestry rhetoric is widely adopted by the environmental movement, there will be continued political confusion about forests, and an inability to achieve consensus at both national and international levels.

Following on the failure of the International Panel, the UN established a lower-key International Forum on Forests to keep the discussion alive. Hopefully, as the importance of forestry becomes more widely appreciated, an agreement will eventually be achieved and the extreme anti-forestry views will fade from favor. This would do a lot to end the present climate of boycott threats and accusations that do not reflect a fair assessment of the situation. The idea that all countries -- producers and consumers of forest products -- should operate on a level playing field appeals to everyone who wants to see fairness as well as firmness built into world forestry regulations.

An international agreement on sustainable forestry will have to address a number of topics. Some of the most important are:

• The protection and conservation of wilderness and biological diversity in forests. Can nations agree to set aside a certain percentage of their land for protection from development? Some countries, particularly in Europe and Asia, have already developed most of their landscape. Can they restore some of these areas to a semblance of the original ecology? Other countries, such as Canada, Brazil and Russia, still have a large percentage of their land in original forest. How much of this can reasonably be preserved while maintaining a vibrant economy? Is it possible for countries with little wilderness to finance wilderness protection in countries that have a high percentage of original forest remaining?

• Protection of soil, water and air. Forests are essential for the building and maintenance of soil health. They cleanse the air of pollutants and take up carbon dioxide. Forested watersheds provide clean water for fish, wildlife, and human communities. Can we agree on international standards for the protection of these essential elements that support all life on earth?

• Conversion of native forests to plantation forestry with exotic species. In some regions, particularly but not excluded to the Southern Hemisphere, tree species from other regions are better suited to commercial forestry than the native species. Plantations of exotic tree species often result in more alteration to the native biological diversity than if native species were used. In many cases where exotic tree species are used they are planted on agricultural lands that were cleared of native tree species many years ago. Should this form of plantation forestry be encouraged to meet global wood requirements?

• Protection of aboriginal people and involvement of local communities in forest management. Many of the forces driving today's economy are global in nature. How can we serve international markets and foster international cooperation while at the same time protecting the rights of local people? This is a major challenge for all human enterprise. How does sustainable forest management fit into the larger global picture in terms of human rights and social issues?

• Conversion of forest lands to agriculture and human settlement. Is it possible for countries to agree on land use plans regarding the amount of forested areas that will be protected from conversion to other uses? Can developing countries control the rate of deforestation for subsistence farming and housing given their rapid growth in population?

• Silviculture, forest renewal, and forestry practices. A key requirement of sustainable forest management is the rapid renewal of healthy, productive forests that can provide habitat for as many native species as possible. Given the great diversity of forest types, from tropical rainforests to cold boreal forests, is it realistic to try to define common criteria for successful forest renewal? How could countries agree that different practices are better in one region than in another?

• Monitoring, compliance and enforcement of international agreements. What would the "International Tree Police" look like? Can nations agree to an independent monitoring arrangement and what sanctions would be imposed on countries failing to comply with international agreements?

• Funding for reforestation and sustainable forest management. Many developing countries are unable to afford the training and investment required for reforestation and development of sustainable forestry practices. Will the developed countries be willing to fund these efforts in both their own regions and in countries that need assistance?

Breaking Through To The Popular Culture

Take the last tree and shove it up the hole in your culture

Leonard Cohen – 1998

There was a time when the forest industry enjoyed the admiration of society. Paul Bunyan, Smokey the Bear, and hard working lumberjacks were respected for the roles they played in providing us with wood and protecting us from fire. This respect has been severely eroded by the anti-forestry movement, which portrays foresters and loggers as either tools of greedy capitalists or unthinking destroyers of the environment. How can this trend be reversed so the general public once again respects the hard work done to provide society with its most renewable material resource?

Throughout its long history, the forest industry has been a producer of raw materials, first lumber and then pulp and paper. These commodities are generally sold into the wholesale market where they are then passed on to the ultimate consumer by other companies who specialize in construction, furniture, cardboard boxes, printing paper, tissues etc. Because of this, the forest industry has developed what might be called a "wholesale culture" as opposed to a "retail culture." That was fine so long as the general public accepted the forest industry as a positive part of the economy. For the forest industry, sales and marketing was a relatively private matter of visiting customers and making sales of lumber and pulp at the wholesale level. But now that the general public has been sensitized to the environmental issues surrounding forest practices and the production of forest products, it is necessary for the forest industry to behave as though it is in retail rather than wholesale. This requires a broad cultural shift, a very difficult process for such a large industry with a long tradition of supplying wholesale markets with no need to advertise or appeal to the general public.

What does it mean to shift from a wholesale to a retail culture? There are two essential ingredients; a major change in perspective and a much greater financial commitment to public awareness. Let's begin with the change in perspective.

Like many professions, the forest industry in relatively self-centered. We work with, eat with, play with and otherwise spend a lot of time with other people in the same business. This can lead to an attitude that is somewhat self-congratulatory and dismissive of other opinions and ideas. In shifting from a wholesale to a retail culture, it is necessary to get "outside the box" and to see oneself in the context of the much larger popular culture; the worlds of media, current affairs, entertainment, politics, education and advertising. Industries that depend on retail sales must keep up with the latest trends in fashion, music, and speech (slang). Prior to the emergence of environmental concern about the impacts of forestry, there was no need for loggers who cut trees for a living to explain themselves in popular terms. "I'm a Lumberjack and I'm OK" was good enough for most people. Today's loggers need a Ph.D. in biodiversity conservation and a degree in journalism to debate the subject effectively. At the very least they need people with these credentials to represent them in the court of public opinion.

A term that is frequently used to describe public acceptance of an industry or company is "social license". It is not enough to have a legal license in the form of permits and land-use agreements even if there is 100% compliance with the law. It is also necessary to have a social license to operate which means gaining and maintaining public support. This is especially true if the operations are on public land but it also applies to private land where public values are effected. The only way to maintain a social license is to communicate with the broad public, and to do it more effectively than your critics.

Sightseers inspect a herd of sea-lions basking on a boom of logs at Fanny Bay on Vancouver Island. Tourism, wildlife, and forestry can often co-exist and even enhance one another.

The critics of the forest industry are waging a major public campaign, backed by hundreds of millions of dollars in donations and grants, to take away the social license the industry once enjoyed. This campaign is being waged in the popular culture, gaining support from Hollywood movie stars,[*] song writers, senior politicians in all parties, opinion leaders in the

---

[*] Oliver Stone, the Hollywood director, was quoted as stating that British Columbians were "the real Natural Born Killers", referring to his extremely violent film of the same name.

media, and a huge segment of the general public. Many people in the forest industry are dismayed by the amount of misinformation and even hatred that is directed towards their line of work. They wonder why the public is buying into the anti-forestry rhetoric. It is precisely because the forest industry is not matching the campaign against them. Never mind why these groups are out to damage or destroy the hewers of wood, they are real and they must be reckoned with, or the industry will suffer further loss of support.

The average level of spending by retail business on advertising and communications is 3% of gross annual sales. Many businesses, such as clothing, cosmetics, soft drinks, and cars, spend much more than the average. The forest industries of the United States and Canada have annual sales of about US$200 billion. Therefore if they just spent the average for retail business there would be a US$6 billion budget for advertising and public education. That's a lot of airtime on TV and a lot of print in magazines and newspapers. There is no doubt that public opinion could be effected if good creative talent was combined with the honest truth in a campaign to restore faith in forestry.

Let's look at some of the techniques used by the retail sector and see which ones might best serve the forest industry. Trees and forest products are useful and interesting but they are not particularly glamorous or exciting. How can we get the public's attention in a world so over-loaded with information? I believe the most effective program would involve recruiting champions to deliver key messages through a coordinated media campaign.

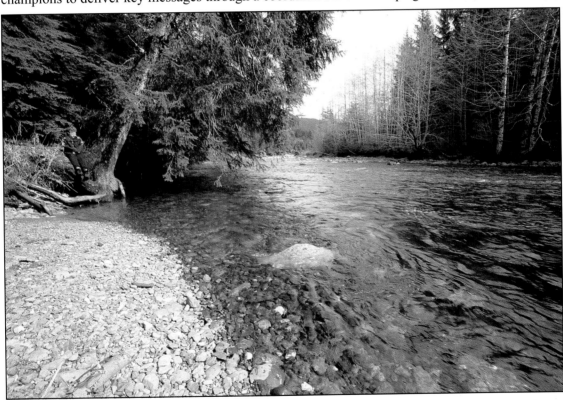

Clear, cool water, filtered by the surrounding forest, makes an ideal habitat for spawning salmon. Salmon and other fish species are healthiest in landscapes dominated by forests.

It is helpful to look at some of the more successful promotional campaigns in other sectors. One of the best involving a commodity is the "Got Milk?" campaign funded by the dairy industries. The formula is simple enough, a celebrity appears in a full-page ad or TV commercial wearing a "milk mustache" and giving a short testimonial about the benefits of drinking milk. In February 1999, the celebrity was Mark McGuire, all-time champion home run hitter in major league baseball. He had the milk mustache and was sporting his baseball bat, made of wood. I thought to myself, "Why doesn't the forest industry hire Mark McGuire to "go to bat" for them?"

After all, the instrument of his fame is fashioned from ash trees growing sustainably in the Appalachian Mountains.

The practice of sponsoring champions in sport and entertainment is well established as a successful way of attracting attention to a consumer product. Nike, the sport shoe and clothing manufacturer, has sponsored both Michael Jordan of basketball fame and Tiger Woods who attracted a whole new audience to professional golf. There is nothing particularly glamorous about casual footwear, but when sports icons are used to market them young people line up to pay exorbitant prices.

Some years ago Pepsi-Cola hired Michael Jackson, then at the pinnacle of his career, to help them fight the "Cola wars" against Coca-Cola. Hundreds of millions, perhaps billions, of dollars were spent on advertising designed to convince the public that one brand of caramelized soda water is better than the other. There is absolutely no socially redeeming value in this competition; it is perhaps even negative for health reasons. Both companies know that if they ever stopped spending the other Cola would win the war, it would be that simple. Proof positive that if you want to influence public opinion you had better be willing to match your detractors, dollar for dollar.

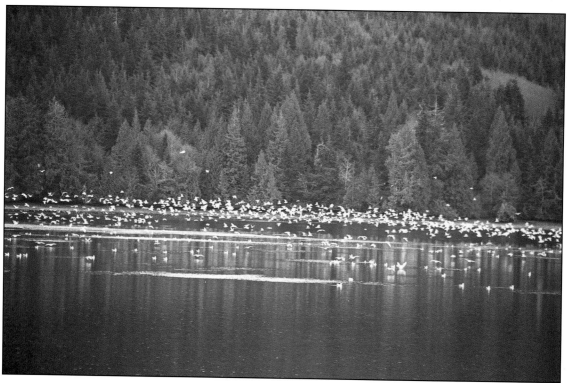

Gulls feed on herring eggs spawned on eel grass across the bay from my Winter Harbour home. The forest behind has grown back from logging in the 1930's and '40's.

The forest industry, on the other hand, has an incredibly positive story to tell. It produces our most renewable material resource, maintains habitat for thousands of species, removes carbon from the atmosphere, and provides a wide range of consumer goods without which life as we know it would be impossible. This story has not been told to the popular culture in ways that people can easily understand. Environmentalists focus on trees turned into toilet paper in order to give the industry a bad smell, and on ugly landscapes in order to associate forestry with death and destruction. There is no choice but to counter these negative messages with positive ones, and the forest industry has no lack of opportunity to do so.

What if the forest industry were to sponsor a sports star like Wayne Gretzky, much loved in both his native country, Canada, and in his adopted home, the United States. A campaign could be created that focussed on two priorities, literacy and reforestation. Literacy is the foundation of an educated, free and prosperous society. Reforestation can help heal the environment and provide much needed fuel and building materials. Wayne could be the public spokesperson for the industry, appearing as a champion for these causes. The industry could provide paper, printing and expenses for literacy programs. They could build nurseries to provide seedlings and they could establish sustainable forest plantations where people could learn to grow trees. These programs could be featured in a major advertising campaign with Wayne scoring goals for the betterment of society. While this is only an example of what could be done, I believe it is a realistic possibility.

Nothing short of a program of this magnitude will deliver social license to an industry that has been painted as the "Dark Side" in a global propaganda campaign of Star Wars dimensions. If we want to get back on the right side of The Force we must fight like Jedi Knights with a cause, the causes of freedom, sustainability, living biodiversity, and truth in science and reason. Clearly this requires a cultural shift of major proportions. Let's get on with it!

As 1999 draws to a close there is finally good news emerging on the communications front. Kelly McCloskey, a professional forester who heads the Canadian Wood Council, has initiated the "Wood is Good" campaign, a generic, North America-wide program to promote the environmental and other benefits of using wood. Industry leaders in the United States and Canada have signed on and the initial fundraising has begun. The first objective is to meet the challenge of the steel industry, now spending about $20 million per year on TV and print ads to convince people they should build their houses with steel rather than wood. Ironically, the ads claim that steel is better for the environment than wood, that it would be better to recycle eight used cars than to cut down a forest. No mention is made of the massive energy consumption of the electric-arc furnaces used to melt car bodies, never mind the associated dioxin emissions from burning the plastic. Wood is Good will provide a counter to the steel industry's campaign, giving the public a more balanced view of the choices they can make. Hopefully it will grow into programs that can effectively counter the "use less wood" policy of the major environmental lobbies. Perhaps they will eventually see the error of their ways and join with foresters, ushering in a new era of renewable energy and materials. Wood is not only good, it is the best.

When I was a leader in the Greenpeace movement I often reminded my fellow environmentalists that "our job is to work ourselves out of a job." The same is true of all social movements. Eventually society either accepts, or rejects, the principles of the movement and people move on to other pursuits. I feel the same way about my efforts to promote the sustainability and renewability of forestry and wood. I am sometimes amazed by the fact that this seems more difficult than my original work to promote awareness of ecology and the environment. But life is full of surprises so I will just take it in my stride and continue to communicate my beliefs until I work myself out of a job again.

Epilogue

As I sit writing in my Winter Harbour home I am looking across the bay at the lush forest growing on the hills. The area is a combination of second-growth coming back after logging by my grandfather and others in the 1930s and thick hemlock and alder stands that originated with blowdown early in the century. The blowdown stands were too young to cut in 1930 but they are now reaching commercial size. There are a few scattered old spruce and cedars that survived the blowdown and the logging.

All the forest I can see from my house is zoned for commercial forestry and much of it will eventually be cut, in my lifetime if I'm lucky enough. I accept this even though it will change the way things look across the bay. But I must admit I am not looking forward to the change. Even after decades of experience in forests and forestry I still prefer the look of a beautiful green forest to that of a recent clearcut. In the end, our sense of aesthetics and our emotional attachments dictate much of how we feel about change in the environment. I know in my mind that logging will not destroy the forest and that my opinion of the way a clearcut looks is not all that important to the trees that will grow back over the years. If my feelings are mixed it is a healthy expression of an inability to know for certain what the future really holds for my family, my community, or my world.

I am very pleased that the hills across the bay won't be logged the way they did it in the old days. Then there was no concern for anyone's "view," partly because everyone was so busy working they didn't have time to look up and appreciate it. The foresters who decide on where and when to cut the forest I can see from my house will be required to plan according to a Forest Practices Code[9] that is designed to ensure sustainability, consideration of visual impact and rapid forest renewal. Perhaps those same foresters will read this book and realize that they should do everything very, very carefully, according to the Principles of Sustainable Forestry. [10]

Forests are the most complex systems that have ever existed on this planet. They house the majority of the earth's species and they provide products that are essential to the survival of civilization. If you desire a rich and rewarding life, study forests There is no environment that offers more wonder or insight. And plant a few more trees if you have the time.

May the Forest be With You

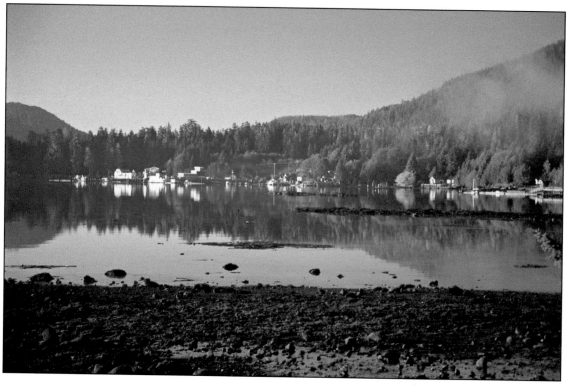

My home town, the tiny hamlet of Winter Harbour on Vancouver Island, has been inhabited for thousands of years. The people there will always depend on the resources of the forest and the sea.

REFERENCES

1 Greenpeace submission to the UN Inter-Governmental Panel on Forests, September 11-15, 1995 New York.
2 See: http://www.ran.org/ran_campaigns/old_growth/taking_action.html
3 See: http://www.sierraclub.org/forests/backgrou.htm
4 Paul Ehlich and Anne Ehrlich, The Betrayal of Science and Reason, Island Press, 1996, Washington, DC, p. 47
5 Jeffrey Kluger, Discover the World of Science, Vol. 16, Number 5, May 1995
6 See: http://www.harima.co.jp/naval/naval_e.html
7 New York Times, April 18, 1995, paid advertisement, International Coalition to Save British Columbia's Forests.
8 Beth Lanski, Daily Variety, April 20, 1995.
9 Forest Practices Code, BC Ministry of Forests, 1994.
10 BC Forest Alliance, Principles of Sustainable Forestry, February, 1993.

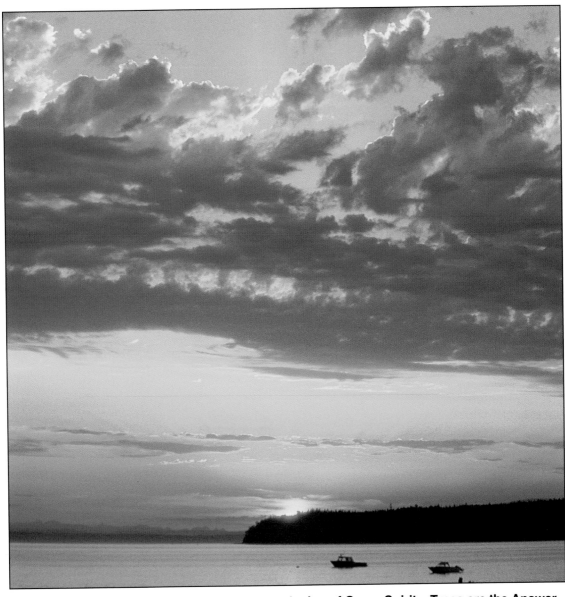

Sunset over a forested island signals the conclusion of Green Spirit – Trees are the Answer.

INDEX